VIETNAM'S
Economic
Policy
SINCE
1975

The Institute of **Southeast Asian Studies** was established as an autonomous organization in May 1968. It is a regional research centre for scholars and other specialists concerned with modern Southeast Asia, particularly the multi-faceted problems of stability and security, economic development, and political and social change.

The Institute is governed by a twenty-two member Board of Trustees comprising nominees from the Singapore Government, the National University of Singapore, the various Chambers of Commerce and professional and civic organizations. A ten-man Executive Committee oversees day-to-day operations; it is chaired by the Director, the Institute's chief academic and administrative officer.

The **ASEAN Economic Research Unit** is an integral part of the Institute, coming under the overall supervision of the Director who is also the Chairman of its Management Committee. The Unit was formed in 1979 in response to the need to deepen understanding of economic change and political developments in ASEAN. The day-to-day operations of the Unit are the responsibility of the Co-ordinator. A Regional Advisory Board, consisting of a senior economist from each of the ASEAN countries, guides the work of the Unit.

VIETNAM'S *Economic Policy* SINCE 1975

VO NHAN TRI

 ASEAN Economic Research Unit
INSTITUTE OF SOUTHEAST ASIAN STUDIES

Published by
Institute of Southeast Asian Studies
Heng Mui Keng Terrace
Pasir Panjang
Singapore 0511

HC
444
.V593
1990

All rights reserved. No part of this publication may be reproduced, stored in a retrieval system, or transmitted in any form or by any means, electronic, mechanical, photocopying, recording or otherwise, without the prior permission of the Institute of Southeast Asian Studies.

© 1990 Institute of Southeast Asian Studies
First reprint 1992

The responsibility for facts and opinions expressed in this publication rests exclusively with the author and his interpretations do not necessarily reflect the views or the policy of the Institute or its supporters.

Cataloguing in Publication Data

Vo Nhan Tri.
   Vietnam's economic policy since 1975: a critical analysis.
   1. Vietnam-Economic policy.
   I. Institute of Southeast Asian Studies (Singapore)
   II. Title.
HC444 V87 1990 sls90-4956

ISBN 981-3035-54-4 (soft cover)
ISBN 981-3035-60-9 (hard cover)

Typeset by International Typesetters
Reprinted in Singapore by Prime Packaging Industries Pte Ltd.

Contents

Preface ix

Chapter 1 Legacy of the Development Model of North Vietnam, 1955–75 1

Chapter 2 Reunification and "Socialist Transformation", 1975–80 58

Chapter 3 The Third Five-Year Plan, 1981–85 125

Chapter 4 Economic "Renovation", 1986–90 181

Chapter 5 Conclusion 241

"La première loi qui s'impose à l'historien est de ne rien oser dire de faux, la seconde d'oser dire tout ce qui est vrai"

CICERON, *DE ORATORE*

Preface

The present work is the result of my collection of data and reflections on Socialist Vietnam's economy since I left the country in late 1984 after spending sixteen years in Hanoi and nine years in Ho Chi Minh City after "Liberation".

Gathering material and particularly statistical data for this book was indeed a hard and time-consuming task, because there were no readily available Vietnamese documents and reference books in libraries or even specific research centres. Very often, I had to read interminable annual reports of Vietnamese leaders to find some useful figures or interesting remarks. As for articles written by Vietnamese economists and published in the journal *Nghien Cuu Kinh Te* (Economic Research) they were most of the time insipid because their aim was to demonstrate, at least until 1985, the *a priori* correctness of the Party's economic policy. However, since 1986–87 this journal began to disclose from time to time some interesting figures and facts about the Vietnamese economy, but at the same time it was difficult to find issues of this journal in most of the libraries in the West which usually subscribed to it.

Thus, searching for Vietnamese statistical data, which belonged to the domain of pathological secrecy, was a very frustrating task.

The General Statistical Office in Hanoi published two series of statistics: one for public purposes, entitled *So Lieu Thong Ke* (Statistical Data), and one "top secret" (*Tai Lieu Toi Mat*) meant for high-ranking cadres, entitled *Nien Giam Thong Ke* (Statistical Yearbook). Generally, the former was patchy and incomplete whereas the latter was more systematic and comprehensive. Nevertheless, one could not find in the latter figures concerning the state budget or foreign aid, which were (and still are) ultra-secret. However, since 1987, the *Statistical Yearbook* has been available for public consumption although some sensitive tables contained in it previously have now been deleted! The publication of these statistics was (and is) generally very late, often with a lag of two or three years.

In this book, as much as possible, the *Statistical Yearbook* has been used instead of the *Statistical Data*. However, the reader should consider all official data with great reserve. For even the Council of Ministers has warned, in their Instruction No 295/CT (14 November 1983) that many units of production and branches have given inadequate statistics. Worse still, some of them deliberately gave false statistics in order to demonstrate "achievements" (see the journal *Thong Ke*, no. 12 [Hanoi, 1983], p. 1, and no. 8 [1987], p. 1). The Party newspaper has been reiterating time and again the necessity to improve the overall quality of statistics and the end of false reports (*Nhan Dan*, 22 February and 12 September 1985; 15 August and 6 December 1986; 24 May 1988). In an unusual article published in its 24 February 1988 issue, this newspaper even disclosed five categories of false statistics with a view to highlighting "achievements".

One of the Vietnamese leaders, Vo Van Kiet, complained that "false statistics lead to wrong policies" (*Nhan Dan*, 21 February 1986). As for Le Duc Tho, he warned that "if reports are false, and statistics erroneous, they become even more dangerous" (*Tap Chi Cong San*, no. 5 [1986], p. 20) for they mislead the Party leadership. In brief, even Party leaders have admitted that they were (and are) mystified by their own mystification!

Primary Vietnamese sources are mainly used in this book, including unpublished Party and government material. The book is divided into four chapters. In chapter 1 I try to analyse and assess the legacy of the Stalinist-Maoist developmental model of North Vietnam during the 1955-75 period. I would like to warn students of Vietnamese affairs that the present assessment supersedes what I had written in my earlier book *Croissance Economique de la Demokratique Republique du Vietnam 1945-65* (Hanoi: ELE, 1967), and other articles on the Vietnamese economy published in Vietnam as well as in the Soviet Union and France during the years 1960-80. For these publications obviously were written under conditions in which, paraphrasing Shakespeare in *King Lear*, I had to write not what I felt but what I had to write. There were at that time, besides self-censorship, several layers of censorship made by the Party and government machinery including that of the Economic Department of the Ministry of Public Security. I was asked to cut large passages of my works which were not palatable to the Vietnamese authorities and to present a rosy economic picture.

In chapter 2, I analyse the consequences of the "Northernization" of South Vietnam after a precipitate "reunification" and the overhasty "socialist transformation" in agriculture and industry during the Second Five-Year Plan (FYP) (1976-80).

In chapter 3, I analyse the performance of the Third FYP (1981-85) during which Vietnam had to implement, after the Chinese attack in February 1979, "two strategic tasks" (instead of one before), namely, "building socialism and defending the socialist homeland".

In the last chapter, I analyse the changed road to development effected by the new Secretary-General Nguyen Van Linh since his accession to supreme power at the Sixth Party Congress (December 1986). His policy is, in fact, a dialectical unity of continuity *and* change (or "renovation" as he put it). It is worth noting, however, that while advocating economic "renovation", Linh also warns that it should remain "within the realm of socialism" and only "aim at its better attainment". This incipient "renovation" process covers not only the internal but also external aspects of the Communist Party of Vietnam's (CPV) economic policy during the Fourth FYP (1986-90).

In the general conclusion I briefly recall great turning points in the economic history of Vietnam since its forced reunification, and try to extract the human significance of its tumultuous economic experience.

I am indebted to Pierre Brocheux, Marie-Agnes Crosnier, Nguyen Thi Dieu, Francoise Direr, Fumio Goto, Ngo Manh Lan, Edith Lhomel, Lam Thanh Liem, Vo Hoang Mai, David Marr, Tadashi Mio, Tsutomu Murano, Nguyen Duc Nhuan, Truong Quang, Lewis Stern, Ikuo Takeuchi, Carlyle Thayer, and Richard Vokes, for sending me useful materials or copies of their own articles from Australia, England, France, Holland, Japan and the USA at various times. I profited greatly from discussions with colleagues and friends such as Georges Boudarel, Victor Funnell, Tetsusaburo Kimura, John Kleinen, Tadashi Mio, Nguyen Thanh Nha, Bui Xuan Quang, Ton That Thien, Jayne Werner, and Christine White.

I would like to extend my appreciation also to the Institute of Southeast Asian Studies in Singapore for providing me a Research Fellowship for two years to complete this book, to the personnel of its library, and to the typist for typing my manuscript with unfailing good humour.

February 1989   V.N.T.

chapter 1

Legacy of the Development Model of North Vietnam, 1955–75

As the Hanoi leadership sought to impose the very same development model experienced in the North (the Democratic Republic of Vietnam or DRV) upon the reunified country after 1975, it might be useful to recall firstly some salient features of the Vietnam Workers' Party's (VWP) economic policy and performance during the twenty-year period preceding the reunification of the country. This period embraced the first Reconstruction (1955–57), the "Socialist Transformation" (1958–60), the First Five-Year Plan (1961–65), the war years and the second Reconstruction (1965–75).

In the interests of consistency, this account will focus only on three principal sectors of the DRV's economy, namely, agriculture, industry and handicraft, and foreign aid and trade, which are indispensable for the comprehension of the post-reunification economic policy.

Agriculture
In the field of agriculture the analysis will be primarily concerned with agrarian reform and co-operativization (or collectivization).

Regarding agrarian reform, the details of the implementation of the land reform proper (from December 1955 to July 1956) and its bloody "errors" need not be repeated here as many Vietnamese authors as well as foreign observers have already dealt at length with this topic.[1] The following account will be limited to briefly *reexamining* two important issues related to the VWP's policy of land reform which was, as everybody knows, greatly inspired by the Maoist paradigm, and implemented under the close guidance of Chinese advisers.[2]

First Issue

Is it correct to assert, as the communique of the famous Tenth Central Committee Plenum (Second Congress) held in September 1956 did, that "the policy line of the Central Committee had basically been correct" and "the direct cause of the serious errors lay in shortcomings in the work of directing the implementation [of land reform]"?[3] It was reported that, as a result of land reform, 810,000 hectares were confiscated or expropriated (together with 1,846,000 farm tools, 106,448 heads of cattle and 148,565 houses) and then redistributed to 2,104,138 peasant households involving 8,323,630 peasants (72.8 per cent of the rural population),[4] implying a figure of less than 0.4 hectares of land per peasant household. It is worth noting that half of the abovementioned 810,000 hectares had already been distributed on a temporary basis before the land reform proper.[5]

This result had been achieved at considerable human cost, however. In order to carry out this reform, the Central Land Reform Committee (whose chairman was Pham Van Dong, Vice Premier of the DRV, and vice-chairmen were the VWP's General Secretary Truong Chinh, Minister of Agriculture Nghiem Xuan Yem, and Central Committee member and Vice-Minister of Agriculture Ho Viet Thang) had had recourse to "an anarchic campaign of terror"[6] which had taken the lives of 15,000 innocent people. This figure was extracted from a top secret report written by the Party Committee of the Ministry of Public Security and addressed to the Central Committee in 1956 which this writer discovered in the Archives of the Party Central Committee in Hanoi in 1961.[7] However, some veteran Party members who had participated in the land reform campaign told this writer that the above-mentioned figure of innocent victims was certainly underestimated. It is worth noting that this figure concerned only the innocent victims. The total number of people who were executed during the land reform exercise was definitely much higher. To this, one has to add a great number of people who were unjustly imprisoned,[8] forced to commit suicide because of fear, anger or humiliation, or became insane. Oh, Peasants! What a lot of crimes (not "errors") the Party has committed in your name!

After thirty years, the scars left by the "frightening way in which Land Reform was carried out"[9] still remain in the memory of the northern peasants. Even as recently as 1985, an Overseas Vietnamese living in France who made a trip to his native village still heard senior villagers talking about the "red terror" during the land reform "with quavers in their voice".[10]

In October 1956, the Party chose General Vo Nguyen Giap, the prestigious victor at Dien Bien Phu, as spokesman for its public *mea culpa* and the correction of land reform "errors" which had been "serious, widespread and prolonged".[11]

Western writers on land reform "errors" have usually mentioned only General Giap's report[12] following the famous Tenth Plenum of the VWP Central Committee, but overlooked the very interesting internal report delivered by Dr Nguyen Manh Tuong, an honest and courageous intellectual, at the National Congress of the "Fatherland Front" in Hanoi on 30 October 1956, in which he inspected the land reform "errors" from a politico-juridical point of view. According to the latter, the fundamental causes of "errors" were the haziness of the Party's conception of "Friends" and "Foes", the complete contempt for legality and juridical expertise and, above all, the lack of democracy.[13]

But let us go back to General Giap. In a passage worth citing at length, he revealed:

> Because we [the VWP's leadership] did not make investigations, we thought the proportion of landlords in our society was rather high; . . . we committed many serious errors in the demarcation of classes [which was very hazy in any case]. It was not just that in many areas some rich peasants or upper middle peasants were classified as landlords; there were even places where poor

peasants and agricultural laborers were classified as landlords. ...[14]

Because all landlords were mechanically considered enemies, in some places Resistance landlords were also considered enemies; because we did not distinguish the anti-Resistance activities of a small number of diehard landlords, the situation became tense ... the enemy was overestimated, and it was thought that there were enemies everywhere. When suppressing [enemies], we emphasized determination but did not emphasize caution..... The landlord class, considered as a class ... must be overthrown. But looking closely at the political attitude of each individual landlord, [we see that] there are a number of small and medium landlords who, although economically they exploit by feudal means,[15] politically have a certain degree of nationalist spirit.... We must discriminate in our treatment of each type of landlord [but in fact the Party did not] ... The policy of suppressing sabotage was incorrectly applied, and this further widened the area of struggle (i.e., repression);[16] and, as a result, many innocent people were classified as reactionaries, were arrested, punished (*xu tri*), kept under formal surveillance (*quan che*), besieged and completely isolated (*bao vay*) ... [Giap should have added also: executed] . ... [In the Party], aside from aware workers [there are also] outstanding elements of the peasantry, the petty bourgeoisie, and the revolutionary intellectuals, including some from bourgeois and landlord backgrounds who have participated enthusiastically in the revolution.... We must attach appropriate importance to class stand but absolutely avoid falling into "class-ism" and thinking that [social] class stand determines [or should determine] everything (...)

... Because we investigated too little and overemphasized "class-ism" in regard to the former chapters of the Party, the government, and the various mass organizations, we often slighted or denied achievements in the Resistance, and only attached importance, in a distorted fashion, to achievements in the anti-landlord struggle during the mass mobilization for rent reduction and the land reform. As a result we did not correctly evaluate the former organizations; there were even places where we thought that ... enemy organizations had infiltrated our own organizations. Therefore, the deeper our attacks on the enemy went, the more they were misdirected; when we attacked the landlord despots and saboteurs, we attacked within our own ranks at the same time. A number of Party members, cadres and families which had worked with the Resistance and the revolution as well as many good [peasant] association members . . . were regarded as reactionaries, kept under formal surveillance, besieged, or wrongly punished.[17] The errors in the reorganization of the [Party rural] chapters were the most serious committed in the whole land reform.[18]

The above quotation clearly shows that the Party's policy *per se* was not flawless, particularly its "class-ism" which, as a Western observer rightly pointed out, "was one of the fundamental causes of the land reform errors".[19] For instance, according to this stand, "any action of the landlords [and so-called landlords] that could by any stretch of the imagination be attributed to counter revolutionary sentiments was so attributed".[20] In contrast, "the fact that a person was a poor peasant, and thus inherently good, was considered adequate grounds for making that person a cadre in the absence of any demonstrated ability to perform the functions of the position in question".[21] Le Van Luong, a Party leader in charge of the reorganization of the Party rural chapters during the land reform, had said explicitly that it was all right to promote labourers and poor peasants to posts for which they were not fully qualified, if they had the proper spirit![22]

At the time that "leftist errors" were actually being committed, the VWP's Seventh Plenum (March 1955) stressed, however, that the implementation of the land reform had been too moderate, too "rightist",[23] and resolved to " . . . oppose rightism and leftism, but opposing rightism is basic". This Party stand ineluctably spurred a campaign against supposed rightist errors that eventually led to an immense wave of catastrophic leftist excesses. Moreover, Truong Chinh and Ho Viet Thang had also told land reform cadres that they should not worry about the poor peasants committing leftist excesses if given a free hand![24] The Ninth Plenum of the VWP Central Committee (April 1956) did not alter this "leftist" line either. As late as May 1956, the Party's newspaper was still criticizing many land reform cadres for "leaning to the right".[25]

All these facts indisputably show that, contrary to the assertion of the communiqué of the Tenth Central Committee Plenum, many important aspects of the Party's policy were well and truly incorrect. Moreover, how could the Party's policy be "correct" when the Central Committee itself acknowledged that "there were shortcomings in the thinking of [its] leadership",[26] or as Giap said, that "there were leftist errors with regard to [its] ideology"?[27] In addition to the Party's policy "errors" there were also excesses stemming from the implementation of the "Central Land Reform Committee" itself and its local chapters, which were anyway, according to Truong Chinh himself, "under the Party's leadership"[28]

What were the principal "leftist errors" in the implementation of land reform? According to Giap:

> .... It was correct to emphasize decisively overthrowing the landlord class, but the error lay in attacking [it] ... without carrying out the policy of differentiation — in not having consideration for the families of landlords who had worked with the revolution and for the families of landlords whose children had served as soldiers or cadres...
> ... While carrying out attacks on the enemy, we overemphasized attacking decisively..., and did not emphasize the necessity for caution and for avoiding unjust punishment of innocent people; therefore we expanded the area of attack... , and made widespread use of excessive repressive measures...[29]

Mechanically transplanting the Chinese experience into Vietnam, the leadership of the "Central Land Reform Committee" ordered land reform cadres to find at all costs *"four to five per cent"* of landlord households in *every* commune.[30] In fact, after the correction of "errors", more than half the people who had been wrongly classified as landlords were reclassified.[31] But meanwhile a sizeable number of them — who had been described as "landlord despots"[32] — had been, alas, sentenced to death by the so-called "People's Tribunals"[33] and already executed. The execution of these landlords was regarded as "a good method to enhance the power and influence of the peasants".[34]

At that time, the "Central Land Reform Committee" put out the unbelievable — but true! — watchword:

> Let TEN innocent people die rather than let ONE enemy escape (*Tha Chet Muoi Nguoi Oan Con Hon De Sot Mot Dich*).[35]

The Party's newspaper acknowledged afterwards that most people who were condemned during the land reform (as "landlord despots", and "reactionaries", etc.) had been wrongly condemned.[36] Concerning the "leftist errors", Giap also said:

> ... In carrying out land reform in areas with many religious people, we ... violated the policy of respecting the people's freedom of religion and worship ...
> After peace was reestablished, [in 1954] policy emphasized restricting the area of struggle [read "repression"] and using more administrative methods but in practice attack and struggle spread broadly. Policy forbade methods of "vigorous interrogation" to extract confessions (*truy buc*) but in practice these methods became widespread.[37]

From the preceding pages it is crystal clear that the above-mentioned leftist "errors" (in fact, crimes) stem from *both* the incorrectness of the Party's policy *and* its implementation by the land reform committees at various echelons. The "subtle" distinction between the Party's policy — which was supposed to be "basically correct" — and its implementation, which was acknowledged as incorrect, had one specific purpose: to let it be understood that the Party was infallible (*Infaillibilité oblige!*).

The fact remains that *"leftism"* has represented since then *a predominant aspect of the Party's economic policy* which wrought havoc in the Vietnamese economy both before and after the reunification of the country in 1975.

Second Issue

Were the "Communist leaders candid about their ... intentions"[38] in designing the land reform? Were they really "not engaged in some Machiavellian scheme"?

To answer this question, it might be opportune to refer to what a Party economist at the Institute of Economy in Hanoi had to say. In the Party's perceptions, he emphasized, Vietnamese agriculture had to go through *three stages* during its development process: *first*, "to give land to the tillers" through a radical land reform scheme, thus satisfying the long-time desire of the small peasants for possession of land. This first step was, however, regarded by the Party from the very beginning only as a *temporary* measure. *Secondly*, to transform the small-scale individual peasant economy into a large-scale socialist agriculture based on the collective ownership of the peasant-cooperators. And *thirdly*, to transform socialist agriculture based on the collective ownership of the peasants into one based on the ownership of the whole, that is, the land is ultimately nationalized.[39] Indeed, according to Article 19 of the 1980 Constitution of the Socialist Republic of Vietnam "the lands, forests, etc. . . . are under ownership of the entire people" and, therefore, the peasant-cooperators have only the usufruct of the land (see Article 20 of the same Constitution).

In other words, the Party gives the land to the peasants *once* from one hand and takes it back *twice* with the other hand (indirectly through collectivization, and then directly through nationalization)! (This might probably serve as a lesson for the peasants in the Third World — in the Philippines, for instance.)

Machiavellian or not, the fact remains that the Party has managed, through the lure of land reform, galvanized the peasant-porters (*dan cong*) and the peasant-soldiers to heroically march to the front during the war against the French, "contribu[ting]", in Giap's words "a decisive part to the historic victory of Dien Bien Phu",[40] thus paving the way for the Party to return to power in 1954.[41]

At that time it was never suspected that the Party leadership had already a master plan of collectivization ready for use!

* * *

With the re-establishment of peace following the Geneva Accords in 1954, North Vietnam reportedly entered the stage of "socialist revolution".[42] This, according to Secretary-General Le Duan, included two fundamental tasks which were closely interrelated, namely, "socialist transformation" and "socialist construction". In the first period of socialist revolution, the VWP took "socialist transformation as the central task, while [also] taking the first step in socialist construction".[43]

At its Fourteenth Central Committee Plenum (November 1958), the Party regarded agricultural co-operativization (or collectivization) as the main link in the whole process of socialist transformation.[44]

Instead of examining in detail the collectivization drive here[45] it will be more appropriate to focus on the analysis of the most important aspects of the Party's policy in this domain, and its impact on agricultural production.

One of the characteristics of co-operativization in North Vietnam was that it preceded agricultural mechanization. "We must lead the peasantry and agriculture immediately to socialism without waiting for a developed industry though we know very well that without the strong impact of industry, agriculture cannot achieve large scale production and new relations of ... production cannot be consolidated", said Le Duan. And he continued:

> With socialist collective ownership, with the reorganization of labour on a large scale to carry out water-control work, soil improvement..., with the application of the achievements of the green revolution and limited help from industry, we are fully capable of taking our country's agriculture ... on the path of large-scale socialist production, at a time when industry is still built up....
>
> ... To start the process of socialist construction by establishing the system of collective ownership [in agriculture] ... is a peculiarity of the process of our country's historical development.[46]

In spite of the fact that the VWP loudly swears loyalty to Marxism-Leninism, the abovementioned stand undoubtedly runs counter to the precepts of K. Marx and V.I. Lenin,[47] for both of them made it clear that (according to Le Duan himself), "without a [large] industry, the cooperatives could not be consolidated".[48] However, the Party's stand was quite in accordance with Mao Zedong's standpoint which argued that "collectivization could partially substitute for [agricultural mechanization] in the short-run by maximizing the output and productivity potential of traditional inputs and technology".[49]

It is worth noting that recently, a Party economist indirectly questioned the correctness of the collectivization before mechanization policy, by emphasizing that Lenin's viewpoint was that "the development of industry . . . is the most important prerequisite of building socialism in the countryside".[50] He also noticed that twenty-four years after the "basic completion" of co-operativization (1960), the majority of the agricultural producers' co-operatives in North Vietnam still had only rudimentary means of production (ploughs and draught animals), and agriculture continues to remain backward for it has always been experiencing a dramatic shortage of tractors and other industrial inputs. Thus, he said, the "socialization of production in agriculture" has so far been carried out "only for form's sake".[51]

In the absence of an adequate industrial base, the Party should have carried out co-operativization cautiously and slowly, but, in fact, it did not! According to the same economist, the Party should have followed Lenin's recommendation concerning the socialist transformation in the countryside by starting first with the formation of co-operatives centring on *trade and credit*, which would create the basis for peasant support and participation in proto-socialist institutions and eventually for basic cultural and economic changes which would facilitate the gradual setting up of co-operatives in the domain of *production* later on. In fact, a number of trading and credit co-operatives were set up in North Vietnam before the collectivization drive but they had little scope and impact on agricultural production.[52]

Like in China under Mao (with the exception of the "people's communes"), the co-operativization process in North Vietnam has gone through three stages: the temporary and permanent mutual-aid (or labour exchange) teams, the elementary (or low-level, that is, semi-socialist) co-operatives, and the advanced (or high-level, that is, socialist) co-operatives. The mutual-aid teams (MAT) were regarded by the Party as organizational frameworks which allowed individual peasants to help each other in resolving immediate problems in production (water conservancy, lack of labour and draft power, shortage of farm implements, and so forth) while keeping intact the individual ownership of the means of production. They were also considered a transitional form of organization — which allegedly contained "sprouts of socialism"

— leading to the setting up of agricultural producers' co-operatives later on.

After 1953, the MATs flourished alongside land reform. In March 1956, a national conference called for the development of MATs as the main force for promoting agricultural production. After the discovery of "errors" during the land reform exercise, however, the number of MATs declined sharply. Then, following a resolution issued by the VWP in September 1957 on the restoration and development of MATs, a major drive to develop MATs occurred during the 1957 tenth-month harvest. A further drive was launched during the 1958 tenth-month harvest.

As a consequence, 65.7 per cent of the peasant households were included in the MATs by the end of 1958, compared to only 21.9 per cent by the end of 1957.[53] However, the then Secretary-General Truong Chinh acknowledged that "the mobilization of the masses to take part in the [mutual aid] teams usually had the character of pressure".[54] General Giap also "admit[ted] that the labour exchange movement has not imprinted itself deeply on the [rural] masses . . . " by the end of 1958.[55]

In spite of that, the VWP decided at its Fourteenth and Sixteenth Central Committee Plena (held in November 1958 and April 1959 respectively) to rapidly switch over from the MATs to the elementary agricultural producers' co-operatives (EAPCs).[56] In the latter, the co-operators pooled and used collectively their land, draught animals and large farm implements while still owning them privately; they were paid for their work and also a rent for their property investment.[57]

In a major speech at the National Assembly in May 1959 — which followed the Sixteenth Plenum — Truong Chinh showed dissatisfaction with the slow progress of co-operativization, criticized those who stressed that "the [co-operativization] movement must be proceeded cautiously", and called for a "closer guidance of the movement".[58]

In late 1958, 4,800 co-operatives were formed comprising only 4.7 per cent of peasant households. But by the end of June 1959, there were 16,200 co-operatives including 21.3 per cent of peasant families. Then, following an important agricultural conference held in September 1959, a further acceleration of collectivization in the last three months of 1959 was launched. By the end of 1959 there were reportedly 28,775 co-operatives (overwhelmingly EAPCs) which included more than 45 per cent of all peasant families[59], representing an increase of nearly ten times compared with the end of the previous year! Truong Chinh acknowledged, however, that in 1959 "in some localities [actually in many localities] the co-operatives were set up in a hurry, without a good preparation of the mind of the [rural] masses; the problems which were worrying the masses were not completely thrashed out; education in policies was not properly attended to; the professional training of the staffs of the cooperatives was not carefully undertaken . . ."[60]

In spite of that, there was little change in the scope of collectivization in the first three months of 1960, although consolidation of existing co-operatives was emphasized. In August 1960, the Secretariat of the VWP's Central Committee passed a resolution calling for the completion of elementary level co-operativization by the autumn harvest and for enrolling 70–75 per cent of all peasant households in elementary and advanced co-operatives by that time. By the end of September 1960, more than 75 per cent of peasant families were reportedly in elementary and advanced co-operatives, and the proportion rose to 85.8 per cent — of which 73.4 per cent joined the EAPCs — at the end of 1960,[61] which was substantially above the planned targets. At that time, the co-operativization process was regarded as "basically completed". Thus, during a period of only two years, the proportion of peasant households pushed into the EAPCs went from 4.7 per cent at the end of 1958 to 73.4 per cent by the end of 1960.

At the same time, there had been pressure since 1959 to switch over from the elementary to advanced agricultural producers' co-operatives (AAPCs). In the latter, land payment was eliminated, all means of production became common property and each member was paid solely according to the labour performed for the co-operative. Theoretically, an EAPC was transformed into an AAPC only when there existed at least two conditions, namely, a stabilized or higher production, and an improved management. In practice, however, this was not always so. The fact remains that by the end of 1960, about 12.4 per cent of peasant households were hurriedly pushed into the AAPCs, compared with 2.4 per cent in the previous year. This collectivization drive was heavily inspired by Mao Zedong's experience, *including* his "leftist" mistakes.[62]

In spite of the fact that the Party had proclaimed that "voluntarism" was "the most important" of the "three principles of the movement for agricultural co-operation"[63] [the two others being "mutual benefit" and "democratic management"], that one should "never compel [the middle peasants] to participate in the cooperatives",[64] in fact, the peasants were rapidly pushed into the EAPCs by a combination of subtle manoeuvres with crude coercion.

Restricted access to the free market to buy basic industrial inputs and consumer goods, on the one hand, and to sell agricultural commodities, on the other, made it very difficult, if not impossible, for the peasants to maintain their economic independence. Special privileges — such as a favoured rate of agricultural tax (a reduction of up to 40-50 per cent of the regular tax rates), cheap credit, exclusive rights to purchase industrial inputs, seeds, and basic consumer goods, entrance to higher education for children, and so forth — were offered to peasants if they joined the co-operatives. More often than not, farmers were forced to join the co-operatives, as the Party's newspaper admitted: "Some comrades and cadres have not yet understood the [principle of voluntarism] and therefore there have been commandism and coercion of peasants into [joining] the cooperatives."[65]

It would be too easy to blame the village level cadres, but they acted only under strong pressure from the district officers[66] in order to meet the high targets set with a fixed deadline, which had been sent down from above. This explains why "voluntarism" in theory actually meant coercion in practice. The divorce between the Party's proclaimed "liberal" policy in theory and its tough implementation in practice, in this case as well as in other cases which will be discussed later on, is a common phenomenon in Vietnam, and this ambiguity was (and is) deliberately fostered.

Needless to say, this forced co-operativization ran counter to Marx's and Engels' precepts which emphasized that peasants should be persuaded to join agricultural co-operatives through economic incentives and voluntarily.[67] As for Lenin, he put the point at issue well in a prescient statement: "... *coercion would ruin the whole cause*. What is required here is prolonged educational work. We have to give the peasant, who ... is a practical man and a realist, concrete examples to prove that cooperation is the best possible thing ... *Nothing is more stupid than the very idea of applying coercion in economic relations with the middle peasants*" (emphasis added).[68] He also insisted that "the transition to the new form of agriculture [that is, collectivization] may ... proceed slowly".[69]

Here, once again one can see that in practice the VWP's co-operativization policy completely contravened the recommendations of Marx, Engels and Lenin in spite of the fact that it always swears loyalty to Marxism-Leninism.

In retrospect, thirty years after the collectivization drive, the Party's journal recently acknowledged that it was a "shortcoming" at that time to "hurriedly switch over from mutual-aid teams to agricultural producers' cooperatives" in a "very short period of time".[70] This "shortcoming" was allegedly due to a "a simplistic conception of socialist transformation ... plus an over hasty and subjectivist thinking (deriving from Utopian socialism)".[71]

The journal also admitted that, in the process of setting up the agricultural producers' co-operatives, contrary to Lenin's precept, the principle of voluntarism was violated "in many places".[72] The Party's self-criticism also included the infringement of the principle of gradual transformation from elementary to advanced organizations in trying to take short cuts during the co-operativization process, and the tendency to hurriedly collectivize the draught animals.[73]

After 1960 the Party made every effort to rapidly switch over from the EAPCs to the AAPCs. The percentage of peasant households joining the EAPCs fell from 73.4 per cent in 1960 to 25.1 per cent in 1965, then to 3.6 per cent in 1970 and to 2.5 per cent in 1975 in favour of the AAPCs, the percentage of which increased dramatically from 12.4 percent in 1960 to 65 per cent in 1965, then to 91.1 per cent in 1970 and to 93.1 per cent in 1975.[74]

This overhastiness to change over from the EAPCs to the AAPCs when conditions were not yet ripe was recently regarded also as a "shortcoming".[75] Parallel to this tendency, since the Fifth Plenum of the Central Committee (Third Congress, July 1961) an effort was made to merge the initial small agricultural co-operatives into larger ones, first of the size of a hamlet (*Thon*), and later of the size of a commune (*Xa*, covering 3-4 *Thon*).[76] On the average, the number of peasant households per co-operative increased from 60 in 1960 to 136 in 1968, covering 100 hectares of land. In 1974, Le Duan suggested that the "average size of cooperatives [could] be stabilized at around 200 hectares of cultivated land, but the crops must be multiplied, so that the acreage under crops [would] be equal to some 500 hectares". "Besides", he continued, "the cooperatives [should] switch from scattered . . . production to planned production under unified direction at *district* level"[77] (emphasis added). This successive enlargement of agricultural co-operatives was also acknowledged recently as a "shortcoming".[78]

The forced co-operativization has, of course, brought about a resistance on the part of the peasants, although a non-violent one, probably because there was not a strong class of "rich peasants", and also because the people in North Vietnam have always been docile, and more or less resigned to their fate.

In the early days of co-operativization, many peasants reportedly adopted a "one foot in, one foot-out" tactic, that is, they reluctantly joined the co-operatives but at the same time were ready to withdraw from them as soon as there was a good excuse to do so.[79]

Many peasants tried to sell some of their draught animals before joining the co-operatives. It was reported that some cadres at the district and provincial levels even advised their families to do so.[80] Some of these draught animals were subsequently slaughtered, consequently reducing the already scarce draught power even further. When cadres pushed the peasants — particularly the "rich" and "middle" ones — to breaking point, they slaughtered their buffaloes,[81] and even cut down their fruit trees.

In retrospect, the Party's journal recently admitted that all the above-mentioned mistakes — euphemistically described as "shortcomings" — related to the co-operativization policy "more or less dampened the peasants' enthusiasm for work and exerted a harmful effect over agricultural production".[82] One of the important factors which did not encourage the peasants to work was the system of remuneration implemented in an AAPC.

Following the implementation of the "work-day" and the "work-points" systems in the mid-1960s, the "three-point contract" system was put into practice from 1970.[83] In the latter system, the AAPC signed contracts first with "specialized teams" for tilling, irrigation, seed selection, manuring and plant protection, then signed "three-point contracts" with the "production brigades" for the remaining jobs.

These "three-points" included contractual output, production costs, and work-points. In its turn, the "production brigade" assigned work to its members, specified the norms for each task, and fixed the number of work-points to each member accordingly. However, this "three-point contract" system had a fundamental flaw, given that the grass-root farmers were not economically motivated to work for they were not directly linked to the final product. (It was the "production brigades" and not the grass-root farmers which benefited from the crop). Therefore, little attention was paid to the quality of work, and generally the co-operative members shirked work or neglected farm work for more lucrative side-line occupations, including trading. A working day at that time amounted to only 4-5 hours on the average!

Besides, as an agricultural economist wrote, "the average value of work days (in an AAPC) reached only about 0.5 *Dong*, of which food grain represented barely 1 kilogram.... Consequently, the co-operative member's life experienced many difficulties.... Obviously, with such an amount of money and food grain for a work day,... [he could not meet the basic needs] of his family".[84] Recently, the Party's journal acknowledged that the above-mentioned work points system was a "too advanced form of management compared with the low level of the productive forces", and that it "clearly dampened the enthusiasm for work of the collectivized peasants".[85]

All this explains why the co-operative members devoted more attention to their family plot than to the co-operatives. The Party's newspaper complained, for instance, in this respect that "although the crop was ripe, a number of cooperative members continued to busy themselves with their trade or with planting vegetables or their [family] plots or land. Cadres were unable to mobilise many people to go harvesting".[86]

Why? Simply because the family plot — which represented only 5 per cent of the collective property granted to the co-operative member as an usufruct — generated some 51.8 per cent of his total income in 1965 and 54.3 per cent in 1975, whereas 95 per cent of the co-operative's property brought him only 39.2 per cent and 34.6 per cent respectively.[87] Faced with the situation in which even "during times of pressure [such as harvest time], many cooperatives could mobilize only 70% to 75% of their [members] who worked with low efficiency",[88] many AAPCs, particularly in the Vinh Phu province, thought of a way out by allowing their production brigades to subsequently sign "the three-point contracts" with individual peasant households, named "contracts with households" (*Khoan Ho*).

By subcontracting land and other production means to households, they hoped to encourage their members to work harder, for their reward was directly related to the result of their work. But these "contracts with households" were severely condemned by the Party's chief ideologue, Truong Chinh, in November 1968 in these terms:

> [The] contracts with households are in reality a return to the individualistic way of working. They destroy the meaning of agricultural cooperatives and turning them into a mere form.

He continued:

> The idea that 'any method of production that increases the social product is acceptable', is not the view of ... the Party. Indeed, in the agriculture of the North today there are only two production formulae: collective production and individual production. The former moves toward socialism .... The latter creates an economy of small commodity production. This economy, every day and every hour, gives rise to capitalism .... This is the main reason why we have to continue to reform the relations of production in agriculture.[89]

Truong Chinh's stand was adopted as official Party policy at that time, and for the following ten years household subcontracting was ideologically taboo, a position which strikingly resembled the Maoist stand on the same controversy in China in 1961.[90] The Party consequently clamped down on the practice in Vinh Phu province and dismissed its provincial Party committee's Secretary.

However, more than ten years later, with the attempts at economic reform in 1979, the "contract with households" system was, out of necessity, taken up again, slightly modified and then applied nation-wide from 1981. Had this initiative not been clamped down in 1968, the agricultural situation in North Vietnam would certainly have been much better since then.

One of the proclaimed goals of collectivization was that it would result in higher productivity and production through better utilization of existing techniques and the application of new techniques. In other words, co-operativization would *ipso facto* "clear the way for the development of the productive forces" in agriculture.[91] "With the change of relations of production [that is, collectivization], with cooperation in labour", said Truong Chinh, "... our peasants are not only able to increase production but also apply the advanced experiences of the brother countries ..., particularly the experiences of China in improving farming techniques".[92] As for Le Duan, he even asserted at a conference on crop production in September 1959 that "the Chinese Revolution has set a good example: with determination and diligence, with or without modern tractors, the peasants [could] still increase the yield [total yield of field with two harvests] to 10 tons of paddy per hectare".[93]

What was the impact of the above-mentioned policy on agricultural production? North Vietnam's agricultural production during the 1958–75 period is presented in Table 1.1. The official data — which for various reasons should be used with caution[94] — shows that, with the exception of 1959, a year of very favourable climatic conditions, the average paddy (husked rice) yield remained below the level of 1958 (2.04 tons)[95] for twelve consecutive years; however, between 1972 (2.24 tons per hectare) and 1975 (2.12 tons), it exceeded the level of 1958, but only marginally. From 1958 to 1975, that is, during seventeen years of actual co-operativization, the average paddy yield increased by only 3.9 per cent. The yearly total paddy yield on two-crop land also generally remained below 5 tons per hectare during the whole period 1958–75, with the exception of 1974 (5.17 tons),[96] whereas the target set by Le Duan in 1959 was 10 tons per hectare!

Thus, *paddy production* remained *below* the 1958 level (4.58 millions) during the whole period of 1958–75, with the exception

TABLE 1.1
North Vietnam's Agricultural Production, 1958–75

	1958	1959	1960	1961	1962	1963	1964	1965	1966
Paddy Production (m. tons)	4.58	5.19	4.18	4.39	4.39	4.11	4.43	4.55	4.13
Paddy per capita (kg)[a]	304	335	261	281	256	232	243	240	212
Subsidiary Production (paddy equiv. m. tons)[b]	0.38	0.57	0.52	0.81	0.79	0.90	1.09	1.02	0.97
Total Staples Production (m. tons)	4.96	5.77	4.70	5.20	5.17	5.01	5.52	5.56	5.10
Total Staples per capita (kg)	331	372	293	314	301	283	302	294	262
Paddy Yield (100 kg/ha) (average harvest)	20.4	22.9	18.4	18.4	18.2	17.4	18.2	19.0	17.3
Population (million)	15		16.10					18.63	

TABLE 1.1 (cont'd)
North Vietnam's Agricultural Production, 1958–75

	1967	1968	1969	1970	1971	1972	1973	1974	1975
Paddy Production (m. tons)	4.29	3.71	3.91	4.46	4.12	4.92	4.47	5.49	4.78
Paddy per capita (kg)[a]	214	179	184	204	184	215	190	228	194
Subsidiary Production (paddy equiv. m. tons)[b]	1.11	0.92	0.80	0.82	0.80	0.82	0.72	0.79	0.72
Total Staples Production (m. tons)	5.40	4.63	4.71	5.28	4.92	5.74	5.19	6.28	5.50
Total Staples per capita (kg)	269	224	222	242	220	250	221	261	224
Paddy Yield (100 kg/ha) (average harvest)	19.6	17.8	18.2	20.2	19.9	22.4	21.4	24.2	21.2
Population (million)		20.21				22.70		23.94	24.55

[a] One kg of paddy (unhusked rice) gives an average of 0.65 kg of rice after husking.

[b] Subsidiary crop production data were converted to paddy data at the ratio of: 1 kg paddy = 0.7 kg maize = 2.3 kg sweet potatoes = 2.3 kg manioc = 0.5 kg soybeans (*So Lieu Thong Ke, 1960–63* [Hanoi, 1963], p. 64).

SOURCES: *Tinh Hinh Phat Trien Kinh Te Va Van Hoa Mien Bac Xa Hoi Chu Nghia Viet Nam 1960–75* (Hanoi: Tong Cuc Thong Ke, 1978), pp. 117–20 (rounded up figures) or calculated on the basis of data therein; and official data cited in A. Vickerman, *The Fate of The Peasantry, Premature Transition to Socialism in the DRV*, Monograph series No. 28 (Yale University Southeast Asia Studies, 1986), p. 279.

of 1959 (5.19 million tons), 1972 (4.92 million tons), 1974 (5.49 million tons), and 1975 (4.78 million tons). It varied between 3.71 million tons in 1968 and 5.49 million tons in 1974.

Compared with 1958, paddy production increased by only 4.36 per cent whereas the population grew by 63.6 per cent in 1975. If one takes into consideration the subsidiary crops also, that is, maize, sweet potatoes, manioc, soybeans, and so forth) one can see that the total staples production (or total crop production, that is, paddy plus subsidiary crops) fluctuated between 4.63 million tons (1968) and 6.28 million tons (1974, a year of good harvest) during the 1958–75 period. *Compared with 1958, the total staples production increased by only 10.9 per cent whereas the population was augmented by 63.6 per cent in 1975!* During the period under review, the total staples production per capita had a tendency to decline, and, with the exception of 1959, could never have caught up with the level of 1958 (331 kg). In 1975, it amounted to only 224 kg(!), far below the minimum level of subsistence (officially estimated at 300 kg).

In a directive issued by the Central Committee at the time of the "Conference on the Reorganization of Agricultural Production" in Thai Binh province in August 1974, the Party made an assessment of the situation in these terms: "The productivity of many products has not increased, or has increased very slowly; the cultivated area has decreased; agricultural production has failed to meet the people's demand for grain and foodstuff, and to provide sufficient raw materials for industry."[97]

Why, in spite of the Party's all-out effort to "achieve a stable solution of the food problem"[98] did the total crop production in general and the paddy production in particular increase only marginally during the 1958–75 period, and in any case at a tempo which was very far behind population growth? How was it that, "by the mid-1970s, North Vietnam's agriculture fell into recession", "a reality that no one can deny"?[99]

There were many reasons but the most important ones were: the misallocation of state investments at the expense of agriculture, the unequal exchange between the state and the peasants, the disincentives ensuing from the "three-point contract" system, and the deliberate limitation of the household economy.

The state investments in "agriculture and silviculture" were far less than those made in "industry" during the 1960–75 period, as seen in Table 1.2.

As a share of the total, budgetary investments in "agriculture and silviculture" went down from 15.2 per cent in 1958[100] to 10.3 per cent in 1960, then climbed up to 17.9 per cent in 1965, and then went down again to 15.6 per cent in 1975. On the whole, it fluctuated between 10.3 per cent (1960) and 17.9 per cent (1965) during the 1960–75 period. In other words, the share of "agriculture and silviculture" in the total amount of state investments is obviously too small compared with the share of industry (in the broad sense of the word, that is, "industry" *plus* "capital construction" or building industry) in a predominantly agricultural country like North Vietnam: 10.3 per cent compared with 46 per cent in 1960; and 15.6 and 42.9 per cent respectively in 1975. This misallocation of state investments was one of the principal errors of North Vietnam's strategy of economic development during the period in question, an error which seriously signed away its economic prospect. This error — which ensued from the dogma of the priority given to heavy industry at the expense of agriculture — was also recently acknowledged by the Party's theoretical and political journal itself.[101]

Besides, if one inspects the structure of state investments in agriculture (excluding forestry), one can see that an important part of these investments went to "state farms and other installations", even at the expense of "irrigation", which was of major significance for the agricultural co-operatives: in 1960, 52.8 per cent went to the former whereas only 23.4 per cent went to the latter; in 1975 their share represented 32.7 per cent and 28.3 per cent respectively.[102]

The Party's newspaper admitted in 1974 that "in many [State farms] there [were] more personnel, more machines and materials supply, and more State investments than in the pre-war period [prior to 1965]; yet there [had] not been a production increase, labour output [had] decreased, and there [had] been losses in production";[103] their productivity was even below that of the pre-war level.[104]

Another reason which explained the stagnation and recession in agriculture was the unequal exchange between the State trading

TABLE 1.2
State (or Budgetary) Investments by Sectors of the National Economy (1960–75)
(In million dong and per cent)

	1960 A	1960 B	1965 A	1965 B	1974 A	1974 B	1975 A	1975 B
Total Amount of Investments of which:	669.7	100	959.1	100	1,822.7	100	2,049.8	100
Industry	256.7	38.3	363.9	37.9	641.6	35.2	761.7	37.2
Capital Construction (that is, Building Industry)	51.6	7.7	23.2	2.4	140.5	7.7	116.2	5.7
Agriculture & Silviculture, etc.	69.0	10.3	171.6	17.9	321.6	17.6	319.5	15.6

A = million dong
B = percentage of the total
SOURCE: *Tinh Hinh Phat Trien Kinh Te Va Van Hoa Mien Bac Xa Hoi Chu Nghia Vietnam 1960–75* (Hanoi: Tong Cuc Thong Ke, 1978), pp. 97–98.

agencies and co-operative members to the detriment of the latter in the case of "two-way contract purchases" for quota procurement.[105] The question of urban-rural terms of trade, that is, the difference between State-prescribed prices for agricultural goods and official retail prices of industrial inputs and consumer goods always constituted a thorny issue in the economic relations between the peasants and the State.[106] On the whole, the State had a tendency to buy agricultural goods cheaply from the former and sell high-priced industrial goods (industrial inputs as well as consumer goods) to them. Recently, a Party economist acknowledged that "the 'price scissors' between agricultural prices and industrial prices increasingly widened to the detriment of the peasants", and he rightly emphazied that "this phenomenon exerted harmful influence on the development of agricultural production".[107]

In addition to the "price scissors", the acute shortage of industrial consumer goods — due chiefly to a deliberate negligence of light industry in favour of heavy industry — also contributed to dampen the peasants' motivation for increasing agricultural production.

As regards the "three-point contract" system — which "did not create a driving force for [agricultural] production"[108] and did not prompt the grass-roots co-operative members to work — it has already been dealt with in the preceding pages. Concerning the limitation of the household economy — under the pretext of allowing more labour to be devoted to "brigade production" of the co-operative which, if better organized, would yield production and productivity increases, and limiting intra-peasantry differentiation which allegedly would lead inexorably to "the appearance of the spontaneous tendency to capitalist development"[109] — suffice it to say that, as in China under Mao,[110] this policy, perceived by the Party as a means of consolidating the agricultural co-operatives, led, however, to a stagnation of agricultural production, and the peasant's lack of enthusiasm for work, while at the same time it became harder to consolidate the co-operatives.

Contemporary reports generally emphasized the limited mobilization of labour by agricultural co-operatives, the low labour productivity and derisory value of work-days, and hence the lack of production incentives.[111] Vice-Premier Hoang Anh reluctantly acknowledged that "many cooperative members [had] been attracted to household economic activities and the free market; and [consequently] the management of the cooperatives ... [had] encountered more difficulties".[112] The Party's newspaper even admitted that "in many localities, cooperatives [were] declining; some of them [had] collapsed or [were] only carrying out activities for form's sake".[113]

From the preceding pages, it is clear that North Vietnam's agricultural policy during the period in question — regarding agrarian reform as well as co-operativitization — was greatly inspired by Maoist thought and practice (with the exception of people's communes), including his "leftist mistakes".[114] As far as co-operativization was concerned, the "leftist mistakes" mainly consisted in, besides the blatant under-investment in agriculture, the forced pace of collectivization, overhastiness in switching over from mutual-aid teams to elementary producers' co-operatives, and then to advanced producers' co-operatives, rapid enlargement of co-operatives, work-points system of remuneration, unequal exchange between the State and the peasants, and limitation of the household economy.

Like the Maoist collectivization, North Vietnam's co-operativization led to a crisis of agriculture and the peasants' lack of enthusiasm for work, mainly because the Party expected too much from a revolutionary change in the "relations of production" [including not only the system of ownership but also the system of management and income distribution].[115] It did not realize at all that "a change in the relations of production much too fast for the growth of productive forces would *impede or even undermine* the latter" (emphasis added).[116]

Recently, a Vietnamese economist admitted that the big gap between the "advanced relations of production" and the "backward productive forces" was "the chief error" of collectivization which seriously held back agricultural production in North Vietnam.[117]

Such was the real situation of collectivized agriculture in this country by the mid-1970s. Some Western scholars, however, continued to assert that "the [North] Vietnamese collectivization process represent[ed] the most successful in the socialist third world"![118]

Industry and Handicrafts

Parallel to collectivization, the Party also advocated the stepping up of the "socialist transformation of private industry and commerce" at its Fourteenth and Sixteenth Central Committee Plena held respectively in November 1958 and April 1959.[119]

In view of North Vietnam's economic backwardness, the Party decided to make use of the national bourgeoisie for a certain period of time in order to boost the country's economy. That was why it advocated a policy of "gradually utilizing, restricting and transforming" it.[120] This policy of "peaceful transformation of private industry and commerce" was in accordance with Marx's and Engels' precepts which pointed out that, under given conditions, the proletariat might adopt a policy of "redeeming" the means of production of the bourgeoisie. Lenin also proposed to "buy off" a section of the bourgeoisie through "state capitalism" after the Russian October Revolution. From Lenin's viewpoint, there were two kinds of "state capitalism", depending on the ruling class: bourgeoisie or proletariat.[121]

In the second case, which was also the Vietnamese case, state capitalism meant a "capitalism which we [the "workers' state"] shall be able to restrict, the limits of which we shall be able to fix".[122] And this concept was made more explicit by Mao Zedong when he defined "state capitalism" as "a capitalist economy which for the most part is under the control of the People's Government and which is linked with the state-owned socialist economy in various forms.... It is a particular kind of capitalist economy.... It exists not chiefly to make profits for the capitalists but to meet the needs of the people and the State. [It] takes on a *socialist character* to a very great extent and benefits the workers and the State" [emphasis added].[123]

Like in China in the 1950s[124] "state capitalism" in North Vietnam comprised two forms. The *elementary form* consisted of private enterprises working with raw materials supplied by the government and selling the manufactured goods to the latter. (In this way the State managed to control the circulation of their products, cut off their ties with the market and, to some extent, direct their production; in other words, their economy was controlled and directed by the State). The *advanced form* consisted of "joint state-private enterprises" in which the means of production and capital funds were transferred to the State, and the former owners received for their capital a fixed "interest" rate of 6-8 per cent per annum for industrial enterprises. (This so-called "interest" was, in fact, a redemption of the former owners' assets, which was paid in instalments over a certain period of time. Generally, the value of these assets was greatly reduced by the State at the time of their evaluation when the change-over to "joint state-private enterprises" was effected.)

Such "joint state-private enterprises", except for the fact that the former owners were still drawing a fixed "interest", were not much different from state-owned enterprises. They were regarded as "semi-nationalized" and "basically socialist in nature". When the payment of fixed "interest" to the former capitalists was terminated a few years later, all "joint state-private enterprises" were incorporated into the state sector, that is, they became fully nationalized. Ultimately, the *raison d'etre* of the "peaceful transformation of the private industry and commerce" through various forms of "state capitalism" was to lure private enterprises into continuing their business in the course of "socialist transformation" instead of suspending operations or slashing production.

It is worth noting that in North Vietnam, the elementary form of "state capitalism" had already been implemented during the 1955–57 period, that is, before the campaign against the national bourgeoisie had officially started. Then, from October 1958 onwards, the Party launched a drive for an accelerated reconversion of private industrial (and commercial) enterprises into "joint state-private enterprises", particularly from mid-1959 until the end of 1960. By that time it was reported that the "Socialist transformation" of private industry (and commerce) was generally completed: "783 households of capitalist manufacturers (or 100%), [and] 826 households of capitalist traders (97.1%) . . . subjected to transformation have taken the socialist path".[125]

At that time, the Party, which was greatly inspired by Mao Zedong's thought in this domain, perceived that it was necessary to "abolish capitalist relations of production"[126] as soon as possible for "private capitalist economy and national bourgeoisie are the [targets] of socialist revolution" in spite of the fact that the capitalist sector could still play a positive role, given that the level of "productive forces" was still very low in the country. However, in retrospect, it recently acknowledged that this policy was a "mistake". Drawing the lessons of the "past mistakes", in an important Resolution issued in July 1988, the Party's Politburo asserted that in general "it is necessary to vigorously and unlimitedly develop the . . . small-scale business, and private capitalist businesses in the urban as well as in the rural areas . . . ."[127]

The fact remains that the overhasty elimination of the capitalist sector at that time considerably delayed North Vietnam's economic development for a long time.

* * *

Parallel to the socialist reconversion of private industry and trade, the Party Central Committee also advocated the "co-operativization of handicraft" at its Fourteenth Plenum (1959). Generally, the handicraft sector produced the major part of consumer goods and farm implements, while it absorbed the surplus labour from the agricultural sector. In 1957, it reportedly produced 64.7 per cent of consumer goods, 13 per cent of exported goods, and accounted for 63.7 per cent of gross output value in the manufacturing sector,[128] and hence its crucial importance in the North Vietnamese economy.

Three forms of co-operativization under the direction of the state sector were envisaged: (1) "production teams"; (2) "supply and marketing co-operatives" which supplied raw materials to and purchased products from its members. These co-operatives detached handicraftsmen from private commercial capital and attached them to the state sector, and in this sense they were regarded as "semi-socialist" in nature; and (3) "handicraft producers' co-operatives" in which private property was transformed into collective property, with payment to members according to their work and the collective income. Adopting the principle of equal pay for equal work, these co-operatives became "collective enterprises of a socialist nature".

The drive towards handicraft co-operativization started from late 1958 onwards and was reportedly "basically completed" at the end of 1960. By that time it was reported that "over 260,000 artisans have joined the cooperatives, or 87.9% of those submitted to [socialist] transformation".[129] However, in retrospect, the Party acknowledged that "there were many shortcomings"[130] in this overhasty co-operativization process. And one of these "shortcomings" was that the Party let a number of renowned traditional branches of handicraft gradually disappear.

It is worth noting that the blind emphasis put on concentrated production and unified management at that time ran counter to the scattered and localized nature of the handicraft sector. As a result, the people's lives were adversely affected as lack of competition in the market brought about a drop in quality and variety in the handicraft products. But, the principal mistake was the Party's dogmatic perception according to which handicraftsmen, like peasants, "[had] more or less the spontaneous tendency to capitalism", hence the necessity to rapidly "restrict and eliminate" this tendency[131] by forcibly and hastily pushing them into various forms of co-operatives and eliminating the individual producers.[132]

In retrospect, the Party's Politburo recently admitted that "erroneous viewpoints [on this score]... have at times and in some places, weakened the productive forces and resulted in the disappearance of many branches of artistic handicrafts ..."[133]

Generally speaking, forced socialist transformation of industry and the handicraft sector during the period under review undoubtedly delayed the development of North Vietnam's potential for production for at least some decades.

* * *

Together with the completion of the "socialist transformation" of private capitalism and the handicraft sector, the Party carried out "socialist industrialization" which began with the First Five-Year

Plan. At the Third Party Congress (September 1960), Secretary-General Le Duan emphasized that "socialist industrialization of the North consist[ed] in . . . giving priority to the rational development of heavy industry, and *at the same time* striving to develop agriculture and light industry" (emphasis added).[134] By "rational development of heavy industry", the Party meant the building up of a new material-technical base with a view to boosting agriculture and light industry on the one hand, and ensuring its own development on the other.[135]

This direction towards the systematic development of heavy industry was afterwards concretized at the Seventh Plenum of the Party Central Committee (Third Congress, June 1962) which stated specifically that North Vietnam should strive to transform itself from a backward economy into a modern one approximately within a decade![136]

In February 1970, in a speech delivered on the occasion of the fortieth anniversary of the foundation of the Party, Le Duan changed slightly the formulation of "socialist industrialization" as follows: to give priority to the rational development of heavy industry *based on* [instead of "at the same time" as stated in 1960] the growth of agriculture and light industry".[137] And he explained:

> . . . In order to build a heavy industry, there must be prerequisites to be created by agriculture and light industry. These are the labour force, consumer goods, primitive accumulation and the market . . . . Thanks to our own resources [which were in fact non-existent!], the help of the socialist countries, and international co-operaton, we can speed up primitive accumulation and solve complex problems of science and technique . . . . Right from the beginning, we can appropriate a part of the national income and labour force for the building of a heavy industry . . . . However, we must be fully conscious that heavy industry can only vigorously advance when agriculture and light industry have become its firm bases . . . . If we promote heavy industry without aiming at pushing forward agriculture and light industry, we shall, in practice, not only fail to develop heavy industry but also worsen the existing economic imbalance, create more difficulties, and check the advance of our national economy as a whole.[138]

Unfortunately, it was precisely that disastrous result which happened in reality in North Vietnam during the period under review, in spite of this rhetoric. Le Duan's rhetoric was somehow reminiscent of Mao Zedong's stand in his famous 1956 speech *"On the Ten Great Relationships"* that "while emphasis should be placed on heavy industry, special attention should be paid to the growth of agriculture and light industry".[139]

It might be useful to stress here that, contrary to some of Mao's hagiographers who construed his above-mentioned speech to be a radical departure from the Stalinist industrialization policy based on heavy industry, Mao himself pointed out that emphasis on agriculture and light industry would not be harmful to the development of heavy industry; on the contrary, the surplus from these sources could help finance heavy industry. And he even claimed that his method of developing heavy industry "[would] lay a more solid foundation for the development of heavy industry".[140]

It is worth noting that both Mao Zedong and Le Duan's viewpoints bore a great resemblance to those already advocated by Nicolai Bukharin during the Soviet industrialization debate of the 1920s who envisaged a *balanced* relationship between agriculture and industry, and viewed agriculture and light industry as the foundation for the development of heavy industry and the economy in general.[141]

However, in spite of what Le Duan had said in theory, the fact remains that in practice since 1958, heavy industry developed in a lopsided manner during the whole period under review — including the war years[142] — at the expense of agriculture and light industry, as in China under Mao.[143]

The over-emphasis on industry compared with agriculture on the one hand, and on heavy industry compared with light industry on the other, was clearly reflected in the allocation of state investments as shown in Table 1.3.

As a share of the total, state investment in industry (excluding the building industry) represented 38.3 per cent in 1960 and 37.2 per cent in 1975, whereas in agriculture (excluding forestry) they constituted only 10.3 and 13.2 per cent respectively. Within industry

TABLE 1.3
Allocation of State Investments in
Industry and Agriculture, 1960–75
(In million dong)

	1960	1965	1974	1975
Total Volume of State Investments	669.7	959.1	1,822.7	2,049.8
Industry (*excluding* the building industry or "capital construction") of which:	256.7	363.9	641.6	761.7
Group A (i.e., heavy industry)	193.7	318.5	490.4	574.9
Group B (i.e., light industry)	63.0	45.4	151.2	186.8
Agriculture (*excluding* Forestry)	69.0	158.8	281.8	271.0

SOURCE: *Tinh Hinh Phat Trien Kinh Te Va Van Hoa Mien Bac Xa Hoi Chu Nghia Viet Nam 1960–75* (Hanoi: Tong Cuc Thong Ke, 1978), pp. 97 and 103.

itself, the share of heavy industry represented 75.4 per cent of the volume of state investments in industry both in 1960 and 1975, whereas that of light industry constituted only 24.5 per cent for the same years.

Theoretically, most of the investments in heavy industry should go, in order of importance, to mechanical engineering in order to equip agriculture and light industry with tools of various kinds, energy, building materials, metallurgy and chemicals.[144] But, in fact, in 1965 they went, in order of importance, to energy, metallurgy, chemicals, and only lastly to mechanical engineering. However, in 1975, there was a change in order of importance: energy, mechanical engineering, metallurgy, and chemicals.[145]

Nevertheless, there were serious imbalances not only between industry and agriculture, between light and heavy industry but also within the different branches of heavy industry itself, which did not allow the latter to play its presumed leading role with respect to agriculture, light industry and the national economy as a whole.

Undue emphasis on heavy industry — which by far exceeded the material and financial capability of the national economy, even if foreign aid was taken into consideration[146] — has greatly constrained the growth of agriculture and light industry,[147] and hindered, in the last analysis its own development. As a result, at the macro-economic level, it ineluctably led to serious economic imbalances. Besides, the development of heavy industry in a country having poor infrastructure and lacking a pool of skilled workers also brought about numerous problems.[148] In spite of this, the Party leadership gave priority to the development of heavy industry at the expense of agriculture and light industry. Why? Simply because it was strongly imbued with the dogma according to which capitalist industrialization started with the building of light industry whereas socialist industrialization should start with heavy industry. (Actually, the transition from an agricultural to an industrial society usually begins with the building of light industry and agriculture; and only after a certain stage of development of light industry and agriculture can the priority be given to heavy industry).

Another important reason was that the Party leadership decided to "build an independent and relatively comprehensive national economy"[149]; therefore it was necessary, right from the very beginning of the transition period to socialism, "to lay the foundations of Vietnam's own heavy industry", in other words, to give priority to the development of heavy industry.

Only in 1986 did the then Secretary-General Truong Chinh admit, in a very important speech delivered at the Tenth Hanoi Party Congress, that "[the Party leadership's] fondness for developing heavy industry on a large scale that exceeded [the country's] real capabilities" was one of the "errors of leftist infantilism".[150]

This strategic "error", which was also recently acknowledged by the Party's theoretical and political journal,[151] *led astray the whole course of economic development in North Vietnam during the period under review.* Had the Party completely reversed the order of priority in its strategy of economic development from the very beginning, that is, given priority to agriculture, then light industry, and lastly heavy industry — agriculture, and consequently light industry would have developed more rapidly, resulting in a quicker improvement in the standard of living of the working people, and greater financial revenue which could ultimately contribute to the development of heavy industry as well. This would have meant undoubtedly a broader road towards economic progress, one with a continual rise in agricultural and industrial production, and an increasing quantity of foodstuff and consumer goods for the people in general.

In the course of "socialist industrialization" the Party advocated, among other things, the combination of the development of centrally-run industry with state local industry. "We must", said Le Duan, "develop industries... in a planned and guided way, with the aim of providing the local population with certain means of production, consumer goods and building materials which are in general demand, and... supplementing the output of centrally-run industries".[152] The local industry played an important role not only in its contribution to production, and as a link between industry and agriculture in every region of the country in time of peace[153] but also and particularly in time of war when local production became crucially important given that the centrally-run industry was heavily damaged by U.S. bombing.[154]

In the preceding pages, the main aspects of the industrialization policy were passed in review. It is necessary now to go through the performance of the industry and handicraft sector during the 1957–75 period. However, before going into details, it might be helpful to recall that official data on the output of industry and handicraft usually suffered from two defects: double counting in the calculation of ex-factory prices because total value instead of added value was used; and different mark-ups of consumer goods and producer goods prices which led to distortions and made it difficult to evaluate correctly the gross output values.[155]

It was reported that, in 1959 constant prices, the gross output value of industry and handicraft increased by 76.3 per cent in 1960 compared with 1957. Industry *per se* (which represented 41.3 per cent and 57.1 per cent of the total industrial output respectively in 1957 and 1960) increased by 143.8 per cent, whereas handicraft (which had been disrupted by "socialist transformation" and neglected in spite of the fact that it represented 58.7 per cent and 42.9 per cent of the total industrial output respectively in 1957 and 1960) increased by only 28.8 per cent during the same period.

One should, however, bear in mind that the starting point of modern industry was very low in 1957 (the last year of the reconstruction period) and this was the main reason for the dramatic increase in the gross industrial output during the three-year plan period.

It is worth noting also that, compared with 1957, heavy industry and light industry increased their gross output value respectively by 164.5 per cent and 50.3 per cent in 1960, in constant 1959 prices. One can see that the priority given to the development of heavy industry was implemented even before the Party had formally advocated it at its Third National Congress in September 1960.

As for the state-run industrial sector which received the major portion of public investments, it grew by 243.3 per cent in 1960, compared with 1957 in constant 1959 prices.[156] However, "socialist industrialization" actually started on a large scale only with the First Five-Year Plan, that is, from 1961 onwards.[157] From 1960 to 1975 the gross industrial and handicraft production calculated in constant 1970 prices evolved as shown in Table 1.4.

The figures show that total gross industrial output (industry and handicrafts) continually increased from 1960 to 1965, then declined during the war years 1966–68, climbed up again in the following three years of relative peace, then slumped again in 1972 because of the devastating U.S. bombing, and then climbed up again after the Paris Agreement in 1973.

Compared with 1960, it increased by 89.4 per cent in 1965 and 236.2 per cent in 1975. Within this total, industry grew much faster than handicraft: in 1975 the former increased by 339 per cent whereas the latter, which was virtually stagnant during the 1960s, increased by only 100.8 per cent compared with 1960.

If one compares both the trend and fluctuations of the total value of gross industrial output on the one hand, and of the gross agricultural output (excluding forestry) on the other[158] one can clearly see the dominant constraint imposed on industry and handicraft by agriculture. The fluctuations in the growth rate of total gross industrial output mirrored, albeit with a time-lag, that of the gross output of agriculture. The table also shows that in accordance with Party policy, the gross output value of heavy

TABLE 1.4
Industrial and Handicraft Production Indexes, 1960–75

Year	Total Industrial Output (Industry+ Handicraft)	Group A Gross Industrial Output	Group B Gross Industrial Output	Group A Share	Group B Share	Industry Gross Output	Handicraft Gross Output	Central Gross Output	Local Gross Output	Central Share	Local Share
1960	100.0	100.0	100.0	33.7	66.3	100.0	100.0	100.0	100.0	40.2	59.8
1961	114.4					124.8	101.4	125.9			
1962	143.4					163.8	118.1	168.8			
1963	155.5					181.7	121.6	188.5			
1964	173.5					212.8	121.9	222.7			
1965	189.4	241.5	162.9	42.9	57.1	240.8	121.7	251.0	148.0	53.3	46.7
1966	184.0					231.1	122.0	232.5			
1967	159.8					194.6	114.3	175.3			
1968	169.3					215.5	108.6	193.6			
1969	184.6					236.4	116.4	212.6			
1970	200.4					259.6	122.4	232.7			
1971	232.3					305.0	136.2	279.6			
1972	206.1					261.7	132.4	226.9			
1973	241.6					303.5	158.4	261.4			
1974	291.4	376.2	248.5	42.9	57.1	376.2	178.6	343.0	257.0	44.9	55.1
1975	336.2	439.0	284.2	43.4	56.6	439.0	200.8	411.2	287.0	46.7	53.3

SOURCE: *Tinh Hinh Phat Trien Kinh Te Va Van Hoa Mien Bac Xa Hoi Chu Nghia Viet Nam 1960–75* (Hanoi: Tong Cuc Thong Ke, 1978), pp. 65, 66, 67, 78, 79.

industry (Group A) always grew faster than that of light industry (Group B) during the whole period under review, including the war years 1965–68;[159] in 1975 they increased by 339 per cent and 184.2 per cent respectively, compared with 1960.

The share of heavy industry increased from 33.7 per cent in 1960 to 43.4 per cent in 1975 whereas that of light industry fell from 66.3 per cent to 56.6 per cent respectively. (The latter continued to decrease even during the war years in spite of the apparent emphasis on light and local industry). The centrally-run industry output grew much faster than the local (or regional) industry during the period under review: they increased by 311.2 per cent and 187 per cent respectively in 1975, compared with 1960. The share of local industry fell from 59.8 per cent in 1960 to 46.7 per cent in 1965, then rose to 53.3 per cent in 1975.

It is worth noting that the shares of state and "joint state-private" sectors in total gross industrial output continually grew from 52.4 per cent and 4.9 per cent respectively in 1960 to 66.8 per cent and 6 per cent in 1965. Since then, they have been lumped together (one might infer from this that since 1965 all the "joint state-private" industrial enterprises were fully nationalized), and their share reached 72.9 per cent in 1975.[160] Correlatively, the share of the "collective sector" decreased from 37.7 per cent in 1960 to 24.8 per cent in 1975, while that of the "individual sector" also fell from 4.6 per cent to 2.3 per cent respectively. The "capitalist sector", which represented 0.4 per cent in 1960, has, however, disappeared from the economic scene since then, despite the proclaimed policy of maintaining the existence of non-socialist sectors for a certain period of time. The rapid decrease and elimination of the non-socialist sectors undoubtedly contributed to the severe shortage of consumer goods at a time when the state sector was far from able to meet the basic needs of the people.

In spite of the dramatic growth of the total gross industrial output (due chiefly to a very low starting point), the per capita output of a number of important industrial products was still insignificant in 1975.

It is worth noting that there was frequent official criticism of the low-quality and substandard production of industrial goods[161]

TABLE 1.5
Per Capita Output of Selected Industrial Products

		1960	1975
Electricity	(kwh)	15.9	54.6
Clean coal	(kg)	161.2	210.7
Cast iron	(kg)	0.5	3.9
Bicycles	(per thousand)	1.4	2.5
Cement	(kg)	25.3	15.1
Sawn wood	(cubic metres)	0.045	0.034
Cardboard and paper	(kg)	0.35	0.87
Matches	(boxes)	11.4	6.9
Sleeping mats		0.33	0.32
Cloth and silk	(metres)	6.0	4.4
Salt	(kg)	7.3	9.1
Sea fish	(kg)	5.6	3.9
Fish and other sauce	(litre)	2.3	2.3
Sugar and molasses	(kg)	2.0	0.8
Beer	(litre)	0.2	1.1
Cigarettes	(packets)	4.6	10.6
Laundry soap	(kg)	0.3	0.35

SOURCE: *Tinh Hinh Phat Trien Kinh Te Va Van Hoa Mien Bac Xa Hoi Chu Nghia Viet Nam 1960–75* (Hanoi: Tong Cuc Thong Ke, 1978), p. 83.

on the one hand, and poor economic results of the state enterprises on the other.[162]

On the whole, in 1975 North Vietnam was still an overwhelmingly agrarian economy; "Industry" (excluding "Capital Construction") accounted for only 27.9 per cent of the Produced National Income (*Thu Nhap Quoc Dan San Xuat*) whereas "Agriculture and Forestry" represented 40.4 per cent.[163]

Foreign Aid and Trade

Industrialization in Vietnam would have been impossible without a substantial amount of foreign aid from the socialist countries, particularly from the Soviet Union and the People's Republic of China (PRC). Unfortunately, only a few figures concerning foreign aid — which was regarded as a state secret — have been disclosed from time to time, and very often these figures did not tally with each other. It was reported that during the 1955–65 period, the total amount of economic aid from the socialist countries (excluding those given under the agreements signed in February 1965 after the start of U.S. bombing) to North Vietnam reached 3,330 million old rubles of which 1,520 million were in grants, and 1,810 million in concessional long-term loans.[164]

During the war years, the socialist countries' economic assistance — all in the form of grants — "ranged from US$270 million to US$1 billion annually" according to one of the Vietnamese leaders, Mr Le Duc Tho.[165] After the Paris agreements, according to Mr Tran Phuong, then Vice-Chairman of the State Planning Committee, in a lecture given behind closed doors at the Party's Central School of Economic Management in Ho Chi Minh City, the CMEA's (Council for Mutual Economic Assistance) economic assistance granted to "North Vietnam before 1975 [reached] Rubles 400 million *per annum*, equivalent of US$700 million".[166] Later, in an interview with a foreign correspondent, in 1985, he said that "Chinese economic aid, all of it in grant form, amounted before 1976 to US$300 million a year".[167] In other words, before 1975 North Vietnam received about US$1 billion in economic aid per annum from all the socialist countries (CMEA and the PRC).

To give the reader an idea of the importance of this aid in North Vietnam's state budget, it might be useful to quote the following figures taken from a "top secret" statistical document (see Table 1.6). From this table one can see that the share of foreign economic aid in total budgetary revenues ranged between 21.5 per cent and 26.5 per cent during the 1960–64 period, then suddenly rose to between 42.3 per cent and 68.9 per cent during the war years 1965–72. In the second reconstruction period (1974–75) it varied between 54.9 per cent and 60.6 per cent. Thus, in spite of the Party's frequent Maoist-style assertion of "self-reliance", particularly in the 1960s and early 1970s, the above figures clearly show a heavy dependence of North Vietnam on foreign economic aid.

Regarding Soviet economic aid specifically, it was reported that in July 1955, the USSR assisted North Vietnam with a grant of 400 million old rubles, 75 per cent of which was for capital investment projects and the remainder for commodity aid. In

TABLE 1.6
Share of Foreign Economic Aid in the Total Budgetary Revenues, 1960–75

	1960	1961	1962	1963	1964	1965	1966	1967
Internal Revenues	77.6	76.9	74.1	73.5	78.5	57.7	39.0	33.4
Foreign Aid (grants & loans)	22.4	23.1	25.9	26.5	21.5	42.3	61.0	66.6

TABLE 1.6 (cont'd)
Share of Foreign Economic Aid in the Total Budgetary Revenues, 1960–75

	1968	1969	1970	1971	1972	1973	1974	1975
Internal Revenues	31.1	31.5	32.4	36.0	39.7	40.1	39.4	45.1
Foreign Aid (grants & loans)	68.9	68.5	67.6	64.0	60.3	59.9	60.6	54.9

SOURCE: *Nien Giam Thong Ke 1982 (Tai Lieu Toi Mat)* (Hanoi: Tong Cuc Thong Ke, 1983), p. 77.

addition, the USSR sent some 1,000 specialists and technicians to Hanoi and undertook the training of about 10,000 Vietnamese in the Soviet Union.[168] The USSR promised under this first agreement to assist North Vietnam in about 90 projects — some 25 of which were classified as major — in heavy industry (electric power, mining, mechanical engineering), light industry (tea-processing, fish cannery) and agriculture (tractors and agricultural machines for agricultural producers' co-operatives).[169] As for commodity aid, it included chiefly foodstuffs, cotton and synthetic cloth, pharmaceuticals, petroleum, fertilizer, and pesticides.

In the First Five-Year Plan period (1961–65), the USSR assisted North Vietnam with a grant of 20 million rubles and a loan of 430 million rubles.[170] Under a five-year assistance agreement signed in Hanoi (23 December 1960), the USSR promised to fund nearly 100 projects, about half of which were considered major. These included electric power plants, mines, mechanical engineering plants, a radio transmitter for Hanoi Radio, an automobile repair plant, and various projects on 37 state farms.[171] A supplementary agreement was signed in September 1962 involving the agricultural sector in particular (water conservancy; tractors; agricultural machinery and equipment for state farms; assistance in developing animal husbandry and industrial crops, and so forth).

During the war years and reconstruction period (1965–75), it was reported that the Soviet Union "provided [North Vietnam] 1.5 billion rubles in aid (consisting of 253 million in grants and the remainder in loans).[172] Suffice it to recall here the statement of ex-Vice-Premier Tran Quynh concerning the strategic importance of Soviet aid during these war years: "Economic and military assistance [from the USSR] was one of the decisive factors leading to the total victory of our people".[173]

As a final gesture of generosity, the Soviet Union cancelled all the debts incurred by North Vietnam before and during the war. About that, the Party's newspaper wrote: "Following the signing of the Paris Agreements in 1973 . . . the Soviet Communist Party and government declared the cancellation of all past debts . . . while continuing to give us economic and technical aid [for post-war economic reconstruction]."[174]

Concerning Chinese economic aid during the period under

review, unfortunately very little information is available. During the 1955–60 period, it was reported that the PRC assisted North Vietnam with 900 million yuan in grants and 300 million yuan in long-term loans. In 1961, the PRC loaned North Vietnam 141.75 million new rubles.[175] From 1954 to 1978, the PRC also funded 450 projects, of which 339 were completed by March 1978.[176] These included rice-husking factories, sugar refinery, paper mill, matches factory, electric bulbs and thermos factory, monosodium glutamate factory, porcelain factory, magnesium phosphate factory, chemical plant, shipyard, iron and steel complex in Thai Nguyen, and so forth. The PRC was also involved in bridge and railroad reconstruction, and supplied equipment for mines, radio network and state farms. Apart from these, the PRC also assisted North Vietnam with 700 million yuan in commodity aid during the war years and reconstruction period (1965–75), which included foodstuffs, textiles and cotton cloth, petrol, cars, ships, locomotives and wagons, and a large quantity of various consumer goods.

In addition, the PRC reportedly sent to North Vietnam 20,000 advisers, specialists and technicians during the 1950–78 period.[177] Apart from that, the PRC disclosed that during the 1955–76 period, it also gave to North Vietnam "more than US$600 million" for its activities related "to the liberation struggle of South Vietnam".[178]

All in all, according to Chinese sources, "in the past three decades or so ... the total value of China's aid to Vietnam, military, economic [and] in foreign exchange [the latter concerned probably the foreign exchange intended for the "liberation struggle of South Vietnam"] exceeded 20 billion US dollars".[179] Unfortunately, no separate figure concerning Chinese economic aid alone is available for the 1955–75 period. All one knows is that before 1976, Chinese economic aid to North Vietnam amounted to US$300 million *per annum*, as mentioned earlier.

The socialist countries' economic assistance was destined mainly for financing the continuous trade deficits (see Table 1.7). The figures in the table show that, compared with 1960, the value of exports increased by 28 per cent in 1965, decreased significantly during the war years 1966–73, and then went up again in 1974 and 1975. In 1975, it increased by 82.4 per cent, compared with 1960.

As for the total value of imports (that is, imports in the strict commercial sense of the word plus foreign aid imports) it kept on

TABLE 1.7
Balance of Trade of North Vietnam, 1960–75
(In "Rubles – U.S. dollars")

Year	Value of Exports	Imports Value of Imports	of which Commercial Imports	Trade Deficit
1960	71.1	116.5	84.7	45.4
1961	73.7	130.8	64.6	57.1
1962	81.0	135.0	88.9	54.0
1963	85.1	143.4	91.8	58.3
1964	97.1	137.4	102.0	40.3
1965	91.0	237.3	132.2	146.3
1966	67.8	370.9	171.8	303.1
1967	45.6	418.5	117.3	372.9
1968	42.9	465.5	91.7	422.6
1969	42.6	512.2	39.7	469.6
1970	47.7	425.7	32.4	378.0
1971	61.4	458.5	32.3	397.1
1972	40.7	362.5	34.8	321.8
1973	67.4	484.5	58.3	417.1
1974	110.7	694.9	120.3	584.2
1975	129.7	784.4	194.9	654.7

SOURCE: *Nien Giam Thong Ke, 1982* (Tai Lieu Toi Mat) (Hanoi: Tong Cuc Thong Ke, 1983), p. 311.

increasing during the whole period under review, particularly since 1965. Compared with 1960, it increased by 17.9 per cent in 1964, 339.6 per cent in 1969, and 573.3 per cent in 1975. However, if one considers only commercial imports (that is, excluding foreign aid imports), one can see that, compared with 1960, they increased slowly from 1962 to 1966, then began to decrease, particularly during the years 1969–73; they rose again in the last two years, 1974 and 1975. Compared with 1960, commercial imports increased by 130.1 per cent in 1975, whereas total imports (that is, including foreign aid imports) grew by 573.3 per cent as mentioned earlier.

It is worth noting that the share of foreign aid imports in the total value of imports increased from 27.3 per cent in 1960 to 75.2

per cent in 1975. As for the trade deficit, it grew by more than fourteen times from 1960 to 1975. In 1975, exports covered only 16.5 per cent of imports, compared to 61 per cent in 1960. Looking at the structure of exports, calculated in "Rubles - US dollars", one can see that in 1960 "industrial and mining products" (that is, coal, apatite, tin, cement, and so forth) represented 47.9 per cent, with handicraft commodities at 24.6 per cent, and "unprocessed agricultural goods" at 27.5 per cent; in 1975 they represented 75.1 per cent, 16.4 per cent and 8.5 per cent respectively.[180]

As for the structure of imports (also calculated in "Rubles-US dollars"), one can see that in 1960, the "means of production" (that is, capital and intermediate goods, which consisted of complete equipment, machines and means of transport, tools and spares, fuels, raw and other materials) represented 87 per cent whereas the share of "consumer goods" reached only 13 per cent; in 1975 the former represented 73.1 per cent and the latter 26.9 per cent.[181]

North Vietnam developed trade relations particularly with the socialist countries. In 1960, it exported 87.1 per cent of its commodities to the socialist countries, 11.9 per cent to the Western industrialized countries, and only 1 per cent to Third World countries. In 1975, it exported 70.3 per cent, 27.6 per cent and 2.1 per cent respectively towards the same countries.[182] In 1960, the share of its imports from the socialist countries represented 91.8 per cent, from the Western industrialized countries 6 per cent, and from the Third World countries 2.2 per cent; whereas in 1975 their share represented 82 per cent, 17.3 per cent and 0.7 per cent respectively.[183]

* * *

In the preceding pages, the main aspects of the Stalinist-Maoist strategy of economic development of North Vietnam, particularly during the 1958–75 period were analysed. As one can see, this strategy gave rise to an irrational economic structure in many respects, and serious imbalances at the macro-economic level. Agriculture could not keep up with the needs of national economic development and this was an important factor limiting the overall economic development. Light industry was also unable to meet the basic needs of the people in both rural and urban areas while heavy industry was developed in a lopsided manner at the expense of agriculture and light industry. This was one of the great mistakes committed by the Party leadership during the period under review. This error also adversely affected the development of communications and transport, commerce and service trades.

The above irrational economic structure resulted in generally low economic efficiency and labour productivity, which ultimately led to a decline in the people's standard of living. The Party leadership also failed to really grasp the dialectical relationship between the "relations of production" and the "productive forces" under North Vietnam's specific historical conditions. Exaggerating the extent to which a rapid change in the "relations of production" (which includes the systems of ownership, economic management and income distribution) might influence the development of "productive forces", it erroneously characterized the relationship between the two as the former lagging behind the requirements of growth of the latter, and drew the wrong conclusion that the higher the level of public ownership, the better it would be for the growth of the "productive forces". As a result, overhasty changes were made in the field of "relations of production" — namely, forced collectivization and rapid elimination of all non-socialist economic sectors — which by far exceeded the actual level of "productive forces". However, practice has shown that — in North Vietnam as well as in China under Mao — an overhasty change in the "relations of production" did not promote but rather retarded or even undermined the growth of "productive forces", and consequently that of the production potential of the country. Recently, this overall error was at least acknowledged by some Party scholars.[184]

The combination of all the above-mentioned "leftist" mistakes — which bear a great resemblance to the ones committed in China under Mao[185] — gave rise to "an institutionalized aggravated shortage economy",[186] or more bluntly to "an economic crisis"[187] as a number of Western-watchers (who are more or less sympathetic to the Hanoi government) termed it. However this "economic crisis" was, at that time, somewhat masked by large injections of foreign economic aid. Yet, there were some scholars who suggested that Third World countries could draw "fruitful" lessons from North Vietnam's economic experience.[188] "Fruitful" or not, the fact remains that immediately after the communist military victory in the South (April 1975), the Party leadership tried to impose *at all costs* the Northern model of development upon the South, and this "northernization" of a restive South brought about disastrous results, as the reader will see in the following chapter.

NOTES

1. Tran Phuong "The Land Reform", *Vietnamese Studies*, no. 7 (Hanoi, 1965), pp. 153–97; Vien Kinh Te, *Cach Mang Ruong Dat O Vietnam*, edited by Tran Phuong (Hanoi: Nha Xuat Ban Khoa Hoc Xa Hoi, 1968); Nguyen Xuan Lai, *La Reforme Agraire au Nord Vietnam* (Hanoi: Editions en Langues Etrangeres, 1981); Doan Trong Truyen and Pham Thanh Vinh, *L'edification d'une economie nationale independante au Vietnam 1945–65*, 2 eme edition (Hanoi: Editions en Langues Etrangeres, 1966), pp. 66–76; 93–98; Vo Nhan Tri, *Croissance Economique de la République Démocratique du Vietnam 1945-65* (Hanoi: Editions en Langues Etrangeres, 1967), pp. 123–34; 198–203; Vo Nhan Tri, "La politique agraire du Nord-Vietnam", *Tiers Monde* (IEDES) (Paris, July–September 1960); Quang Truong, "Agricultural Collectivization and Rural Development in Vietnam: A North/South Study (1955–85)" (Ph.D. dissertation, Vrije Universiteit te Amsterdam, January 1987), chap. 2.; Ngoc Luu Nguyen, "Peasants, Party and Revolution. The Politics of Agrarian Transformation in North Vietnam, 1930–75" (Ph.D. dissertation, Universiteit van Amsterdam, September 1987), chap. 5 and 6; Andrew Vickerman, *The Fate of the Peasantry, Premature Transition to Socialism in the D.R.V.*, Monograph Series No. 28 (Yale University Southeast Asia Studies, 1986), chap. 3; Christine P. White, "Agrarian Reform and National Liberation in the Vietnamese Revolution: 1920–1957" (Ph.D. dissertation, Cornell University, 1981); Edwin E. Moise, *Land Reform in China and North Vietnam* (London: The University of North Carolina Press, 1983), pp. 178–268; and A.G. Mazaev, *Agrarnaia Reforma V Demokratitcheskoi Respublike Vietnam* (I.V.L., Moskva, 1959), chap. 2 and 3 (in Russian).
2. It is rather surprising to see that a knowledgeable Vietnam-watcher like P.R. Feray still has doubts as to the authenticity of this historical truth! (See his book, *Le Vietnam* [Paris: Presses Universitaires de France, 1984], p. 80). On that score, see a more correct viewpoint in Edwin E. Moise's book, *Land Reform . . .*, pp. 6–8; 234–35; 227–80.
3. Communiqué of the Tenth Plenum of the VWP Central Committee, *Nhan Dan*, 30 October 1956. See also *Lich Su Dang Cong San Viet Nam* (Chuong Trinh Cao Cap), Tap III, Nha Xuat Ban Sach Giao Khoa Mac Le-nin (Hanoi, 1986), p. 18.

4. Nguyen Xuan-Lai, *La Reforme Agraire* . . . . , p. 22.
5. Tran Phuong, "The Land Reform", p. 191.
6. F. FitzGerald, *Fire in the Lake*, An Atlantic Monthly Press Book (Boston-Toronto: Little Brown and Company, 1972), p. 223.
7. Tibor Mende, one of the shrewd Western publicists who visited the DRV in 1957, estimated at "12 or 15,000 the number of *innocent* executed" (emphasis added) during the land reform (see "Les deux Vietnam", *Esprit* [Paris, June 1957], p. 941). As for President Ho Chi Minh, he admitted to 10,000 deaths in an interview with Ernst Utrecht in Indonesia (see *Journal of Contemporary Asia* 3, no. 2 [1973]: 220; quoted in F. Houtart and G. Lemercinier, *Hai Van. Life in a Vietnamese Commune* (London: Zed Books Ltd., 1984), p. 18.
8. The Hanoi press reported that nearly 20,000 persons were released after the rectification of "errors". See Tibor Mende, op. cit.
9. Adam Fforde and Suzanne H. Paine, *The Limits of National Liberation* (London: Croom Helm, 1987), p. 36.
10. Z.T., "L'Autre Regard: Ma cousine de Huong Son", *Doan Ket* (a pro-Hanoi journal), No. 377 (Paris, February 1986), p. 24.
11. *50 Nam Hoat Dong Cua Dang Cong San Viet Nam* (Hanoi: Nha Xuat Ban Su That, 1982), p. 144. It is worth noting that in the English version of this Party's history it was mentioned only *in passing* the "serious mistakes" of the land reform. See *50 Years of Activities of the Communist Party of Vietnam* (Hanoi: Foreign Languages Publishing House, 1980), p. 131.
12. *Nhan Dan*, 31 October 1956.
13. Dr Nguyen Manh Tuong's report was, however, *not* published by the Hanoi press, but by the Saigon press. See *Cach Mang Quoc Gia* (Saigon), 22 April 1957; and also Le Chau, *Le Vietnam Socialiste: une economie de transition*, edited by F. Maspero (Paris, 1966), pp. 142–44. At the time this writer met him in Hanoi (in 1961) he had fallen into disgrace since 1956 and was completely marginalized by the Hanoi establishment.
14. For more details, see Ngoc Luu Nguyen, "Peasants, Party and Revolution . . .", pp. 327–29; 331–34.
15. According to Vietnamese historians, *feudalism* had been established in Vietnam since the fifteenth century on the basis of the maintenance of rural communes associated with the development of private land and the landowner-tenant relationship. Concerning the difference between Western and Eastern feudalism, see Nguyen Gia Phu, "Thuat Ngu Che Do Phong Kien Va Van De Che Do Phong Kien O Phuong Dong", *Nghien Cuu Lich Su*, nos. 1–2 (Hanoi, 1987), pp. 3–6.
16. The Party acknowledged that the combination of land reform with the repression of so-called "enemy organisations" was a major "error" which increased the confusion, and widened the scope of repression. See Vien Kinh Te, *Cach Mang* . . . , p. 188.
17. On this score, see in particular the play of Hoang Tich Linh, "Com Moi" in *Van*, nos. 16–17 (Hanoi, 23 and 30 August 1957).
18. See *Nhan Dan*, 31 October 1956.

19. Edwin E. Moise, *Land Reform* . . . , p. 232.
20. Ibid.
21. Ibid.
22. *Hoc Tap*, no. 3 (Hanoi, 1956), p. 22.
23. *Nhan Dan*, 14 and 21 June 1955.
24. *Nhan Dan*, 6 April 1955; and 15 June 1955.
25. *Nhan Dan*, 14 May 1956.
26. *Nhan Dan*, 30 October 1956.
27. *Nhan Dan*, 31 October 1956.
28. See Truong Chinh's report at the First National Conference of the VWP, November 1953, in his *Selected Writings* (Hanoi: Foreign Languages Publishing House, 1977), p. 552.
29. *Nhan Dan*, 31 October 1956.
30. See Vien Kinh Te, *Cach Mang Ruong Dat* . . ., pp. 157, 195; and *Nhan Dan*, 6 September 1956.
31. *Nhan Dan*, 18 April 1958.
32. "At least 25% of the total of landlords in *each* commune" were regarded as "landlord despots". See Vien Kinh Te, *Cach Mang Ruong Dat* . . . , p. 131.
33. Concerning the functioning of these "tribunals", see, for instance, Gerard Tongas, *J'ai Vecu Dans L'enfer Communiste au Nord Vietnam* (Paris: Nouvelles Editions Debresse, 1960), pp. 223–24.
34. See the memoirs of ex-Politburo member Hoang Van Hoan, *Giot Nuoc Trong Bien Ca (Hoi Ky Cach Mang)* (Nha Xuat Ban Tin Vietnam, 1986), p. 361.
35. Quoted by Nguyen Manh Tuong, in *Cach Mang Quoc Gia* (Saigon, 22 April 1957). See also Le Chau, *Le Vietnam Socialiste* . . . , p. 143; and G. Boudarel, *Sudestasie*, no. 52 (Paris, 1988), p. 63.
36. *Nhan Dan*, 8 December 1956.
37. *Nhan Dan*, 31 October 1956. Concerning the "errors" of the land reform, see also Hoang Van Hoan, *Giot Nuoc* . . . , pp. 361–63.
38. Edwin E. Moise, *Land Reform* . . . , p. 9.
39. Vien Kinh Te Hoc, *May Van De Ly Luan Va Thuc Tien Cua Cach Mang Quan He San Xuat Trong Nong Nghiep Nuoc Ta*, edited by Nguyen Huy (Hanoi: Nha Xuat Ban Khoa Hoc Xa Hoi, 1985), pp. 55–56; 118; 120–21. It is worth recalling that already in 1917 V.I. Lenin proclaimed in his *April Theses* the necessity of "Nationali[zing] of all land in the country under control of local councils of agricultural labourers' and peasants' deputies" (quoted in Robert Wesson, *Soviet Communes* [New Brunswick, N.J.: Rutgers University Press, 1963], p. 38). On the same score, see also V.I. Lenin, *Alliance of the Working Class with the Peasantry* (Moscow: Foreign Languages Publishing House, 1959), pp. 180–81.
40. Quoted by Tran Phuong, "The Land Reform", p. 189.
41. In this respect, the VWP has strictly followed V.I. Lenin's recommendation according to which, in a peasant society, an astute proletarian party should use the peasantry — a revolutionary force which was "imbued with a far more spontaneous revolutionary spirit" and a more "passionate desire to

destroy the landlord regime" than the more calculating industrial proletariat — for its own ends. See V.I. Lenin, *The Agrarian Programme of Social Democracy in the First Russian Revolution 1905–1907* (Moscow: Progress Publishers, 1977), pp. 168; 191–94.

42. See Le Duan's Political Report of the Central Committee, in *Third National Congress of the Vietnam Workers' Party*, Documents, Vol. I (Hanoi: Foreign Languages Publishing House, 1960), pp. 65–66.

43. For details, see ibid., p. 70. See also Le Duan, *Selected Writings* (Hanoi: Foreign Languages Publishing House, 1977), pp. 233–84; and Truong Chinh, *Selected Writings* (Hanoi: Foreign Languages Publishing House, 1977), pp. 591–98.

44. Dang Lao Dong Viet Nam, *Nghi Quyet Hoi Nghi Trung Uong Lan Thu* 14, (Hanoi, 1959), pp. 15; 24. See also Le Duan's Political Report, p. 75.

45. For a selective bibliography on this score, see *Lich Su Dang Cong San Viet Nam*, Tap III, pp. 39–43; 71–74; 101–3; 148–52; 173–77; 187–88; 196; 199.
Vien Kinh Te Hoc, *35 Nam Kinh Te Viet Nam (1945–1980)*, edited by Dao Van Tap (Hanoi: Nha Xuat Ban Khoa Hoc Xa Hoi, 1980), pp. 125–30; 135–58.
The Dat, *Nen Nong Nghiep Viet Nam Tu Sau Cach Mang Thang Tam Nam* 1945 (Hanoi: Nha Xuat Ban Nong Nghiep, 1981), pp. 63–162; 221–31.
Truong Dai Hoc Kinh Te Ke Hoach, *Giao Trinh Lich Su Kinh Te Viet Nam* (Hanoi, 1978), pp. 183–85; 204–6; 211–13.
"Economic Policy and National Liberation War", *Vietnamese Studies*, no. 44, (Hanoi, 1976), pp. 158–91.
Vo Nhan Tri, *Croissance Economique . . .*, pp. 273–98; 403–33.
Vo Nhan Tri, "Razvitie Ekonomiki DRV", *Narody Azii I Afriki*, no. 3 (Institute of Oriental Studies, USSR Academy of Sciences, Moskva, 1970) (in Russian).
Melanie Beresford, *Vietnam. Politics, Economics and Society* (London and New York: Pinter Publishers, 1988), pp. 130–40.
Adam Fforde and Suzanne Paine, *The Limits of National Liberation*, pp. 100–26.
Max Spoor, "The Economy of North Vietnam. The First Ten Years 1955–64" (M.Ph. thesis, Institute of Social Studies, The Hague, January 1985), chap. I.
Nguyen Tien Hung, *Economic Development of Socialist Vietnam, 1955–80* (New York and London: Praeger Publishers, 1977), pp. 57–61.
Leon Lavallee, *L'Economie du Nord Vietnam 1960–70*, no. 94 (Tome I., Centre d'Etudes et de Recherches Marxistes, Paris, 1971), pp. 25–30; 73–77.
Le Chau, *Le Vietnam Socialiste . . .*, pp. 161–224; 352–72.
Quang Truong, *Agricultural Collectivization . . .*, pp. 49–130.
Ngoc Luu Nguyen, "Peasants, Party and Revolution . . .", pp. 385–581.
Andrew Vickerman, The Fate of the Peasantry . . ., pp. 117–344.

46. Le Duan, *Selected Writings*, pp. 497–98; 501.

47. Ibid., pp. 495–96. V.I. Lenin held in particular that collectivization of agricultural production would become feasible only at such time when technological revolution could provide the basis for rural petty commodity producers to create more advanced socialist forms.

48. Ibid., p. 496.
49. A. Vickerman, *The Fate of the Peasantry* ..., p. 9. For an interesting discussion on this viewpoint, see ibid., pp. 9–11.
50. Tran Duc, "Tim Hieu Viec Van Dung Ke Hoach Hop Tac Hoa cua Le-Nin O Viet Nam", *Tap Chi Cong San* (The Party's theoretical and political journal), no. 3 (Hanoi, 1988), p. 27.
51. Ibid., p. 28.
52. Ibid., pp. 28; 30.
53. See Vietnamese sources quoted by A. Vickerman, *The Fate of the Peasantry* ..., p. 128.
54. Truong Chinh, *Resolutely Taking the North Vietnam Countryside to Socialism Through Agricultural Co-operation* (Hanoi: Foreign Languages Publishing House, 1959), p. 14.
55. *Nhan Dan*, 20 November 1958.
56. *Lich Su Dang Cong San Viet Nam*, Tap III, p. 41.
57. See the Statute of EPACs in *Etudes Vietnamiennes*, no. 2 (Hanoi, 1964), pp. 175–88.
58. See Truong Chinh, *Resolutely Taking the North Vietnam Countryside* ..., p. 21.
59. Vietnam News Agency (Hanoi), 15 February 1960.
60. See Truong Chinh, *Resolutely Taking the North Vietnam Countryside* ..., p. 19.
61. Vietnamese sources quoted by A. Vickerman, *The Fate of the Peasantry* ..., p. 278.
62. Xue Muqiao, *China's Socialist Economy* (Beijing: Foreign Languages Press, 1981), pp. 35–38; 56–66; Zhang Yulin's article in *China's Economic Reforms*, edited by Lin Wei and Arnold Chao (Philadelphia: University of Pennsylvania Press, 1982), pp. 126–28. See also Mark Selden's articles in *The Transition to Socialism in China*, edited by M. Selden and V. Lippit (Armonk, New York: M.E. Sharpe, Inc., 1982), pp. 58–80; and in *China's Changed Road to Development*, edited by N. Maxwell and B. McFarlane (Oxford, New York: Pergamon Press, 1984), pp. 3–6; and Hugh Deane, "Mao's Rural Strategies: What went wrong?" *Science and Society*, no. 1 (Spring 1985), pp. 104-10.
63. Le Duan, *Third National Congress* ..., Vol. I, p. 77.
64. Ibid., p. 76.
65. *Nhan Dan*, 3 August 1959, and 13 August 1959.
66. See the complaints of these cadres in *Nhan Dan*, 2 February 1960. Le Duan once disclosed that some grass-root cadres requested the higher echelons to allow them to issue commands so that they could implement the Party's policy when dealing with the peasants in *Cach Mang Xa Hoi Chu Nghia O Viet Nam* (Hanoi: Su That, 1976), Tap I, p. 110.
67. According to K. Marx, during the process of "socialization of the land", one should make the peasant see his situation improve immediately and therefore come to accept collective ownership by himself and for economic reasons. (See Hal Daper, *Karl Marx's Theory of Revolution, vol. II: The Politics of Social Classes* [New York: Monthly Review Press, 1978], p. 409). As for F. Engels,

he insisted: "We shall do all that can be done to ease the lot of the small farmer and smooth his way during the transition to co-operation, once he has decided to adopt his course. And even if he still has not made up his mind, we will grant him a prolonged period for reflection..." (Quoted in Theodore Bergmann, *Farm Policies in Socialist Countries* (Westmead: Saxon House and Lexington Books, 1975, p. 253).

68. V.I. Lenin, *Alliance of the Working Class* ..., pp. 276, 282–83.
69. V.I. Lenin, *The Land Question and the Fight for Freedom* (Moscow: Progress Publishers, 1972), p. 65.
70. Tran Duc, "Tim Hieu Viec ... ", p. 30.
71. Ibid.
72. Ibid.
73. Ibid.
74. A. Vickerman, *The Fate of the Peasantry* ..., p.278.
75. See Tran Duc, "Tim Hieu Viec ... ", p. 30.
76. *Nhan Dan*, 3 June 1960.
77. Le Duan, *Selected Writings*, p. 512.
78. Tran Duc, "Tim Hieu Viec ... ", p. 30.
79. Ha Dang's article in *Nhan Dan*, 13 August 1959.
80. Dao Viet Thuong's article in *Nhan Dan*, 23 February 1959.
81. Ngo Thuyen's article in *Hoc Tap*, no. 7 (1963), p. 77.
82. Tran Duc, "Tim Hieu Viec ... ", p. 30.
83. For details, see Nguyen Yem, "Contracted Work and Contracted Produce in Agricultural Cooperatives", *Vietnam Courier*, no. 3 (Hanoi, 1981), pp. 14–15.
84. Le Trong, "Ve Thu Lao Lao Dong Trong Hop Tac Xa Nong Nghiep", *Nghien Cuu Kinh Te*, no. 3 (Hanoi, 1980), p. 26.
85. Tran Duc, "Tim Hieu Viec ... ", p. 31.
86. *Nhan Dan*, 11 December 1968.
87. *Tinh Hinh Phat Trien Kinh Te Va Van Hoa Mien Bac Xa Hoi Chu Nghia Viet Nam 1960–75* (Hanoi: Tong Cuc Thong Ke, 1978), p. 180.
88. *Nhan Dan*, 5 June 1970.
89. See his speech in *Nhan Dan*, 29 and 30 January 1969; and *Hoc Tap*, no. 2 (Hanoi, 1969), pp. 12–13. See also G. Boudarel's article in *La Bureaucratie au Vietnam* (Paris: l'Harmattan, 1983), p. 84; and Christine White's article in *Revolutionary Socialist Development in the Third World*, edited by Gordon White et al. (UK: Harvester Press Publishing Group, 1983), p. 249.
90. A. Lefebvre, "La Politique Rurale de la Chine", *Notes et Etudes Documentaires*, La Documentation Francaise, no. 4766 (Paris, 1984), pp. 57–61.
91. Vien Kinh Te Hoc, *35 Nam Kinh Te Vietnam* ..., pp. 128; 130. Concerning higher productivity, see ibid., p. 126.
92. Truong Chinh, *Resolutely Taking the North Vietnam Countryside*..., pp. 43–44.
93. This conference was reported in BBC, *Summary of World Broadcast (SWB ES)*, No. 338, 26 September 1958, p. 53.
94. A. Fforde and S. Paine, *The Limits of National Liberation*, p. 106; and Nguyen Tien Hung, *Economic Development* ..., pp. 126; 128, 130. Besides, it was

common knowledge that before as well as after 1975 agricultural co-operatives usually had three account books: the first for the state, the second for the co-operative members (which was "closer to reality"), and the third was kept secret among the members of the management committee (see Nguyen Duc Nhuan, "The Contradictions of the Rationalization of Agricultural Space and Work in Vietnam", *International Journal of Urban and Regional Research*, no. 7 [March 1983], p. 372). As for Truong Chinh, he complained that "many agricultural producers' co-operatives have filed inaccurate efficiency returns", *Nhan Dan*, 27 February 1974. On the other hand, according to *Nhan Dan*, 19 June 1974, "statistical data concerning paddy yield and production volume [in the state farms] [were] exaggerated to magnify achievements, but they [were] trimmed down when the time came to fulfill grain deliveries."

95. In November 1958, the Party decided to switch over from MATs to EAPCs, and *this switch-over represented an important turning point* ("as a qualitative change" in Marxist terminology) *in the whole process of co-operativization*.
96. 1960: 3.59 tons; 1965: 3.91 tons; 1970: 4.31 tons; 1975: 4.49 tons per hectare. See *Tinh Hinh Phat Trien . . .* , p. 119.
97. BBC, *SWB WS*, No. 796, 28 September 1974, p. A16.
98. Le Duan, *Third National Congress . . .* , Vol. 1, p. 122.
99. Acknowledgement made by Chu Van Lam, "Khoan San Pham Va Che Do Kinh Te Hop Tac Xa Trong Nong Nghiep", *Nghien Cuu Kinh Te*, nos. 1 and 2 (1988), p. 33. At the Sixth Central Committee Plenum (September-August 1979), the Party also admitted that "during the past ten years, North Vietnam's agriculture has almost stagnated". Quoted by Le Trong, "Ve Thu Lao . . . ", p. 25.
100. Official source cited in A. Vickerman, *The Fate of the Peasantry . . .* , p. 191.
101. Tran Duc, "Tim Hieu Viec . . . ", p. 31.
102. Calculation based on official data mentioned in *Tinh Hinh Phat Trien . . .* , p. 103.
103. *Nhan Dan*, 24 May 1974.
104. *Nhan Dan*, 3 May 1974.
105. For more details concerning the procurement prices, see Nguyen Duong Dan, *Kinh Te Nong Nghiep Xa Hoi Chu Nghia* (Hanoi: Nha Xuat Ban Nong Bghiep, 1983), pp. 137–43; and Vu Huy Bang's article in *Etudes Vietnamiennes*, no. 13 (Hanoi: 1967), pp. 154–56.
106. Christine White, "Agricultural Planning, Pricing Policy and Cooperatives in Vietnam", World Development 13, no. 1, pp. 99–113; A. Fforde and S. Paine, *The Limits of National Liberation*, pp. 108–10; Ngoc Luu Nguyen, *Peasants, Party and Revolution . . .* , pp. 537–41; A. Vickerman, *The Fate of the Peasantry . . .* , pp. 171–72; 184–85, 251–52; 258.
107. Tran Duc, "Tim Hieu Viec . . . ", p. 31.
108. Chu Van Lam, "Khoan San Pham . . . ", p. 34.
109. Truong Chinh, *Resolutely Taking the North Vietnam Countryside . . .* , p. 11. As for Le Duan, he asserted in 1960 that "the peasants, the handicraftsmen . . . are toiling people . . . But at the same time, they are small producers . . . (and)

have a more or less spontaneous tendency to capitalism . . . We must of necessity educate them . . . at the same time devis[e] appropriate measures to cut their economic ties with the bourgeoisie in order to restrict and eliminate their spontaneous tendency to capitalism" (*Third National Congress* . . . , Vol. 1, pp. 80–81). Again, in 1974, he emphasized, at the Thai Binh Conference on Agriculture that "small production by itself begets capitalism daily and hourly" (*Selected Writings*, p. 522).

110. Xue Muqiao, *China's Socialist Economy*, p. 38.
111. See, for instance, *Nhan Dan*, 17 April 1974.
112. See his report at the Thai Binh Conference on Agriculture in August 1974 (BBC, *SWB WS*, No. 803, 1 October 1974, p. C.3).
113. *Nhan Dan*, 27 February 1974.
114. Zhan Wu and Liu Wenpu's article in *China's Socialist Modernization*, edited by Yu Guang Yuan (Beijing: Foreign Languages Press, 1984), pp. 214–15; and Zhang Yulin's article in *China's Economic Reforms*, pp. 126–30.
115. Truong Chinh, *Selected Writings*, pp. 593–94.
116. Xue Muqiao, *China's Socialist Economy*, pp. 38 and 237.
117. Chu Van Lam, "Khoan San Pham . . . ", p. 35. See also Nguyen Ngoc Long, "Chong Benh Kinh Nghiem, Giao Dieu, Doi Moi Tu Duy Ly Luan", *Tap Chi Cong San*, no. 5 (1988), p. 36; and Tran Duc, "Tim Hieu Viec . . . ", p. 32.
118. Carmen Diana Deere, "Agrarian Reform, Peasant and Rural Production . . . ", in *Transition and Development. Problems of Third World Socialism* (New York: Monthly Review Press, 1986), p. 119.
119. *50 Years of Activities of the Communist Party*, pp. 133–34. On this score, see also Bui Cong Trung, *Mien Bac Viet Nam Tren Con Duong Tien Len Chu Nghia Xa Hoi*, 2nd edition (Hanoi: NXB Su That, 1961), pp. 117–28; Vien Kinh Te Hoc, "35 Nam Kinh Te . . . ", pp. 79–84; *Lich Su Dang Cong San* . . . , pp. 43–49; Vo Nhan Tri, *Croissance Economique* . . . , pp. 220–27; 298–315; and E.P. Glazunov, *Pryeobrazovanye Chastnoy Promyshlyen-nosti I Torgovli Vo Vietname* (Nauka, Moskva, 1981), chaps 3 and 4 (in Russian).
120. *Lich Su Dang Cong San* . . . , pp. 23; and 45.
121. V. I. Lenin, *Selected Works*, Vol. IX (London: Lawrence and Wishart, 1946), p. 238.
122. V. I. Lenin, *Selected Works*, Vol. 11 (New York: International Publishers, 1952), pt. 2, p. 644; and *Oeuvres Choisies*, in 2 volumes (Editions de Moscou, 1954), t. 2, p. 665.
123. *Selected Works of Mao Tse Tung* (Peking: Foreign Languages Press, 1977), Vol. 5, p. 101.
124. Xue Muqiao wrote "China was the first country in which the proletariat succeeded in 'buying off' the bourgeoisie and transforming capitalist economy through State capitalism" (*China's Socialist Economy*, pp. 26–27). Concerning the various forms of Chinese "State Capitalism", see ibid., pp. 27–32. See also Chu Yuan Cheng, *China's Economic Development. Growth and Structural Change* (Boulder, Colorado: Westview Press, 1982), chap. 5.
125. *50 Years of Activities of the Communist Party* . . . , p. 136.

126. Le Duan, *Third National Congress* . . . , Vol. I, pp. 78–79.
127. *Nhan Dan*, 19 July 1988.
128. *Lich Su Dang* . . . , p. 48.
129. *50 Years of Activities of the Communist Party*, p. 136.
130. *Lich Su Dang* . . . , p. 49.
131. Le Duan, *Third National Congress* . . . , Vol. I, pp. 80–81.
132. Van Tung, "Phat Trien Manh Tieu, Thu Cong Nghiep", *Tap Chi Cong San*, no. 8 (1987), p. 6.
133. *Nhan Dan*, 19 July 1988.
134. Le Duan, *Third National Congress* . . . , Vol. I, pp. 85; 117–18.
135. *Lich Su Dang Cong San* . . . , Tap III, p. 77.
136. Ibid., pp. 74–77; and *The Road to Happiness and Prosperity*, Resolution of the 7th Plenum (Hanoi: Foreign Languages Publishing House, 1963).
137. Le Duan, *Selected Writings*, p. 246.
138. Ibid., pp. 247–49.
139. Xue Muqiao, *China's Socialist Economy*, p. 9.
140. Mao Tse-Tung, "On the Ten Great Relationships" (Peking: Foreign Languages Press, 1977), pp. 4–5. See also Robert Bideleux, *Communism and Development* (London and New York: Methuen, 1985), pp. 135–36; and R. Kalain, "Mao Tse Tung's 'Bukharinist' Phase", *Journal of Contemporary Asia* 14, no. 2 (1984): 148–52.
141. N. Bukharin, "Notes of an Economist", reprinted in *Economy and Society* 8, no. 1 (November 1979): 481, 492; A. Erlich, *The Soviet Industrialization Debate* (Harvard University Press, 1960), p. 82; and Stephen Cohen, *Bukharin and the Bolshevik Revolution* (Oxford University Press, 1977), pp. 179–80.
142. See "Economic Policy and National Liberation War", *Vietnamese Studies*, no. 44 (Hanoi: 1976), pp. 192, 198, 205.
143. Xue Muqiao, *China's Socialist Economy*, pp. 8–12; Ma Hong, *New Strategy for China's Economy* (Beijing: New World Press, 1983), pp. 37, 42; and Rosalie L. Tung, *Chinese Industrial Society After Mao* (Toronto: Lexington Books, 1982), pp. 19–20, 64–69.
144. Le Duan, *Selected Writings*, pp. 249–52.
145. For more details, see *Tinh Hinh Phat Trien Kinh Te Va Van Hoa Mien Bac Xa Hoi Chu Nghia Viet Nam 1960–75* (Hanoi: Tong Cuc Thong Ke, 1978), p. 103.
146. Regarding the importance of foreign aid in connection with the building of a modern industry, Nguyen Duy Trinh said: "The fraternal [i.e., socialist] countries have in particular granted us all-sided aid in funds, equipment, raw materials, technique and technicians: thanks to this aid, we have . . . speeded up the development of industry and of the whole national economy [during the three-year plan] . . . In the First Five-Year Plan period, we will continue to ask for overall assistance from the Soviet Union, China and other fraternal countries in the building of key projects" [particularly in heavy industry], "the building of a number of establishments in light industry . . . , the development of state farms . . . ." See his report on the tasks of the First Five-Year Plan in *Third National Congress of the Vietnam Workers' Party, Documents*, Vol. II (Hanoi: Foreign Languages Publishing House, 1960), pp. 28, 54. See also Irene Norlund, "The Role of Industry in Vietnam's Development Strategy, *Journal of Contemporary Asia*, no. 1 (1984), p. 98; and

Andrew Vickerman, "A Note on the Role of Industry in Vietnam's Development Strategy", *Journal of Contemporary Asia*, no. 2 (1985), p. 225.
147. Concerning the mutual constraints between agriculture and industry, see, in particular, Nguyen Xuan Lai, "Interdependence between Agriculture and Industry", *Vietnamese Studies*, no. 27, pp. 123–76; and A. Vickerman, "A Note on the Role of Industry ... ", pp. 226–27, 229. As for the constraint constituted by the chronic shortage of state-supplied "complementary inputs" (lack of marketed agricultural surplus: foodstuffs; raw materials, etc . . .) needed to operate the new industrial capacity, see Adam Fforde's paper on "Industrial Development in the Democratic Republic of Vietnam and the Historical Background to Developments during the Post-Reunification Period" (Department of Economics, Birkbeck College, London, January 1986), pp. 2–3; and also A. Fforde and S. Paine, *The Limits of National Liberation*, pp. 38–41.
148. Melanie Beresford, *Vietnam* . . . , pp. 141 and 143.
149. Nguyen Ngoc Long, "Chong Benh Kinh Nghiem, Giao Dieu, Doi Moi Tu Duy Ly Luan", *Tap Chi Cong San*, no. 5 (1988), p. 35.
150. *Nhan Dan*, 20 October 1986.
151. Nguyen Ngoc Long, "Chong Benh Kinh Nghiem . . . ", p. 35.
152. *Third National Congress* . . . , Vol. I, p. 119. See also p. 86.
153. Concerning the advantages of local industry in general, see Michael Ellman, *Socialist Planning* (Cambridge University Press, 1979), p. 138. Regarding the local industry in North Vietnam, see Nguyen Duc Nhuan, "Désurbanisation et Développement régional au Vietnam (*1954–1977*) (Paris: Centre de Sociologie Urbaine, n.d.), pp. 84–89; 103; 120–122.
154. "Economic Policy and National Liberation War", *Vietnamese Studies*, no. 44 (Hanoi, 1976), pp. 197–204.
155. Max Spoor, *Economy of North Vietnam* . . . , p. 101.
156. Official data quoted in Vo Nhan Tri, *Croissance economique* . . . , pp. 316–17.
157. Vien Kinh Te Hoc, *35 Nam Kinh Te Viet Nam* . . . , pp. 85–98.
158. *Tinh Hinh Phat Trien Kinh Te Va Van Hoa Mien Bac Xa Hoi Chu Nghia Viet Nam 1960–75*, pp. 65, 78, 111.
159. "Economic Policy and National Liberation War", *Vietnamese Studies*, no. 44 (Hanoi, 1976), p. 209; and A. Vickerman, "A Note on the Role of Industry", p. 228.
160. *Tinh Hinh Phat Trien Kinh Te Va Van Hoa Mien Bac Xa Hoi Chu Nghia Viet Nam 1960–75*, p. 79.
161. *Nhan Dan*, 11 August 1968, complained, for instance, that "in many areas, between 30% and 60% of agricultural tools and machines are out of order due to the fact that they are of poor quality".
162. See Nguyen Nien's article in *Luat Hoc*, no. 2 (Hanoi, 1973), p. 46.
163. *Tinh Hinh Phat Trien Kinh Te Va Van Hoa Mien Bac Xa Hoi Chu Nghia Viet Nam 1960–75*, p. 56.
164. *Nhan Dan*, 8 September 1963. Concerning the amount of aid from the socialist countries, calculated in dong and given by the Ministry of Finance

in Hanoi to this author, see Vo Nhan Tri, *Croissance Economique* ... , p. 555 (nearly 4,229.8 million dong, of which nearly 1,524.6 million were in grants and 2,705.2 million in long-term loans).
165. Quoted by P. Quinn-Judge in *Far Eastern Economic Review*, 2 May 1985, pp. 31–32.
166. Tran Phuong, "Chinh Sach Kinh Te Cua Dang Cong San Viet Nam Trong 5 Nam Qua" (Internal Party Document, 27 November 1980).
167. Interview with F. Nivolon, *Far Eastern Economic Review*, 19 December 1985, p. 98.
168. See I. Arkhipov's article in *Pravda*, 2 September 1971 (in Russian).
169. For details, see *Nhan Dan*, 21 July 1980.
170. *Nong Nghiep* (Hanoi), 5 November 1987.
171. For details, see *Hanoi Radio*, 18 January 1964.
172. *Nong Nghiep* (Hanoi), 5 November 1987. For details concerning Soviet economic aid during the 1965–75 period, see Douglas Pike, *Vietnam and the Soviet Union, Anatomy of An Alliance* (Boulder and London: Westview Press, 1987), pp. 115–16; 121; 125–26. The same author also gave *detailed estimates* of Soviet economic and military aid to North Vietnam *in U.S. dollars* for the 1955–86 period (ibid., p. 139). On this score, see also Thai Quang Trung's article in "Behind the Vladivostok Initiative. The Soviet Strategic Reach in Southeast Asia" (A Special Dossier), *Indochina Report* (Singapore, October 1986), p. 14, where estimations in *U.S. dollars* for the 1965–86 period are given.
173. *Nhan Dan*, 18 July 1985.
174. *Nhan Dan*, 12 July 1980.
175. Vo Nhan Tri, *Croissance Economique* ... , p. 554.
176. Hoang Van Hoan, *Giot Nuoc Trong* ... , pp. 341–42.
177. Ibid., p. 345.
178. Ibid., pp. 342–43.
179. People's Daily and Xinhua News Agency Commentators, *On the Vietnamese Foreign Ministry's White Book Concerning Vietnam–China Relations* (Beijing: Foreign Languages Press, 1979), p. 11. See also Hoang Van Hoan, *Giot Nuoc Trong* ... , p. 340.
180. For details, see *Nien Giam Thong Ke, 1982* (Tai Lieu Toi Mat) (Hanoi: Tong Cuc Thong Ke, 1983), p. 317.
181. Ibid., p. 324.
182. Ibid., p. 315.
183. Ibid., p. 320–21.
184. Tran Ho, "Ve Su Lac Hau Ve Nhan Thuc Ly Luan Kinh Te", *Tap Chi Cong San*, no. 2 (1988) pp. 21–22; Vu Nhat Khai "Nang Cao Chuc Nang Phe Phan, Cai Tao Cua Ly Luan Mac-Lenin", *Tap Chi Cong San*, no. 2 (1988), pp. 32-33; Tran Dinh Nghiem, "Ve Che Do So Huu Xa Hoi Trong Thoi Ky Qua Do Len Chu Nghia Xa Hoi", *Tap Chi Cong San*, no. 3 (1988), pp. 33–37. Concerning the Chinese experience on this score, see, for instance, Xue Muqiao, *China's Socialist Economy*, pp. 236–37; and *Social Sciences in China*, no. 1 (March 1988), p. 16.

185. Ma Hong, *New Strategy* ..., pp. 34–46; Su Shaozhi, "Prospects for Socialism: China's Experience and Lessons", in *Socialism on the Threshold of the Twenty-First Century*, edited by Milos Nicolic (London: Verso, 1985), pp. 200–4; and *China's Socialist Modernization*, edited by Yu Guang Yuan, pp. 65, 68, 101.
186. A. Fforde and S. Paine, *The Limits of National Liberation*, p. 71. See also ibid., p. 55.
187. For more details, see Melanie Beresford, "Vietnam: Northernizing the South or Southernizing the North?", *Contemporary Southeast Asia* 8, no. 4 (March 1987): 268–69.
188. Le Thanh Khoi, *Socialisme et Developpement au Vietnam*, IEDES (Paris: Press Universitaires de France, 1978), p. 8.

chapter **2**

Reunification and "Socialist Transformation", 1975–80[1]

During the two decades that followed the Geneva Accords (July 1954), the economics of North and South Vietnam evolved in quite different directions: the former, as discussed earlier, was based on an attempt to construct socialism while the latter was set on the capitalist path of development.

South Vietnam's economy was mainly characterized by a great excess of consumption over production, large budget and trade balance deficits and, last but not least, a heavy dependence on foreign aid.[2] Suffice it to recall here that, according to a knowledgeable American observer, "when communist forces marched into Saigon on April 30, 1975, the [South Vietnamese] economy was in a state of collapse".[3]

It is worth noting that although these two economies have followed diametrically opposite paths of development, they had in common at least three principal characteristics: strong dependence on foreign aid, excess of consumption over production, and a trade balance deficit. Concerning the budget deficit, one can only conjecture about it as far as North Vietnam is concerned because it has never disclosed the details of its budget. However, the symptoms of its budget deficit were quite evident. In the case of South Vietnam, as mentioned earlier, the official data showed a large budget deficit.

Reunification and Transition to Socialism

Before the complete military victory over the South, the Hanoi leadership let it be understood in Vietnam and abroad that the reunification would be carried out step by step during a period of fifteen years.[4] But hardly six months after the collapse of the South Vietnam Government, at the Twenty-fourth Plenum of its Central Committee (Third Congress, August 1975), the Party decided that the South should bypass a period of separate existence and rapidly move towards socialism. As the Resolution issued at the close of this Plenum pointed out, the strategic task of the Vietnamese revolution in the new stage would be "to complete the reunification of the country and take it *rapidly, vigorously and steadily* to socialism" (emphasis added).[5]

With regard to the South, this Resolution emphasized the task of "carrying out at the same time socialist transformation and socialist construction", that is, "closely combining transformation and construction ... in every field: political, economic, technical, cultural and ideological". It also asserted that " ... the sooner the reunification, the more rapidly the all-round strength of the homeland is promoted".[6]

To implement the Party's policy, a so-called joint Political Consultative Conference on reunification was held in November 1975 in Saigon (which was later renamed Ho Chi Minh City by the unified National Assembly at its first session in June 1976). The Conference was attended by representatives of the North headed by Politburo member Truong Chinh and those of the South led by Pham Hung, also a Politburo member and former Deputy Premier in the North who had been sent to the South late in the 1960s to conduct the war against the United States. This Conference was actually a farce for, as a Vietnamese scholar aptly pointed out, it "consisted of the communist party negotiating with itself, with its number two man [that is, Truong Chinh] on one side and its number four man [that is, Pham Hung] on the other".[7]

Truong Chinh, whose address was regarded as the keynote speech of this Conference, put the issue of reunification in these terms:

... At present, completely liberated, should South Vietnam limit itself with the people's national democratic revolution for a period of time before embarking on the socialist revolution and socialist construction? We think that it is not necessary. The great Spring victory ... of this year [30 April 1975] has put a victorious end to the phase of the people's national-democratic revolution in South Vietnam and opened up for the South Vietnamese people a new phase of the revolution with a new strategic task, that of socialist revolution .... The South Vietnamese people should concretely begin the step-by-step socialist transformation of the national economy and the building up of the first foundations of socialism. At the same time, they must complete the remaining tasks of the people's national democratic revolution[8] [that is, rooting out the compradore bourgeoisie in urban areas, and "abolishing the feudal system of land ownership and putting into effect the slogan 'Land to the Tiller' wherever this agrarian problem is still pending in social life"]. ... From the people's national democratic revolution [the Vietnamese people] must go direct to the socialist revolution, by-passing the stage of capitalist development.[9]

Why did the Party decide to *accelerate* political reunification and consequent socio-economic change in the South, in spite of the fact that in doing so, the badly needed Western aid to the South would certainly not materialize? There may have been various reasons but the chief ones were political and economic in nature. Indeed, at that time, some leading Southern members of the Party and the Provisional Revolutionary Government (PRG) voiced their reservations about the tempo of reunification, particularly the mechanical enforcement of the northern model of socialism in the South (or, in other words, "northernizing" the South). They argued that, without *fully* taking into account the latter's specific characteristics, such a decision would inevitably lead to a decline in the Southern economy in general and a rapid deterioration of the living standards of the Southern people in particular, and consequently, their political disaffection from the new regime. Besides, there existed also some vague hope of a coalition government and a neutralist policy among certain sections of the people in the South, particularly the intellectuals.

All these tendencies were, however, regarded by the Hanoi leadership with great suspicion for it feared that they might ultimately lead to the loss of control of the South or, at least, the creation of potential threats of separatism (or, as a French observer put it, of "dangerous autonomism which might lead up to the forming of revolutionary feudalities" in the South).[10] Consequently, the Hanoi Party leadership wanted to curb these "unhealthy" tendencies by accelerating the process of reunification as the longer it took to do so the harder it would be to realize.

Another reason for quickening the reunification process was the lure of the vast potential of Southern agriculture (in the vain hope of solving rapidly the problem of food sufficiency for the whole country), fishing and forestry, as well as the developed consumer goods industry, and the sophisticated transportation and communications system in the South. On this score, it may be useful to recall here what former Premier Pham Van Dong said at the thirtieth anniversary celebrations of the National Day (September 1975):

> It is certain that the South of our country will soon become a prosperous centre for agricultural production and fisheries . . . In addition, [it] has many industrial branches, especially light and food [processing] industries . . . . Communications and transport, and specially the building industry in South Vietnam have substantial . . . capabilities.[11]

Truong Chinh also emphasized that "economic unification will be very beneficial because the economies of the two zones will be able to complement each other . . . . The aggregate strength of the whole country will create great opportunities for . . . redistributing the productive forces and social labour, stepping up socialist industrialization, carrying out . . . the planning of national economy. . . . ."[12]

These domestic attractions of the South were not the only factors, however, as the Hanoi leadership also took into account certain external considerations. The Twenty-fourth Central Committee Plenum Resolution pointed out that national reunification would "raise Vietnam's prestige in the world",[13] and make it, as Secretary-General Le Duan said, an "impregnable outpost of the socialist system, an important factor of ... national independence, democracy, and social progress in Southeast Asia".[14] To put it plainly, this important statement reveals that the Party had the intention of transforming a united Vietnam into a springboard for the support of revolutionary movements in Southeast Asia.

In retrospect, it can be seen that the over-hasty reunification was economically disastrous not because "the South siphoned off resources" [of the North] as has been suggested[15] — in fact, it was quite the opposite that happened — but because, as foreseen, the Hanoi leadership intended to immediately impose at all costs its Stalinist-Maoist model of development on the South without taking into account the latter's social, economic and psychological characteristics.

In this respect, it may be interesting to point out that in 1984 a senior official of the State Planning Committee indirectly admitted that in the past the Hanoi leadership had failed to take into consideration the South's characteristics, and "arbitrarily applied the .... North[ern model] ... to the South's economy" because it "regarded this model as completely adequate".[16] Recently, a Party economist openly acknowledged that one of the Party's "numerous errors and shortcomings" since reunification was the transplantation of the "Northern model and experience" into the South, particularly in the domain of "socialist transformation" and "socialist construction".[17]

The reunification process moved with relative ease after the joint Political Consultative Conference and in December 1975 it was given final ratification in both the North and the South. By January 1976, the South had returned formally to civilian rule and in April 1976, nation-wide elections were held for a new National Assembly composed of representatives of both zones. This National Assembly, not surprisingly, approved the formation of a new Socialist Republic of Vietnam (SRV), which was formally promulgated on 2 July 1976.

Since "the triumph of national people's democratic revolution" (30 April 1975), the country as a whole had entered a new historical stage, the stage of a "transitional period to socialism" in which, according to Le Duan, "the whole country ... fulfills a *single* strategic task of carrying out socialist revolution".[18] However, since the Chinese attack (17 February 1979), Le Duan had stressed that the Vietnamese people must "strive to carry out *two* strategic tasks", namely, "to build socialism [politically, economically and culturally]" and "to stand ready to defend the homeland".[19] In the political report delivered at the Sixth Party Congress (December 1986), the then Secretary-General Truong Chinh also reaffirmed "the continued performance of [these] two strategic tasks", but emphasized that "while giving constant care to the task of national defence, [the] Party ... continues to attach *prime importance* to the task of building socialism"[20] (emphasis added).

The transition period from being "essentially [an] economy of small-scale production [directly] to socialism [that is, to "large-scale socialist production"], by-passing the stage of capitalist development", would be "largely completed within about twenty years",[21] according to Le Duan in 1976, still in the flush of military victory at that time. However, ten years later, the Party's theoretical and political journal acknowledged that

> because [Vietnam] is advancing toward socialism from a very low starting point ..., [and] is utterly poor ... it would be a harmful illusion to think that we [the Party leadership] need only several decades to complete building socialism. Practical experience gained over the past decade shows what disastrous mistakes, subjectivism, hastiness have led to! It is obvious that the transitional period in our country must be a relatively long historical period .... [and will take] several more decades.[22]

At the Sixth Party Congress, Truong Chinh formally admitted that:

> having failed to fully realize that the period of transition to socialism is a relatively long historical process, which has to go through numerous stages; and owing to hastiness and wishful thinking, the Fourth Party Congress, in its desire to bypass necessary stages, did not [correctly] define the targets for the initial stage [that is, the 1981–90 period].
> ... As a result, over the past ten years [1976–86] *we* have made lots of errors in defining the targets and the steps to take in building the material-technical base in socialist transformation

and economic management.... Our mistakes and shortcomings have made the situation even more difficult".[23]

On the same topic, the new Secretary-General, Nguyen Van Linh, recently emphasized:

> .... The transitional period in [Vietnam] must inevitably unfold in different stages, with each of them having its own specific historical tasks .... It lies in the period of transition from capitalism to socialism worldwide, which began with the [Russian] October Revolution. Against this background, two most important factors of the [present] epoch are directly and deeply affecting the transitional period in [Vietnam]. Firstly, it is the unprecedented growth of the socialist power in the world of which the USSR and the Socialist Community serve as the core..., and secondly, the new cycle of scientific and technological revolution which has been taking place since the mid-1970s.... These are factors which make a deep imprint on the domestic and foreign economic and political policies of our country.[24]

The reader has to bear in mind the above-mentioned concept of the "transitional period", particularly its "initial stage", in order to correctly understand the Party's socio-economic development strategy in the following pages.

Remaining Tasks of the "People's National Democratic Revolution"

As mentioned earlier, from May 1975 onwards, Vietnam embarked upon the "socialist revolution" while *at the same time*, trying to "complete the remaining tasks of the people's national democratic revolution" in the South,[25] namely, the "elimination of the compradore bourgeoisie and the vestiges of feudal landlordism" as advocated by the Twenty-fourth Central Committee Plenum.[26]

For the CPV, the Southern bourgeoisie were divided into two categories: the "compradore bourgeoisie" and the "non-compradore bourgeoisie". The former were said to be big businessmen who were "reactionary in politics", that is, who colluded with the United States and the client Saigon administration [political criterion], and made their fortunes in contract work or commerce in support of the U.S.-Saigon administration war effort, and used the economic clout thus obtained to establish monopoly control over certain markets [economic criterion].[27] They were regarded as the "principal social basis" of the Saigon administration, "which in turn relied on [them] to grow rich".[28] As for the "non-compradore bourgeoisie", it was chiefly composed of former small businessmen, skilled handicraftsmen and professionals who allegedly had prospered as a result of the war with the United States. However, a certain number of them also took part in the resistance movement against the Saigon administration.

From the Party's viewpoint, said Nguyen Van Linh, "on the *strategic* plane, the bourgeoisie — either compradore or not — must be eliminated [as a social class] in the course of socialist revolution. However, on the *tactical* plane, the ways of dealing with each of these categories should vary, given that they have different characteristics".[29] Against the "compradore bourgeoisie", the tactics used was the total or partial confiscation of property, whereas against the "non-compradore bourgeoisie" it was "socialist transformation" through various forms of "state capitalism", as it was implemented in the North in the late 1950s. But Linh stressed that this differentiated tactic only represented "two different forms of class struggle" *within* the framework of the dictatorship of the proletariat.[30]

Enforcing the Twenty-fourth Plenum's Resolution, the PRG — which was, in fact, a simple political tool of Hanoi — promulgated its fourteen-point "Declaration concerning Industry and Trade" at a press conference in Saigon on 11 September 1975. The eleventh point of this Declaration stipulated: "All property of compradore capitalists . . . , whether they have fled abroad or remain at home, is . . . confiscated in whole or in part depending on the nature and extent of their offences".[31] Theoretically, the revolutionary government confiscated only their industrial and commercial property (that is, their means of production and business) and left them the necessary means to earn a living. However, in practice, not only was their industrial and commercial property wholly confiscated but also, according to some testimonies given to this writer, their valuable personal items such as jewellery and high-quality watches. Point 10 particularly emphasized that "speculators and economic monopolists [in this case, the "compradore capitalists"] who are causing disturbances to the market . . . will be arrested . . . , [and] their property may be confiscated in whole or in part".

Later on, in July 1976, in a Resolution passed by the Politburo, the Party insisted again on implementing the policy of "eliminating the compradore bourgeoisie".[32]

Early on the morning of 11 September 1975, army units, public security agents, local militia and self-defence units, and communist youth cadres raided the houses of compradore capitalists in Saigon-Cholon and other South Vietnamese cities. It was the beginning of a nation-wide campaign under the code name "X1" which, within a few days, led to the arrest of many "traffickers, and speculators" besides several hundred compradore capitalists. They were charged with illegal profiteering — not only after "Liberation" but also before it — and a variety of other economic offences. This "X1" campaign, which lasted from September 1975 till December 1976, was, according to the official media, "the logical continuation of the military and political campaign against the puppet regime rigged up by US imperialism" on the economic plane.[33]

The actual number of victims of this campaign in Saigon-Cholon and seventeen other provincial cities in the South reached 670 heads of families. However, when the "X1" campaign concluded, only 159 of them — of whom 117 were ethnic Chinese — were officially considered as genuine compradore capitalists.[34] Why had there been such a great margin of error in the arrests? According to the Party "Committee for Transformation of Private Industry and Trade", in the heat of the action the Party had not made a distinction between compradore and non-compradore capitalists, particularly in the provincial cities. In addition, it was also acknowledged that the compradore capitalists — who should have been the only targets at that moment — had been lumped together with the non-compradore capitalists who allegedly had "committed political as well as economic offences". Besides, the "Committee for Transformation of Private Industry and Trade" also admitted that prior to the attack against the "compradore bourgeoisie", the Party did not have enough time to determine precisely and concretely all the criteria which characterized that social class.

It is worth noting that during the "X1" campaign, the "non-compradore bourgeoise" and other private merchants were still excluded from attack. They even received assurances that the "X1" campaign was not a prelude to a general attack against them,[35] whereas, in fact, the elimination of the "compradore bourgeoisie" had already been conceived by the Party as a good precondition for the "socialist transformation" of the non-compradore bourgeoisie at a later stage![36]

As mentioned earlier, the majority of "compradore capitalists" (about 70 per cent) was composed of ethnic Chinese. Therefore, it may be useful to examine briefly here the history of Chinese immigration into Vietnam, in particular into the Saigon-Cholon area where about half of South Vietnam's one million ethnic Chinese lived in 1975. Over the past centuries, large numbers of Chinese from Kwangtung, Fu Kien, Chao Chou, and Hainan came and settled in Vietnam. During the thousand years of Chinese rule, starting from the beginning of the Christian era, Vietnam had received Chinese immigrants coming as occupation troops, administrators, landlords and traders.[37] Under French rule, Chinese immigration to Vietnam was stepped up: between 1925 and 1933, up to 600,000 people came and settled in Vietnam. During the Sino-Japanese war, for various reasons, many Chinese also left their country for Vietnam. And under the Saigon administration, many Chinese from Macao, Hong Kong and Taiwan also came to South Vietnam for business activities and then stayed there.

A fraction of those Chinese which constituted the *Hoa* bourgeoisie collaborated with Western capitalists in tapping the natural riches, exploiting the people, checking the development of Vietnamese capitalism, and became wealthy.[38] Under French rule, the collecting of paddy in the Mekong delta was in the hands of Chinese merchants who resold it to French companies for export. Industrial commodities imported from France by French companies in Vietnam were retailed to the rural population in the South by Chinese merchants, some of them holding exclusive distribution rights.

Later, in the 1960s and 1970s, the United States reportedly made use of the relatively developed trade and service network of the *Hoa* capitalists to meet their military needs. This was a golden opportunity for the *Hoa* compradore capitalists to get rich, particularly from 1965 until 1975. Throughout the war with the United States, by taking advantage of U.S. aid, they expanded not only their trade and services but also their operations in other domains. They controlled almost all key sectors of the South's economy: trade, industry, banking, communications and transport. According to Hanoi, they controlled up to two-thirds of the amount of cash in circulation, 80 per cent of the processing industry, 100 per cent of the wholesale trade, 50 per cent of the retail trade, and 90 per cent of the import-export trade. They completely monopolized the grain business, obtained up to 80 per cent of all credit granted by South Vietnamese banks, owned 42 out of the 60 major companies with a turnover of one billion piasters and more, and accounted for two-thirds of the total annual investments in the South. The business circles called them "crownless kings": rice "king", gasoline "king", scrap-iron "king"; agro-machine "king", wheat flour "king" and so forth.[39]

Their huge materials supply system ensured maximum support for whatever they were engaged in producing. And their deliveries to the market were allegedly calibrated so as to ensure maximum profits. They were able to control the market and prices through their import-export and transport systems, and also through the network of big and small retailers of Chinese stock who acted as their underlings and providers of economic intelligence.

The *Hoa* compradore bourgeoisie in South Vietnam also had the economic and political backing of the Chinese capitalists in the United States, Taiwan, Hong Kong, and other countries in Southeast Asia. Particular mention should be made here of the assistance provided by the Chinese capitalists in Taiwan who constituted the link between the Chinese business communities in Southeast Asia and the *Hoa* compradore capitalists in South Vietnam.

The relationship between the *Hoa* compradore capitalists and the bigwigs of the Saigon administration and army was reportedly very close. The former gave to the latter valuable gifts and shares in industrial and banking firms, and entertained them to lavish banquets and, in plush night-clubs. In turn, the Saigon administration and army elites colluded with the *Hoa* compradore bourgeoisie in order to acquire greater wealth, so forming "the bureaucratic and militaristic wing" of the Southern compradore bourgeoisie.[40]

The most typical representative of the *Hoa* compradore capitalists was undoubtedly Ly Long Than who reportedly had large assets in eighteen major commercial and industrial enterprises (Vinatexco and Vinafilco textile factories, Vinatefinco dye-works, Vicasa steel factory, Nakydaco edible oil factory, Rang Dong sea transport company, a real estate company, a plush hotel, an insurance company and many restaurants) and sixteen banks including the Bank of China, the Agricultural Bank, and the Agriculture-Industry-Commerce Bank.[41] A visitor to Cholon — "a state within the state" before 1975 — could see a multitude of import-export companies, banks, modern high-rise buildings, plush hotels and restaurants owned by the *Hoa* businessmen.

As for the Vietnamese compradore capitalists, the case of Hoan Kim Quy was often made much of. A native of Hanoi where he had an important import-export firm, he went South in 1954, and made his fortune from the manufacture of barbed wire, the operation of a large textile and appliance import company, and the gold trade. He was Director General of Vitako Company, and a major shareholder in several banks. He was also a member of the Upper House, and known for his close association with Nguyen Van Thieu's family.

After the "Liberation", the compradore capitalists, in particular the *Hoa* businessmen, were accused of having engaged in speculation and hoarding of basic commodities and trafficking in gold, diamonds, narcotics and foreign exchange to such an extent that they allegedly made stabilization of the economy impossible. Their main tactics consisted of competing with the state-trading agencies in purchasing goods, especially rare basic commodities, and then selling them in small quantities at exorbitant prices, thus creating an artificial shortage of goods in order to raise prices. By subtle methods, they bribed government employees into illegally siphoning off materials from State warehouses, with which they produced commodities destined for the black market, and evaded taxation.

They were also accused of manufacturing fake goods, including medicine and foodstuff. Moreover, some of them reportedly "continued to maintain connections with counter-revolutionaries".[42] The fact that most of the victims of the "X1" campaign were ethnic Chinese suggests that the revolutionary government wanted to penetrate the *Hoa* community, particularly in Cholon, break up the formidable power structure which governed it. The Party perceived that "to liberate themselves, the Vietnamese people had to struggle not only against the imperialists and feudalists but also against the *Hoa* compradore capitalists. This struggle, therefore, assumed the character of both a class struggle and a struggle for national liberation".[43]

In late 1976, according to a Vietnamese source, large sections of the monopolistic business organizations of the compradore bourgeoisie had been dismantled, including the paddy and gasoline monopolies, groups of metal producers, businesses engaged in importing cotton thread, producers of cloth and clothing, importers of chemical products, producers and merchants involved in fertilizer, insecticide, detergent and plastic markets, and nearly all dealers of precious metals.[44]

On the other hand, all the commercial and industrial firms, banks, and transport companies belonging to the compradore capitalists and businessmen who left the country after 30 April 1975 were confiscated by the State. The proclaimed goal of nationalizing those enterprises — which contributed largely to expanding the State sector — was to "increase their production and business operations . . . ."[45] However, their production and business operations did not increase; on the contrary, they seriously declined particularly because of mismanagement.

It is worth noting that, in spite of the "X1" campaign, the *Hoa* compradore capitalists managed to elude most of the revolutionary regulations at that time, and carry on business as if nothing had changed (for example, controlling the wholesale rice trade, hoarding consumer goods, and especially black-marketeering in gold and foreign exchange). One factor which helped these businessmen carry on as before "was the corruptibility of many communist cadres".[46] Moreover, governmental efforts to seize control of their assets had been thwarted to a great extent by their clever last-minute dispersal of goods and raw materials among underlings and small businessmen who were their former clients.

In correlation with this campaign, another important measure aimed at reducing the economic influence of private business in the South was the introduction of a new currency in September 1975. The old Southern piaster was abolished as a medium of exchange, and replaced by a new Southern dong. (This new currency was not to be interchangeable with the dong in use in the North, as it was described as only temporary until final reunification of the two zones.). In theory, all piasters held by private citizens in the South were to be exchanged for the new currency (at the rate of one dong for 500 piasters) but, in reality, each family possessing less than one million piasters was allowed to exchange up to 100,000 piasters for 400 dong and deposit the remainder in the State bank. Small businesses with certified licences could exchange an additional 300,000 piasters for another 600 dong.[47]

This first currency reform was, however, "largely foiled by smart businessmen [that is, Chinese businessmen] who through clever dispersal of their currency holdings and bribes managed to obtain large sums of the new currency".[48]

Regarding the abolition of the feudal system of landownership, one Vietnamese publicist commented that there was no need for a far-reaching land reform similar to that undertaken two decades earlier in the North, because the power of the landlord class in the South had already been broken as a result of previous revolutionary land reform campaigns in the "liberated areas" in the late 1960s as well as Thieu's "land-to-the-tiller" law in 1970.[49]

Therefore, it was only needed to readjust land holdings, that is, to take the "surplus lands" from "upper-middle peasants, rich peasants and rural capitalists" and allot them to "landless or poor peasants".[50] It is worth noting, however, that "immediately after [this readjustment]" the Party urged to "organize mutual-aid groups for agricultural production" which constituted the first step of collectivization for the main objective of this land readjustment was "to supply [the landless peasant] with a means of production as an indispensable initial asset which [would] allow him to participate in the collective economy".[51]

The Second Five-Year Plan (1976–80)

As said earlier, while completing the abovementioned tasks of the "people's national democratic revolution", the whole country embarked on a new phase of revolution, namely the "socialist revolution" since 30 April 1975. Speaking at a large conference of cadres in Hanoi (at which the writer was present) on the eve of the formal signing of the Paris Agreements on Ending the War in Vietnam (January 1973), the then Premier Pham Van Dong said that under the Party's leadership the Vietnamese people had succeeded in defeating the U.S. imperialists, which was the most difficult task. He then continued with the *non sequitur* remark that there was no reason why the Party could not succeed in building a socialist economy as well, which was perceived as a much easier task. This argument was repeated again and again by other Vietnamese leaders afterwards.

In retrospect, however, the new Secretary-General, Nguyen Van Linh, acknowledged recently that

> With the seething impetus brought about by the triumph over the world's richest and strongest imperialists [in 1975] we [the Party leadersl] thought that we could rapidly and successfully achieve the building of socialism in Vietnam; and we simplistically believed that once we had defeated the [enemy] in an extremely fierce war, it would also be easy for us to succeed in economic construction. [But, in so thinking]we did not take into account two completely different [kinds of] laws [that is, "laws" of war and "laws" of economics] .... [and] as a result ... we have set forth an erroneous development strategy concerning the [macro] economic structure, the mechanism of economic management, and the socialist transformation.[52]

Here, it is relevant once again to recall Pham Van Dong's statement made in April 1977 at a reception given in his honour by the Association d'Amitié Franco-Vietnamienne in Paris: By its military victory in the South in April 1975, Socialist Vietnam has set an example to the Third World. And, he emphasized:

> Now, for the purpose of building a new [social and economic] life, I want to tell you that ... we [the Party leadership] will try to build a better and more beautiful life *in order to demonstrate to all the peoples* who are struggling for their national and social emancipation that any people determined to build a new life will be able to do so .... (emphasis added).[53]

In other words, Socialist Vietnam will set an example to the Third World not only in the military field but also in the socio-economic field. Vietnamese leaders, as one can see, were not flawed by an excess of modesty at that time!

* * *

At its Fourth National Congress held in December 1976, the CPV (the Vietnam Workers' Party [VWP] was formally renamed the Communist Party of Vietnam [CPV] at its Fourth National Congress in 1976) mapped out "the line of building a socialist economy" for the *whole* transitional period to socialism[54] as follows:

> To set up *socialist industrialization* ... and take the economy of (the) country from small-scale production to large-scale socialist production. *To give priority to the rational development of heavy industry* on the basis of developing agriculture and light industry, (and) build industry and agriculture in the whole country into an industrial-agricultural economic structure; build the central[ly-run] economy while developing the regional economies; ... combine [economic construction] with national defence; strengthen ... the cooperation and mutual assistance with fraternal socialist countries ..., at the same time develop our economic relations with other countries ....[55]

Flushed with victory, the Party thought in 1976 that "the process of taking the economy ... from small-scale production to large-scale socialist production [in order to "turn Vietnam into a socialist country with modern industry and agriculture"] shall be largely completed within about twenty years"![56] However, ten years later, the Party realized that Vietnam has [still] to make strenuous efforts for several more decades ["fifty years or even more"] in order to bring to fruition the socialist industrialization".[57]

It was also at this Fourth National Congress that the Party unveiled its Second Five-Year Plan (FYP) (1976–80) for the reunified country.[58]

Seven fundamental tasks were outlined for fulfilment during this FYP:

1. "Concentrate the forces of the whole country to achieve a sudden spurt of *agriculture* ...; vigorously develop *light industry* ... (including handicrafts and small[-scale] industries) ...; improve the *material and cultural life* of the people ....
2. Turn to full account the existing heavy industry capacity and build new bases of *heavy industry* ... in order to serve agriculture ... and light industry first of all ....
3. Use all *the [labour] force* ...; combine central with regional economies; build the district into an agro-industrial economic unit step by step; combine [economic construction] with national defence ....
4. Achieve basic *socialist transformation* in the South ...; vigorously improve trade, prices, finance, and banking operations.
5. Rapidly increase the sources of *export [goods]*, first of all agricultural and light industry products; broaden *economic relations with foreign countries*.
6. Strive to develop education, culture and health work ....
7. Effect a deep change in *economic organization and management* ... on the national scale."[59]

The goals of this Second FYP were indeed very ambitious: 21 million (metric) tons of food (paddy and subsidiary crops converted into paddy); 16.5 million pigs; 1 million tons of salt water fish; 10 million tons of coal; 5,000 million kilowatt-hours of electricity; 2 million tons of cement; 1.3 million tons of chemical fertilizer; 300,000 tons of steel; 450 million metres of cloth; and 130,000 tons of paper, and so forth.[60] In retrospect, the Party leadership acknowledged that "in the years 1976–80 [it] set too high targets for ... development of production" owing to "hastiness and wishful thinking".[61]

Generally, one could explain these over-ambitious objectives by the fact that (1) the Hanoi leadership was over-confident in itself after the military victory, and tended to set planned targets mainly based on "subjectivism, voluntarism in defiance of objective [economic] laws" as Nguyen Van Linh acknowledged,[62] and (2) it also expected to receive a massive amount of foreign aid from the East as well as from the West (Western industrialized countries, including the United States, and international financial agencies), and some foreign investment.[63] However, the overall level of Western aid (in spite of Pham Van Dong's extended tour of Western Europe during the spring of 1977) and foreign investment (despite the promulgation of a relatively liberal foreign investment code in 1977)[64] was rather disappointing.

After a few years of implementation, the Party had to modify the guidelines of the Second FYP, following the Chinese attack against the Northern provinces in February 1979. However, this reorientation was carried out within the framework of the economic policy already defined by the Fourth Party Congress, namely: (1) "to boost production and socialist transformation ..." and, at the same time, (2) "to strengthen and consolidate national defence and [internal] security; to be ready to fight resolutely to defend the homeland", and (3) "to continue to build the material and technical basis of socialism".[65] This process can best be understood by looking at the main branches of the national economy, namely, agriculture, industry and handicraft, and foreign economic relations.

Agriculture

As mentioned earlier, at its Fourth National Congress, the Party contemplated concentrating the resources of the whole country to achieve a leap forward in agriculture. However, it was not until the Second Central Committee Plenum (June-July 1977) that the Party began to "realize the prime importance of agricultural development in the initial stage of socialist construction".[66] At this Plenum, the Party also acknowledged that "for quite a long period .... [it had] dissociated industrial development from agricultural development" instead of conceiving them as "a unified economic structure".

A few years later, in 1980 a Vietnamese leader stressed again "the primary task" of developing agriculture.[67] However, this awareness of the primary importance of agriculture was at that time still hazy and only in theory. In practice, not only was the share of agriculture in the total amount of state investments in the national economy well below that of industry, but it also declined from 20 per cent in 1976 to 19 per cent in 1980 in spite of Pham Van Dong's prediction at the Fourth Party Congress that 30 per cent of the State funds would be invested in agriculture during the Second FYP.[68] This is borne out by Table 2.1.

TABLE 2.1
Sectoral Composition of State Investments, 1976–80

	1976	1977	1978	1979	1980
Total (Millions of dong, at 1970 constant prices) of which:	2,979.4	3,719.7	4,064.5	3,964.5	3,712.9
— Agriculture (% share in total investment)	20.0	23.7	22.7	20.1	19.0
— Forestry (")	2.3	3.2	3.4	2.9	2.7
— Industry (")	31.9	31.3	33.6	39.1	40.7
— Capital Construction (") Etc.	5.4	5.1	5.6	4.5	5.4

SOURCE: *Nien Giam Thong Ke 1982* (Tai Lieu Toi Mat) (Hanoi: Tong Cuc Thong Ke, 1983), pp. 223; 230.

It is worth noting also that from 1976 to 1980 the State funds destined for agriculture increased by only 18.6 per cent whereas those destined for industry grew by 59 per cent.[69] In retrospect, the Party recently acknowledged that it was a great mistake for not concentrating enough State investments on agriculture during the Second FYP,[70] and the consequences of this error were strongly felt in the following five-year plans.

* * *

Regarding the socialist transformation of the countryside, which was another important aspect of the agricultural policy, the Party advocated the "consolidation and perfection" of the current socialist relations of production in the North on the one hand, and the beginning of the revolutionary transformation of the "old" relations of production in the South, on the other. In fact, it was especially a question of socialist reconversion of Southern agriculture. In this respect, the Party envisaged at its Fourth Congress "to develop the work-exchange teams and the solidarity-teams, and build pilot cooperatives" as well as to "immediately strengthen the district level..., [and] prepare the necessary conditions to undertake large-scale cooperativization of agriculture in a steady, rapid ... way".[71]

It was especially since the Second Plenum of the Central Committee (June-July 1977) that the agricultural collectivization (or "co-operativization") was carried out in order to "establish unified socialist relations throughout the country ... [so as] to develop agriculture on lines of large-scale socialist production".[72] The Party also decided at this Plenum that "by the beginning of 1978, each province must have set up a 'pilot' district and some 'pilot' cooperatives".[73]

At this Plenum, the Party also asserted the need "to closely coordinate the [socialist] transformation of agriculture with that of private capitalist trade and industry" in each district. Following this Plenum came a series of Directives of the Central Committee's Secretariat (Directives No. 15 in August 1977; Nos. 28 and 29 in December 1977), and especially the Politburo Directives No. 43 and 57 issued in April and November 1978 respectively which ordered to step up "quickly" and "resolutely" the collectivization of Southern agriculture with the clear intention of pushing the peasants into "production collectives" (that is, the equivalent of elementary agricultural producers' cooperatives in the North) by the end of 1979.[74]

Thus, the collectivization drive was launched on the initiative of the Party leadership itself. But when it came up against fierce reaction by the peasants in the Mekong Delta, Le Thanh Nghi, a Politburo member, squarely laid the responsibility for that action at the local cadres' door:

> A number of cadres' ... hastiness and over- simplification of things ... have created ... adverse consequences .... As a result of their hastiness and over-simplification the building of production

collectives[75] has been done in a hasty, impetuous and unprepared manner, and the peasants in certain areas [not only "in certain areas" alas!] have been forced to join these collectives. This shortcoming ... has caused many production collectives to achieve poor results in their production, to collapse or remain in existence merely for the sake of formality ...[76]

The hastiness of local cadres can be explained mainly by the fact that the upper echelons of the Party and government apparatus always set rather unrealistic target dates for achieving co-operativization when the peasants were still recalcitrant because the so-called advantages of joining the production collectives were not yet evident. Therefore, local cadres charged with pushing the movement were bound to feel that they could meet the target only by "using constraint rather than persuasion", as the Party's newspaper acknowledged.[77] This admission, as well as other recent acknowledgements in the Party's theoretical and political journal[78] belie the assertion of the Party's *History*, according to which "the forms and steps ... taken [in order to bring] the [Southern] peasants to collective production [were] based on [their] willingness."[79]

Recently, in assessing the lessons of the Party's policy concerning collectivization, Truong Chinh, the chief promoter of forced co-operativization in the North in the late 1950s, and ardent proponent of accelerated collectivization in the South, said that in order

> to advance to socialism, the tendency toward private ownership must be eliminated (*sic*). But ... it must be done gradually by raising the level of production socialization while educating our peasants continuously, actively, and persistently, helping them gradually change their way of thinking . . ., and not by giving orders and applying administrative, coercive measures to eliminate this tendency overnight .... Our peasants ... will object if we [the Party leadership] impose on them what is against their legitimate interests and if we force them to yield to our subjectivist will.[80]

The basic reason for forced collectivization in the South was more or less the same as that for the North in the late 1950s which has already been discussed.

Suffice it to recall here that, whereas in the coastal plains of Central Vietnam forced collectivization did not meet strong reaction from the peasants because of certain specific economic and political factors,[81] it brought about a fierce resistance from the restive peasants of the Mekong Delta, including those who actively supported the communists during the war with the United States. This was evident from their boycotting of the co-operative movement, refusing to harvest crops in time, abandoning large stretches of land, slaughtering livestock, destroying fruit trees, selling machines and farm implements before joining the production collectives, and even challenging the cadres-in-charge.[82]

According to an official source, more than 10,000 out of the 13,246 production collectives which had been set up in 1979 collapsed by the beginning of 1980. The same phenomenon also occurred with regard to "pilot co-operatives".[83] The failure of this forced collectivization brought about uncertainty among Party members and local leaders. Hence, Directive No. 93 of the Central Committee's Secretariat was issued (in June 1980) to boost collectivization again as well as correct previous errors. By the end of 1980, it was proclaimed that there existed 3, 729 production collectives and 137 agricultural co-operatives in the South.[84]

However, in retrospect, a Vietnamese economist has acknowledged that "shortcomings and errors" were committed during this collectivization drive. And he continued:

> the main error ... was the mechanical application of the experience of collectivization of some countries which had implemented it before [that is, the USSR and the People's Republic of China]. The [Party leadership's] simplistic views on socialism and on the way to take the peasants to socialism [that is, through collectivization] .... without taking into account the real situation [in the South] ... has not only developed, but on the contrary put a check on the potential possibilities of the ... peasants in the initial stage of the transitional period to socialism.[85]

Recently, some Party scholars have even questioned the correctness of the Party's collectivization policy in the North (in the late 1950s) as well as in the South (in the late 1970s) by making such sweeping statements as the following: "The error of collectivization in the past derived from ... [the belief that] the establishment of 'advanced' relations of production *ipso facto* paves the way to the development of the productive forces .... But the actual situation in agricultural production invalidates this [belief] ...."[86] It is interesting to note that this dogmatic belief is certainly of Maoist inspiration.[87]

Besides forced collectivization, the irrational quota procurement prices fixed by the State also constituted a cause of great dissatisfaction among the Southern peasants. These prices were set at such a low level that "in many localities the peasants refuse[d] to sell their produce to the State".[88] That explains why "during the Second FYP, the State-trading agencies did not succeed in meeting the targets of quota procurements at all; worse still, these quota procurements had a tendency to fall, not only relatively but also in absolute terms".

In 1978, the Party newspaper, *Nhan Dan*, complained that the peasants "wasted rice by using it to distill alcohol or to feed pigs and ducks, while it [was] in short supply in a number of cities".[89] Rice was reportedly used to feed pigs at the rate of 1.5 million tons per year in the whole country, particularly in the Mekong delta.[90] Le Duan himself — who, in 1974, tried to justify more or less the low level of quota procurement prices — reportedly admitted at the time of the Sixth Central Committee Plenum (September 1979) that the quota procurement prices enforced until then "did not prompt the peasants to work with zeal".[91]

As for Truong Chinh, he retrospectively acknowledged in 1986 that: "Had our policies [towards the peasants] — especially ... pricing, circulation and distribution policies — been rational, the peasants would certainly not have given up tilling, would not have pulled up tobacco plants, would not have destroyed sugarcane, and would not have given up hog raising; on the contrary they would have enthusiastically produced more ...."[92]

A Vietnamese economist has also acknowledged that "after the first two years [which followed the "liberation" in 1975], agricultural production slowed down, because of mistakes committed in the policy of forced collectivization and the inadequate prices fixed for farm produce".[93]

The great shortage of consumer goods was also due to the

neglect of light industry and handicraft in favour of heavy industry, which did not encourage the peasants to increase production either. As a Vietnamese publicist succinctly put it, their reasoning was: "If I've eaten my fill and can't buy ten metres of cloth [the current ratio was five metres a year], I'll say, 'Forget it. I won't work any more'."[94]

Moreover, the limitation of the household economy and the implementation of the "three-point contract" system in the agricultural producers' co-operatives (already described in Chapter I), also did not prompt the peasants to produce. A Vietnamese economist had aptly remarked that the lack of due regard to the economic interests of the peasants was the principal factor which explained the poor performance of agriculture in the Second FYP.[95]

Thus, in spite of the emphasis laid upon agriculture, gross agricultural output successively fell in 1977 and 1978 (see below). In December 1978, the Fifth Plenum of the Central Committee was convened in order to, *inter alia*, assess the economic situation of the first three years of the Second FYP. Although the flagging economy was rapidly drifting towards a major crisis at that time (that is, *before* the invasion of Kampuchea),[96] this Plenum did not advocate any drastic remedial measure yet. It was not until September 1979 that the Party Central Committee convened its famous Sixth Plenum (Fourth Congress) to tackle the evident socio-economic crisis which had been exacerbated by the Chinese attack in February 1979. Recently, a senior Party official disclosed that, on the eve of this Plenum the country's situation was regarded by Secretary-General Le Duan himself as "perilous" (*"Hiem Ngheo"*).[97]

The Sixth Plenum decided "to amend a number of policies and measures aimed at ... bringing about a turn in production and livelihood .. ",[98] "strengthening national defence and [internal] security ..., [and] overcoming the negative aspects in economic and social activities".[99]

Overall, the new policies emphasized the necessity of (1) maintaining the five economic sectors (that is, State, collective, joint State-private, capitalist, and individual sectors), particularly the private sectors; (2) providing material incentives to enhance production (particularly in agriculture, consumer goods and regional industry), and to boost exports; and (3) granting more autonomy to province and especially district levels.

It is worth noting that these policies had a certain similarity with the "economic readjustment and reform" advocated by Deng Xiaoping at the historic Third Plenum of the Chinese Communist Party Central Committee (December 1978) as far as tolerance of private sectors, acknowledgement of material incentives, and necessity of decentralization are concerned, despite the pervasive Sino-Vietnamese antagonisms at that time.

The fact remains that at its Sixth Plenum (September 1979) — which represented *the first great turning point of post-war Vietnam's economic policy* — the Party overhauled its policy concerning agriculture and advocated a series of measures aimed at giving a new impetus to agricultural production favouring the peasants' interests, namely:

— stabilizing the level of procurement quotas for paddy for five years and re-evaluating the state-fixed prices for all procurement quotas in order to stimulate production;
— stabilizing the agricultural tax (which theoretically represented 10 per cent of the output) for five years;
— allowing the peasants to sell the remainder of their produce (after the deduction of procurement quotas and agricultural tax) either to state trading agencies at "mutually agreed prices" (which were close to the market prices) or in the free market;
— encouraging family-sized units to produce and sell their goods at "market prices"; and
— allowing individual households to cultivate land unused by the co-operatives (and retaining the harvest in full).[100]

In implementing the Sixth Plenum's Resolution, the Politburo issued, in April 1980, a directive on measures to push ahead production, procurement, distribution, consumption and management of food grain. The overall impact of the abovementioned policy on the evolution of agricultural production during the Second FYP is shown in Table 2.2.

From the table it can be seen that the gross value of agricultural production dropped appreciably in 1977 and 1978. The primary

TABLE 2.2
Evolution of Agricultural Production, 1976–80

	1976	1977	1978	1979	1980
Gross value of agricultural output at 1970 constant prices (million dong)	7,035.8	6,633.9	6,516.2	7,083.1	7,613.6
of which:					
— Cultivation	5,677.8	5,254.8	5,219.9	5,717.2	6,096.3
— Livestock	1,358.0	1,379.1	1,296.3	1,365.9	1,517.3
Staples output (paddy & subsidiary crops converted into paddy equivalent, thousands of metric tons)	13,493.1	12,621.8	12,265.3	13,983.8	14,406.4
of which:					
— Paddy	11,827.2	10,597.1	9,789.9	11,362.9	11,647.4
— Subsidiary crops	1,665.9	2,024.7	2,475.4	2,620.9	2,759.0
Average yield per annum (quintal/ha) of which:					
— Paddy	22.33	19.38	17.92	20.72	20.79
— Subsidiary crops (paddy equivalent)	18.3	17.3	18.8	18.3	19.0

SOURCE: *Nien Giam Thong Ke 1982*, pp. 84, 86, 90, 100, 102.

reason for this was that these were the years of forced collectivization in the South; the subsidiary factor was poor weather conditions. After the drastic change of agricultural policy decided at the Sixth Plenum (September 1979) and also because of favourable climatic conditions, agricultural production recovered in 1979 from the low levels of 1977 and 1978. There was a further increase in 1980. However, on the whole the gross value of agricultural output rose by an average of only 1.9 per cent a year in 1976–80, against a target of 8-10 per cent under the Second FYP.

The total staples output (paddy plus subsidiary crops) fell by 9.1 per cent in 1978, compared with 1976, primarily because of collectivization and unfavourable climatic conditions.[101] Although it increased gradually from 1979 and reached 14,382.6 million tons in 1980 the target set for 1980, in the Second FYP, was 21 million tons — a huge gap between target and performance.

As for paddy production alone, it decreased by 17.3 per cent in 1978 compared with 1976 (for the same reasons mentioned above), then increased gradually in the following two years. However, by 1980, it was still below the level of 1976. If one examines separately the evolution of paddy output in the South (where forced collectivization took place), the negative effect of collectivization was more striking: from 6.37 million tons in 1976 output tumbled down to 5.03 million tons in 1978 (a fall of 21 per cent), then climbed up again to 6.46 and 7.26 million tons respectively in 1979 and 1980 after the change of policy in 1979.[102]

The drastic fall in paddy output in 1977 and 1978 was, however, partly compensated by an increase of 65.6 per cent of subsidiary crops during the 1976–80 period. On the whole, during the Second FYP the total staples output increased by 6.7 per cent whereas the population grew by 9.2 per cent. (However, if only paddy production is considered, it decreased by 1.6 per cent whereas the population increased by 9.2 per cent during the period). Hence, the diminution of *per capita* staples output: from 274 kg in 1976, it fell to 238 kg in 1978, then climbed up again to 268 kg in 1980,[103] while the *minimum* standard for human consumption alone, in Vietnamese conditions (that is, excluding seeds, livestock breeding, and so forth) was officially fixed at 300 kg. Consequently, Vietnam had to import "from 8 to 9 million tons" of food (rice, wheat flour, maize, etc) during the whole of the Second FYP[104] in marked contrast to the Party's expectation to "ensure enough food ... for the whole society, as well as a food reserve" by 1980.[105]

The average paddy yield per annum for the whole country also dropped from 22.33 quintal/ha in 1976 to 17.92 in 1978, then recovered in 1979 from the low levels of the previous years of forced collectivization (20.72 quintal/ha) and levelled off in 1980 (20.79 quintal/ha). It is worth noting that in 1980, it was still far below the 1976 level while the proclaimed goal of collectivization was to increase both yield and production.[106] If one looks at the average paddy yield of the South alone, one can see that the harmful effect of forced collectivization was undeniable: from

21.9 quintal/ha in 1976, production fell to 16.6 quintal/ha in 1978, then increased appreciably after the Sixth Plenum's new policy to reach 21.30 quintal/ha in 1979, and 22.1 quintal/ha in 1980.[107]

Nevertheless, the average paddy yield per annum remained low owing chiefly to inadequate irrigation and drainage, shortage of fertilizers and farm implements, and particularly lack of material incentives to the producers.

As for the production of pigs, after sizeable declines in 1977 and 1978, it increased in the following two years as a result of new specific measures implemented by the government. However, by 1980 it reached only a little more than 10 million heads (compared with 8.958 million in 1976)[108] whereas the target set in the Second FYP was 16.5 million heads, as said earlier.

Industry and Handicrafts

In order to create "an industrial-agricultural economic structure" which was regarded as having "a decisive significance" in the process of building "a large-scale socialist production", the Party decided at its Fourth Congress (December 1976) *"to give priority to the rational development of heavy industry* on the basis of the development of agriculture and light industry"[109] (emphasis added) during the *whole* transitional period to socialism. At that time, the Party had not yet divided this transitional period into smaller stages. It also stressed that industry and agriculture should be integrated into "a single entity, developing harmoniously side by side on the path to large-scale socialist production ..., promoting and serving each other".[110]

This policy of "socialist industrialization" was the direct continuation of one implemented during the First FYP in the North which has already been discussed in Chapter 1. Suffice it to note here that in practice, contrary to the abovementioned Party rhetoric, there was no harmonious or balanced development of industry and agriculture but a boost of industry at the expense of agriculture, and in the industrial sector itself, an over-emphasis on heavy industry at the expense of light industry.

In Table 2.1, it can be seen that the share of "industry" (in the restricted sense of the word, that is, excluding "capital construction" or the building industry) in the total amount of state investments was always bigger than that of "agriculture": in 1980 the former represented 40.7 per cent and the latter only 19 per cent, compared with 31.9 per cent and 20 per cent respectively in 1976. The gap between industry and agriculture would be wider if the share of "capital construction" in "industry" is included. Moreover, during the 1976–80 period, state investments destined for "industry" (excluding "capital construction") increased by 59 per cent whereas those destined for agriculture grew by only 18.6 per cent.[111] In industry itself, the stress laid upon heavy industry at the expense of light industry is clearly shown in Table 2.3

TABLE 2.3
State Investments in Industry, 1976–80
(In million dong)

	1976	1979	1980
Total (million dong)	905.5	1,552.0	1,511.5
of which:	(100.0)[a]	(100.0)	(100.0)
— Group A (i.e., heavy industry)	637.8 (67.1)	1,045.8 (67.3)	1,097.0 (72.5)
— Group B (i.e., light industry)	312.7 (32.9)	506.2 (32.7)	414.5 (27.5)

[a] Figures in parentheses are percentage shares in total investment calculated by the author.
SOURCE: *Nien Giam Thong Ke 1982*, p. 206.

From the table it can be seen that the share of heavy industry in the total amount of state investments grew from 67.1 per cent in 1976 to 72.5 per cent in 1978, whereas that of light industry fell from 32.9 per cent in 1976 to 27.5 per cent in 1980. During the same period, state funds destined for heavy industry increased by 71.9 per cent, whereas those for light industry was augmented by only 32.5 per cent.

The main role assigned to heavy industry during the Second FYP was that it was supposed "to serve agriculture, forestry, fisheries and consumer goods".[112] For this purpose the Party decided to develop in particular the engineering, energy, metallurgy and chemical industries. In retrospect, a Vietnamese economist has acknowledged that allocating so much investment to heavy industry was "inadequate [and] ineffective".[113] In fact, the over-emphasis on heavy industry at the expense of agriculture and light industry was not only "inadequate" but also brought about a lopsided economic structure characterized by great imbalances in the national economy, low economic efficiency and serious waste.

Truong Chinh himself admitted in a very important speech delivered at the Hanoi Party Congress (October 1986) that "the Party's fondness for developing heavy industry on a large scale that exceeded [the country's] real capabilities" was one of the "errors of leftist infantilism".[114] Then, in his political report delivered at the Sixth Party Congress (December 1986) he acknowledged that

> in the years 1976–80, we [the Party leadership] stood for promoting industrialization at a time when the premises for it were not yet available.... We did not pay adequate attention to restoring and [readjusting] the economy, laying [too] much stress on building heavy industry and large-scale projects .... Hence, too many investments but very low efficiency.[115]

Echoing this viewpoint, the new Secretary-General Nguyen Van Linh said recently in one of his speeches:

> We [the Party leadership] have set forth erroneous strategic policies .... As far as the economic structure is concerned, we have paid more attention to developing heavy industry on a large-scale basis and at a high speed and belittled agricultural production, consumer goods industry and exports. We have also made indiscriminate investment in capital construction; as a result our investments have been scattered and their efficiency very low.[116]

Recently, a Vietnamese economist wrote in the Party journal that the "main error ... of socialist industrialization in the past stemmed from the very fact of setting the goal of building an independent and relatively comprehensive economy".[117] Consequently, he continued, "it was necessary to give priority to the development of heavy industry from the very beginning of the transitional period [to socialism] in order to lay the foundations of [Vietnam's] 'own' heavy industry .... This error reached its climax in the 1976–80 period".

As for light industry, the Party's decision was "to concentrate on developing branches catering for the vital necessities of life" and "put an early end of the shortage of daily necessities". For that, "special attention must be given to the restoration and vigorous development of handicrafts and small[-scale] industry ...."[118]

In spite of that rhetoric, handicrafts and small-scale industry were in fact "underestimated" and even "neglected".[119] As a result of the neglect of light industry in general and handicrafts in particular, instead of "an early end to the shortage of daily necessities" there was an increased shortage of basic consumer goods in 1979 compared with 1976! Hence, the remedial measures advocated by the Sixth Plenum in September 1979 (see below).

Regarding the "socialist transformation of private capitalist industry and trade" in the South, the Politburo decided "to actively carry out their reconversion" from July 1976.[120] This decision was confirmed a few months later at the Fourth Party Congress.

Party policy towards the capitalist industry and handicrafts consisted of "using, restricting and transforming" the medium enterprises through "joint State-private enterprises" or "cooperative enterprises", and putting the small enterprises under the management of the State sector on the one hand, and transforming the handicrafts "chiefly by means of cooperativization ..." on the other hand. Nonetheless, in the Party's perception, the "reconverted" enterprises should "operate within the framework of the planned socialist economy and serve the interests of socialism".[121] This "socialist transformation" of capitalist industry and trade was the continuation of the "State capitalism" policy which had already been implemented in the North in the late 1950s. Suffice it to recall here Lenin's statement that in a communist regime "State capitalism would be [already] three-quarters of socialism".[122] Transforming private capitalism into "State capitalism" was, as in the case of North Vietnam before, only the first step of the process of socialist reconversion, while the second step would be a rapid change over from "State capitalism" to socialism, that is, the "reconverted" enterprises would become wholly nationalized.

As a matter of fact, by the beginning of 1977, under relentless fiscal, economic and political harassment, a large fraction of private industrialists was forced to "voluntarily offer" (*sic*) their enterprises to the state, and the latter became *ipso facto* nationalized. Then, following an announcement made by Le Duan in July 1977 that the government would soon seize control over the whole capitalist industry and commerce in the South, a "Committee for the Transformation of Industry and Trade" was set up by the Party Central Committee under the chairmanship of Nguyen Van Linh to direct this campaign of "socialist transformation" under the code-name "X2".

Afterwards, according to a knowledgeable source, in mid-February 1978, the Politburo convened a meeting to decide on the assault on capitalist industry and trade in general and on the Chinese economic power in the South in particular, as well as the toppling of Pol Pot in Kampuchea.[123]

It is worth noting that on the eve of the "X2" campaign, Nguyen Van Linh, accused of "Rightism" at that time, was suddenly replaced as chairman of the "Committee for the Transformation of Industry and Trade" by his deputy Do Muoi, a man who had proved his "ability" when he was in charge of "socialist transformation" in the North in the late 1950s, and was also renowned for his unforgettable motto: "Capitalists are like sewer rats; whenever one sees them popping up one must smash them to death!"[124]

However, by the time the government moved decisively to radically abolish the non-compradore bourgeoisie in general, and the capitalist merchants in particular, on 23 March 1978[125] the victims were essentially "medium and small capitalists".[126] Nevertheless, the "X2" campaign was very brutal, particularly against the capitalist merchants who numbered "nearly 40,000 households".[127] They were prohibited from carrying out commercial activities, and ordered to shift to productive activities (such as agriculture, industry and handicrafts, fisheries and forestry) or to join collective or "joint State-private enterprises".[128] They were also compelled to leave Ho Chi Minh City and other cities; but the rich among them, who offered to invest their funds in setting up industrial "joint State-private enterprises" would be allowed to stay in the cities, while others were obliged to go to the "New Economic Zones" (resettlement areas on virgin land) to start any productive activity by investing their own resources.

In the industrial sector 1,500 large and medium-sized private manufacturers were reconverted into state-run enterprises, thus skipping the intermediate link of "joint State-private enterprises". (This overhasty reconversion was regarded later on as a "mistake"). A total of 150,000 workers in these targeted enterprises were affected by the reconversion which equalled 70 per cent of the labour force working in private enterprises.[129]

Although this campaign was allegedly carried out "uniformly... regardless of nationality and religion",[130] the ethnic Chinese were most affected because of their disproportionately high involvement in business, particularly in Cholon which was regarded as "a strong capitalist heart beating inside the socialist body of Vietnam".[131]

Compared with the "socialist transformation" of capitalist industry and commerce in the North in the late 1950s, this "X2" campaign was much more drastic because capitalist business in the South was economically by far stronger than the one that existed in the North.[132] Furthermore, politically, the Party perceived that there was no longer any need to treat the non-compradore bourgeoisie considerately as the revolutionary power was already in firm command of the whole country.[133]

In May 1978, Hanoi also moved to control privately accumulated wealth by introducing a new currency for the whole country,[134] replacing the different currencies for the two zones — a logical follow-up to the drastic clamp-down on private business. The amount of cash that could be exchanged for new banknotes was strictly limited. Amounts above the legal limit were frozen in savings accounts and could only be used after application to the government authorities.

This monetary reform naturally dealt a further blow to the Southern industrial and commercial bourgeoisie and middle-class.[135] By the summer of 1979 the effects of the economic crisis — which was chiefly due to the brutal "socialist transformation" realized "in a hasty way" and in a "voluntarist style",[136] overhasty elimination of non-socialist economic sectors, lack of material incentives, and economic mismanagement — made themselves strongly felt.

It was against this background that the famous Sixth Plenum of the Central Committee was convened (September 1979). The Plenum issued a Resolution in which it acknowledged that the

> shortage [of basic consumer goods] was serious ... and [their] quality was not up to standard. Certain means of production (ordinary and improved tools, bricks and tiles, etc.) which could have been produced [by local industry] were scarce .... The role of the consumer goods and local industries, especially that of small[-scale] industry and handicrafts was not [viewed correctly] .... The State and collective sectors of the economy were not sufficiently strengthened while *the private sector ... was not brought into full play*[137] (emphasis added).

And, as a remedial measure, the Party decided at this Plenum that "alongside the State sector, other [economic sectors, that is, collective, joint state-private, individual and private sectors] must be maintained". It also "laid great emphasis on [boosting] the handicrafts and small[-scale] industry in the local economy, especially in producing consumer goods ....".

In order to encourage private initiative to push forward the production of consumer goods, the Party advocated that:

> What is being satisfactorily produced by cooperatives will not be hastily taken over by the State; and what is being fruitfully done by localities will be continued by them. As regards individual production ... and services, those people who are performing good jobs and services and are turning out good products will be helped to continue their work under State management policies. If it is considered that some types of state-produced goods can now be better produced ... by the handicrafts and small-scale industry and private capitalists, they must be boldly assigned to the latter.[138]

Other new policies advocated by this Plenum included maintaining alongside the State sector the free market where individual peasants and craftsmen, and handicraft co-operatives could freely sell their surplus goods or products not handled by the State-trading agencies; and generalizing the application of material incentives (premiums, bonuses, rewards, etc.) and piece-work rates.[139]

As one can see, the new policies advocated at this Plenum — in agriculture as well as in industry and handicrafts — more or less reversed the previous ones, particularly in the domain of "socialist transformation". In retrospect, Truong Chinh acknowledged that "the [Party leadership's] desire to achieve [socialist] transformation at an early date by quickly abolishing non-socialist economic sectors" in the South in 1978 was "a leftist error" which was imbued with "voluntarism" and "went against the objective law [of the transitional period to socialism].[140] He also emphasized, in another speech, that

> as far as socialist transformation is concerned, [the Party] must step it up on a permanent, continuous basis [in other words, not in one fell swoop as in March 1978] by adopting adequate forms and steps for each locality and the entire country .... [It] must make the relations of production consistently conform with the nature and level of the productive forces, and determined not to eliminate [the non-socialist economic sectors] quickly out of a sense of impatience, thereby causing production to decrease and the market to decline ...[141]

Then, at the Sixth Party Congress (December 1986), drawing the general lesson from past experiences, he pointed out:

> We [the Party leadership] have not yet clearly and consistently determined the viewpoints ... and policies guiding the work of socialist transformation. There have been manifestations of hastiness: we wanted to do away at once with non-socialist economic sectors, to rapidly turn the private capitalist economic sector into a State-run sector . . . . So far as the content of transformation is concerned, we laid stress on changing the ownership of the means of production, but overlooked the settlement of problems relating to management, organization and the system of [income] distribution. We often resorted to campaigns, like coercive measures, running after quantity, but neglecting quality and efficiency .... Thus, many so-called joint

> State-private enterprises, cooperatives and production collectives [in the South] were established only for form's sake, and were not really based on the new relations of production.[142]

As for the new Secretary-General Nguyen Van Linh, he indirectly criticized the former Party leadership by recalling that:

> Regarding Socialist transformation, we [the Party leadership] were heavily preoccupied with efforts to discard former relations of production and carried out [socialist] transformation in a rush, like conducting a campaign with the aim of promptly achieving nationalized and collective socialist ownership without recognizing the reality of a multi-sector economy. As a backward agricultural country advancing to socialism and being devastated by the decades long war, we did not attach importance to tapping all economic sectors to push forward the productive forces, and failed to regard the development of the latter as our most important task.[143]

In an interview with *Vietnam News Agency*, he succinctly said that the former Party leadership had made a big mistake by trying to suppress the private sector during the "X2" campaign: "Our conception of socialism was simplistic and unrealistic".[144]

In view of all this, it would be useful to examine the impact of the above-described industrial policy on the evolution of the total industrial output (that is, the production of industry *plus* handicrafts, the latter representing between 37.3 and 42.4 per cent of the total)[145] during the Second FYP.

From Table 2.4 it can be seen that the gross value of industrial output increased from 1976 to 1978, then began to decrease from 1979 chiefly as a consequence of "socialist transformation"[146] and other concomitant factors such as shortage of raw materials, spare parts, and energy, on the one hand, and mismanagement, and so forth, on the other. Besides, poor performance in agriculture — owing to both forced collectivization (primarily) and unfavourable climatic conditions (secondarily) — also exerted a strong negative impact on the evolution of industrial production, albeit with a certain time-lag. Compared with 1976, the gross industrial output reportedly increased by 2.5 per cent in 1980. Its average annual

TABLE 2.4
Industrial Production, 1976–80
(In million dong at constant 1970 prices)

	1976	1977	1978	1979	1980
Gross Value of Industrial Output [a,b]	8,208.9 (100)	8,707.7 (106.1)	9,674.5 (117.9)	9,382.6 (114.3)	8,413.6 (102.5)
By Sector [b]					
— State-owned and joint-State-private	100.0	116.6	124.0	112.6	24.1
— Small-scale industry and handicrafts	100.0	88.3	107.4	117.1	116.6
By Group [b]					
— Group A (Heavy Industry)	100.0	115.5 [c]	132.5 [c]	140.5	131.4
— Group B (Light Industry)	100.0	105.8 [c]	110.8 [c]	100.7	87.5
By Type of Management [b]					
— Central Management	100.0	116.6	120.9	105.0	86.6
— Local Management	100.0	97.7	115.4	121.7	115.1

[a] In million dong at 1970 constant prices. Note that in Vietnam's gross industrial output there is a great deal of double-counting of intermediate products.
[b] Indexes (1976 = 100)
[c] Calculations based on data mentioned in *Nien Giam Thong Ke 1980* (Tai Lieu Toi Mat) (Hanoi: Tong Cuc Thong Ke, 1981), p. 167.
SOURCE: *Nien Giam Thong Ke 1982*, pp. 169–76.

increase reached 0.6 per cent, compared to a target of 16–18 per cent[147] under the Second FYP — as wide a gap between target and performance as in agriculture.

It is worth noting that this increase in gross industrial output was only due to the growth of small-scale industry and handicrafts production (an increase of 16.6 per cent in 1980 compared with 1976) which largely compensated for the decline in production recorded in the State-owned and "joint State-private enterprises" (a decrease of 5.9 per cent in 1980 compared with 1976), although the latter were in principle assigned "the leading role" in the industrial sector.

From Table 2.4 it can also be seen that heavy industry increased significantly from 1976 to 1978, began to slow down in 1979, and then began to decrease in 1980. On the whole, from 1976 to 1980, it grew by 31.4 per cent. The consumer goods industry also slowly increased during the first three years of the Second FYP, then sharply decreased from 1979. Overall, in 1980 it had declined by 12.5 per cent compared with 1976. Thus, despite the Party's rhetoric mentioned above, heavy industry was pushed forward at the expense of light industry as well as agriculture. As a result, there was an aggravation of economic imbalances at the macro-level, and an exacerbation of the shortage of foodstuff and basic consumer goods, particularly in the last two years of the Second FYP.

In the centrally-run enterprises labour productivity per worker in general continuously declined during the 1976–80 period: from 16.2 dong in 1977 it fell to 11.1 dong in 1980.[148] In the State sector, industrial enterprises reportedly operated only at 30–50 per cent of their productive capacity. In Table 2.5 the output of some principal industrial products in 1980 is compared with that of 1976, as well as with the targets of the Second FYP.

From the table, it can be seen that except for electricity, all major industrial products had declined in 1980 compared with 1976. As for the industrial performance in 1980 it was far below the targets set by the Second FYP.

Concerning the quality of industrial products, Vo Van Kiet admitted that it was in general mediocre or even "very bad".[149] As

TABLE 2.5
Output of Some Principal Industrial Products, 1976–80

	1976	1980 Targets	1980 Performance
Coal (million tons)	5.7	10	5.2
Electricity (billion kWh)	3.06	5	3.65
Cement (thousand tons)	743.7	2,000.0	636.6
Steel (thousand tons)	63.8	300	63.5
Cloth (million metres)	218.0	450	174.4
Chemical fertilizers (thousand tons)	434.8	1,300.0	361.7
Paper of various kinds (thousand tons)	75.0	130	48.3

SOURCES: *Nien Giam Thong Ke 1982*, pp. 187–89; and *Vietnam Courier*, January 1977, pp. 6–7.

for consumer goods, an article published in a weekly pointed out the health hazards and other problems associated with the decline in the quality of products ranging from fish sauce to cigarettes.[150] Poor economic performance in agriculture and industry was naturally reflected in the evolution of the National Income (or Net Material Product).[151]

Table 2.6 shows that from 1976 to 1980, National Income increased by only 0.8 per cent, whereas the population grew by 9.2 per cent. The average annual increase amounted to 0.2 per cent whereas the target set by the Second FYP was 13–14 per cent.[152] The Second FYP may be construed as a complete failure in this respect. It is worth noting that in 1980, the share of industry in the National Income amounted to 28.1 per cent, compared with 26.5 per cent in 1976, while that of agriculture *and* forestry was 45.4 per cent and 44.5 per cent respectively.[153]

Foreign Economic Relations

Having analysed the most important aspects of the internal economic problems, the discussion will now briefly examine

TABLE 2.6
National Income, 1976–80

	1976		1977		1978		1979		1980	
	A	B	A	B	A	B	A	B	A	B
	12,455	100.6	13,110	105.3	13,257	106.4	13,024	104.6	12,555	100.8

A = in million dong at constant 1970 prices
B = indexes

SOURCE: *Nien Giam Thong Ke 1982*, pp. 64–65.

Vietnam's foreign economic relations, particularly with regard to the question of foreign aid. Generally, Vietnam saw economic aid granted by the USSR and the Eastern European socialist countries as a mainstay of its development plan. Still, it was eager to supplement that support with bilateral aid from the Western industrialized countries and multilateral aid from international agencies such as the World Bank, International Monetary Fund, and Asian Development Bank. As for Chinese aid, there had been many ups and downs during the 1975–78 period. Before 1976, Chinese economic aid, all of it in the form of grants, had amounted to US$300 million a year. In November 1977 when Le Duan visited Beijing, "the Chinese side said (to him that) it would not be able to provide any assistance to Vietnam".[154]

In the second week of May 1978, China increased pressure on Vietnam by telling Hanoi that it was suspending work on twenty-one of its aided projects. Then, at the end of May 1978, China announced the decision to withdraw aid from seventy-two projects in Vietnam. This Chinese decision was, wrote a foreign observer, "an ironic replay of a Soviet move in 1960 when Moscow suddenly suspended its aid projects in China to express anger at Peking".[155] Lastly, on 3 July 1978, China completely cut off its economic aid to Vietnam.[156]

At that time, the CPV's Central Committee issued an internal Resolution violently denouncing Chinese hostility towards Vietnam.[157] After the termination of Chinese aid and the U.S. refusal to help in Vietnam's rehabilitation, Vietnam's ties with the CMEA (Council for Mutual Economic Assistance) countries, particularly with the USSR, grew rapidly.[158]

On 28 June 1978, Vietnam formally joined the CMEA with which it had maintained economic relations since the early 1950s. It was claimed that "as a full CMEA member [Vietnam could] more rapidly rehabilitate [its] war-torn country".[159] Since then, the development of a "comprehensive and long-term cooperation" between Vietnam and the other CMEA countries has been regarded as "the cornerstone of [Vietnam's] international relations".[160]

At the 33rd CMEA session in June 1979, then Premier Pham Van Dong said that Vietnam's entry into the CMEA created conditions for coping with overwhelming economic difficulties at that time, and for speeding up the construction of socialism. At this session, the CMEA pledged to expand aid to Vietnam and adopted an important decision to extend to Vietnam the principal propositions of the "Comprehensive Program of Socialist Economic Integration" for the acceleration of its economic development as it was done in regard to Mongolia and Cuba.[161] This decision was reportedly "aimed at coordinating the efforts of CMEA countries to ... speed up the process of bringing closer together and equalizing the levels of economic development of Vietnam and other socialist countries".[162]

As regards the specific relations between Vietnam and the USSR, it may be recalled that on 18 December 1975, the two countries had signed an agreement on economic and technical assistance for the 1976–80 period.[163] After joining the CMEA in June 1978, a Vietnamese Party and government delegation went to Moscow and signed an important "Friendship and Cooperation Treaty" (3 November 1978) which has a twenty-five-year validity period,[164] and six documents promoting economic, scientific and technological co-operation between the two countries. Through these agreements, the USSR further strengthened its support of Vietnam, both militarily and economically, and Communist Party-level relations between the two countries drew closer. Since then, Vietnam's inclination towards the USSR has been definite.

For Vietnam, this Treaty, which was signed at a time when it embarked on post-war reconstruction "in the face of a two-pronged threat from China" aimed at "helping Vietnam to accomplish two parallel tasks: building socialism and defending the ... homeland."[165] Article 2 of this Treaty stipulated: "The contracting parties will pool efforts for strengthening and expanding mutually beneficial economic, scientific and technical cooperation with the aim of speeding up socialist and communist construction. The Parties will continue *long-term coordination of their national economic plans*, will agree on long-term measures towards developing crucial sectors of the economy, science and technology, and will exchange knowledge and experience accumulated in socialist and communist construction" (emphasis added). As for Article 6, it stated: "... In case either side is attacked or threatened with attack, the two Parties shall immediately consult each other with a view to eliminating that threat and taking appropriate and effective measures to ensure peace and security of both countries". These two articles reflect the essence of this Treaty.[166]

Soon after the signing of this Treaty, the Vietnamese invaded Kampuchea and toppled Pol Pot in late December 1978,[167] which in turn led to the attack of Vietnam by China in February 1979. According to a Vietnamese source, the Chinese attack against six northern border provinces of Vietnam "caused vast destruction estimated at US$1 billion".[168]

Generally, Soviet-Vietnamese economic co-operation takes three principal forms: economic and technical co-operation; scientific–technological co-operation, and trade relations.

During the Second FYP, the Soviet Union provided Vietnam economic and technical assistance in the designing and construction of 94 important economic projects.[169] In 1979, it was reported that enterprises built with Soviet assistance accounted for 25 per cent of the electricity generated in the country, 89 per cent of extracted coal, 100 per cent of the output of tin, sulfuric acid, apatite, and superphosphate, and 61 per cent of metal-cutting machines.[170] On 3 July 1980, a Soviet-Vietnamese agreement was signed on co-operation in geological exploration and extraction of oil and gas in the southern continental shelf of Vietnam.[171] In agriculture, the development of a 50,000 hectare area specializing in the production of natural rubber in the province of Song Be was begun with Soviet assistance. The USSR also helped in increasing the mechanization of Vietnam's agriculture by providing tractors and other farming implements.

As for Soviet-Vietnamese scientific and technological co-operation, it was claimed that since the signing of the Friendship Treaty it had become more purposeful, and more systematically planned, and included a broader spectrum of topics than before. Concerning trade relations, suffice it to point out that during the 1976-80 period, total Soviet exports to Vietnam amounted to 1,713.3 million rubles whereas total Soviet imports reached only 650.8 million rubles.[172] Consequently, the USSR had to grant Vietnam easy credits to cover the trade imbalance (1,062.5 million rubles).

The Soviet Union supplied Vietnam with 46.2 per cent of its needs in machinery and equipment, 8.2 per cent in oil products, 16.6 per cent in wheat and flour, 6.4 per cent in cotton fibre, during the same period. A Vietnamese high-ranking official also disclosed that "(Soviet) assistance ... included large amounts of commodity aid provided at half the prevailing world rates".[173]

What was the amount of Soviet economic aid to Vietnam? Unfortunately, no official figures have been published as it is a State secret. However, according to Nguyen Lam, then Vice-Premier and Chairman of the State Planning Committee, during the second FYP "the Soviet Union provided rubles 500 million (US$757.7 million) in economic assistance each year",[174] that is, 2,500 million rubles or US$3,787.5 million for the 1976–80 period.[175]

Besides the USSR, Vietnam also received economic aid from other CMEA countries. In addition to this, a number of Western industrialized countries such as France (US$366 million), Sweden (US$100 million), Denmark, Norway, Finland, Japan, Australia and Canada also gave economic assistance to Vietnam. However, because of Vietnam's military involvement in Kampuchea most Western countries had suspended their aid programmes by mid-1979. The World Bank had approved a US$60 million loan to Vietnam, but after US$44.6 million had been drawn, it was stopped because of U.S. opposition.[176]

TABLE 2.7
Share of Foreign Economic Aid in Total Budgetary Revenues (1976–80)
(In per cent)

	1976	1977	1978	1979	1980
Total Revenues of which:	100.0	100.0	100.0	100.0	100.0
— Internal Revenues	55.2	65.5	68.0	59.2	59.4
— External Revenues (grants and loans)	44.8	34.5	32.0	40.8	40.6

SOURCE: *Nien Giam Thong Ke 1982*, p. 77.

On the whole, because of its invasion of Kampuchea, "Vietnam lost US$78.5 million in bilateral aid and US$99 million in multilateral aid which had been pledged earlier"[177] — a serious loss for a country in dire need of funds. Despite a certain loss of Western aid, the share of foreign economic aid (grants as well as loans) in the total budgetary revenues was still very significant, as shown in Table 2.7.

Lastly, it might be interesting to note that foreign aid in the form of consumer goods, including humanitarian aid (from international and non-governmental organizations) was (and is) *not* of much benefit to the people as the government always sold (and continues to sell) these goods at high prices which were quite close to those in the free market.

* * *

As regards the evolution of Vietnam's foreign trade during the Second FYP, some official data are given in Table 2.8.

In the table, it can be seen from columns A that *exports* (calculated "in rubles and U.S. dollars") increased from 1976 to 1978, declined in 1979, then climbed up again in 1980, whereas from columns B (calculated in U.S. dollars) they increased from 1976 to 1978 then decreased successively in the following two years.

On the whole, exports increased by 50.9 per cent (columns A) or by 24.9 per cent (columns B) during the 1976–80 period. As regards imports, they continuously increased from 1976 to 1978, and significantly declined in 1980 (columns A and B). However, on the whole, from 1976 to 1980 they grew by 28.1 per cent (columns A) or 2.9 per cent (columns B).

Despite proclaimed efforts to increase exports, however, the trade deficit remained large: 976 million "rubles-US dollars" as against 801.4 millions in 1976 (columns A), that is, an increase of 21.7 per cent, or US$553 millions in 1980, compared with US$604 millions in 1976 (columns B), that is, a decrease of 8.5 per cent.

In the last year of the Second FYP (1980), exports covered only 25.6 per cent of imports if calculated "in rubles–US dollars" or 41.4 per cent if calculated in U.S. dollars.

TABLE 2.8
Vietnam's Foreign Trade (1976–80)

	1976 A	1976 B	1977 A	1977 B	1978 A	1978 B	1979 A	1979 B	1980 A	1980 B
Trade Balance (Deficit)	801.4	604	895.9	686	976.3	677	1,205.6	778	976.0	553
— Convertible Area (Western and Third World Countries)		173		457		333		331		173
— Non-Convertible Area (CMEA Countries)		432		229		344		447		380
Exports	222.7	313	322.5	456	326.9	482	320.5	420	336.0	391
— Convertible Area		90		110		126		102		121
— Non-Convertible Area		223		346		356		318		270
Imports	1,024.1	917	1,218.4	1,142	1,303.2	1,159	1,526.1	1,198	1,312.0	944
— Convertible Area		263		567		459		433		294
— Non-Convertible Area		655		575		700		765		650

A: In "millions of rubles-U.S. dollars" (Vietnamese source)
B: In millions of U.S. dollars (IMF source)
SOURCES: *Nien Giam Thong Ke 1982*, p. 311; IMF, *Socialist Republic of Vietnam, Recent Economic Developments*, 19 December 1980, p. 34; and IMF, *Socialist Republic of Vietnam, Recent Economic Developments*, 18 May 1982, p. 26.

Concerning the structure of exports (calculated "in rubles-U.S. dollars"), it was reported that in 1980, the industrial and mining products represented 64.1 per cent, the handicraft goods 23.1 per cent, and the unprocessed agricultural commodities 12.8 per cent, compared with 68.9 per cent, 15.3 per cent, and 15.8 per cent respectively in 1976.[178]

As regards the structure of imported goods (calculated "in rubles-U.S. dollars"), in 1980 the share of the "means of production" (or capital and intermediate goods, which consisted of complete equipment, machines and means of transport, spare parts, fuels and raw materials) represented 76 per cent of the total whereas that of consumer goods was 24 per cent, compared with 83.2 per cent and 16.8 per cent respectively in 1976.[179]

The greater part of Vietnam's exports (calculated "in rubles and US dollars") was oriented towards the CMEA countries, particularly the USSR: 67.3 per cent of the total in 1980, compared with 59.7 per cent in 1976. As for exports destined for the Western industrialized and Third World countries, they represented 16.8 per cent and 5.8 per cent respectively in 1980, compared with 29.3 per cent and 11 per cent in 1976.[180]

Vietnam's imports (also calculated "in rubles-U.S. dollars"), on the other hand, was reported in 1980 to consist of 57.6 per cent from the CMEA countries, 24 per cent from the Western industrialized countries, and 12.7 per cent from Third World countries compared with 56.4 per cent, 32.8 per cent, and 10.8 per cent respectively in 1976.[181]

It is worth noting that the trade embargo imposed by the United States in May 1975 was one of the important reasons for Vietnam's relative economic isolation from the West. According to a knowledgeable source, "oil exploration, modernization of agriculture and industry, all of the economic programmes Vietnam has tried to implement have been stifled by the American embargo". Concerning particularly oil exploration, the same author wrote: "The US trade embargo against Vietnam not only forbids the American oil industry to deal with Hanoi, but it ensures that oil related technology of American origin does not fall into Vietnamese hands".[182]

The total outstanding of Vietnam's external debt was reported to amount to nearly US$3 billion by the end of September 1980, of which 54 per cent was owing to the CMEA countries.[183] The total servicing cost of this debt reached US$204 million in 1980, that is, an equivalent of 52.1 per cent of total merchandise exports (calculated in U.S. dollars).

Living Standard

The Produced National Income (or Net Material Product) at constant 1970 prices increased by only 0.8 per cent whereas the population grew by 9.2 per cent during the period under review. Consequently, the per capita of National Income decreased, as shown in Table 2.9.

TABLE 2.9
Per Capita National Income (1976–80)

1976		1980	
A	*B*	*A*	*B*
258.1	101	233.7	91

A: Calculation based on official data mentioned in *Nien Giam Thong Ke 1982*, pp. 29 and 64 (in dong, at constant 1970 prices).
B: Official data reckoned according to the U.N. method (in U.S. dollars), mentioned in *So Lieu Thong Ke Cong Hoa Xa Hoi Chu Nghia Viet Nam 1982* (Hanoi, 1983), p. 18.

From the table it can be seen that from 1976 to 1980 the Vietnamese per capita National Income at 1970 constant prices decreased by 7.7 per cent if calculated in dong, or by nearly 9 per cent if reckoned in U.S. dollars according to the U.N. method.

It is worth noting that concerning the per capita National Income reckoned in U.S. dollars there is a large discrepancy between the figures given by the Vietnamese authorities and those of the International Monetary Fund. According to the former, the per capita National Income amounted only to US$91 in 1980, compared with US$101 in 1976, whereas according to the latter, it reached US$160, compared with US$151 in 1976.[184]

The living standard of the working people in the whole country naturally decreased considerably as a result of the economic crisis on the one hand, and the continuous price increases, particularly since December 1979,[185] on the other hand. But, while in the North the fall in the living standard was relatively "mild" as it had been already very low before the Second FYP, in the South it came about with much brutality. A high ranking official in the South recently recalled with bitterness that in late 1977 and 1978, "for the first time in its history, the 'jewel of Asia' — as Saigon [now renamed Ho Chi Minh City] was flatteringly referred to — had to supplement its daily rice ration with sweet potatoes, manioc [and sorghum]".[186]

In a speech delivered in Ho Chi Minh city in mid-1980, Vo Van Kiet also admitted that workers and civil servants' wages "could not even compensate their own labour costs, let alone the reproduction of their labour force".[187] Concerning the economic situation of the workers and civil servants in the North, here are some figures related to their real per capita monthly income (at 1960 constant prices): 12.3 dong in 1980, as against 17.4 dong in 1976,[188] that is, a fall of 29.3 per cent.

A Politburo directive in November 1980 acknowledged that "... production [was] slumping in several ways, and the livelihood of the labouring people ... [was] deteriorating and encountering many difficulties".[189] Indeed, as Hoang Tung, a member of the Central Committee and editor of the Party's newspaper, admitted in early 1980, "the situation [was] particularly serious and painful for urban people and wage earners".[190]

Dr Duong Quynh Hoa, former Health Minister of South Vietnam's Provisional Revolutionary Government concluded, after a survey of child nutrition in the Ho Chi Minh City area, that in the outskirts "28 per cent of pre-school children ... [were] malnourished", and "38 per cent of the children under four years [suffered] malnutrition" inside the city.[191]

To Huu, then first Deputy Premier, confessed to the Australian journalist W. Burchettt in 1980 that "[the Vietnamese] people will be poor and hungry until the end of this century".[192]

In May 1980, a Vietnamese Cabinet Minister told a foreign journalist that he was amazed at the Vietnamese people's "ability to suffer" (*sic*). "In another country", he said, "the government would have changed".[193] This surprising "ability to suffer" is simply due to the fact that people are terribly frightened by the Party's dictatorship which rests on two powerful pillars, namely, a more than one-million strong police corps (according to a highly reliable source) and a 2.599 million-strong "people's army" which took up to "47 per cent" of the budgetary expenditures.[194] If there was no open revolt among wage-earners, there was, however, a general dejection, lassitude, and passive resistance which was reflected, *inter alia*, in the widely discussed novel titled *Dung Truoc Bien* (Standing Before the Sea).[195] The drastic fall of the living standard of the working people went against the Party's proclaimed policy which emphasized at its Fourth Congress that "to improve the people's material ... life [was] the cardinal task of [the] Party and State, and the highest objective of the economic development programme".[196]

Assessing the overall economic situation at the end of the Second FYP, Secretary-General Le Duan frankly admitted — although in general terms — in his political report delivered at the Fifth Party Congress in 1982 that:

> On the economic front our country is ... confronted with many acute problems.... The implementation of the economic plans in the years 1976-80 have not reduced the serious imbalances in our national economy. [In fact, it increased them.] Production rises slowly while the population increases quickly. The Produced National Income is not in a position to meet the needs of social consumption; part of social consumption must be taken from [foreign] loans and [grants] .... There are shortages of food, fabrics and other essential consumer goods. Great shortages exist in the supply of [fuels] and materials, and in communications and transport. Many [state-run] enterprises operate below capacity. There are still great disparities between budget revenues and expenditures, commodities and money [circulation], and exports and imports .... Prices are unstable [read, soaring upwards]. There are still large numbers of people who are unemployed. The livelihood of the working people, especially workers, [civil servants], and peasants ... is fraught with difficulties.[197]

* * *

The socio-economic crisis described above had many causes, endogenous as well as exogenous. The endogenous causes — which were the *fundamental* ones — were primarily the extension of the Stalinist-Maoist economic development strategy from North to South after a precipitate reunification in 1976, and secondarily the unfavourable weather conditions in 1977 and 1978. The Stalinist-Maoist strategy of economic development in the Second FYP, as in North Vietnam before 1975, included top priority being given to heavy industry at the expense of agriculture and light industry; forced and accelerated collectivization, and strong prejudice against household and individual economy; wilful disregard of material incentives *vis-a-vis* producers (peasants as well as workers); brutal "socialist transformation" of private industry and trade, particularly the overhasty elimination of the private sectors in industry and handicrafts as a result of a pervasive misconception according to which the larger and more public the ownership structure, the better and the more socialist; excessive centralized economic planning and disregard of market mechanism; identification of socialism with egalitarianism, and so forth.

The imposition of this strategy of economic development (which had caused widespread damage in the North before 1975) on the restive South brought about a devastating multiplier-effect which eventually dragged along the whole country towards an unprecedented economic crisis which erupted *before* the invasion of Kampuchea and the Chinese attack.

It is interesting to note that recently, in an important article published in the Party's theoretical journal, one high-ranking Party official admitted that although one had to take into account the natural calamities and the damages caused by the Chinese aggression, the socio-economic crisis which broke out in 1978 and 1979 was mainly caused by "the very serious errors" committed by the Party leadership in its economic thinking and macro-economic management. And those *"errors of leftist character"*, he continued, stemmed particularly from *"dogmatism* and ... *Maoism"*.[198] The latter naturally included "subjectivism [and] voluntarism, [that is], a simplistic way of thinking and acting, and impatiently seeking to realize [the Party's] subjective wishes", as acknowledged by Truong Chinh in his political report delivered at the Sixth Party Congress.[199]

Concerning the exogenous causes, the cut-off of Western aid and the U.S. embargo, the war in Kampuchea and the Chinese attack could be regarded as the important ones. However, they only *exacerbated the endogenous causes* which should be considered as the primary ones. This reality was at last acknowledged — but still very vaguely — at the famous Sixth Plenum of the Central Committee in September 1979 which represented, as said earlier, the first great turning point in the Party's post-reunification economic strategy. The new policy advocated by this Plenum was afterwards endorsed and expanded at the Fifth Party Congress, which will be discussed in the following chapter.

NOTES

1. This chapter and the following one are complete revisions of the contents of my monograph, "Socialist Vietnam's Economy, 1975–80. An Assessment," mimeographed (Tokyo: Institute of Developing Economies, 1987).
2. Nguyen Anh Tuan, *South Vietnam. Trial and Experience. A Challenge for Development*, Monographs in International Studies, Southeast Asia Series, No. 80 (Athens, Ohio: Ohio University, 1987), pp. 347–48 (excess of consumption over production); p. 338 (budget deficit); pp.224, 342 (trade deficit); pp. 54–75, 320, 328–29, and 337–38 (foreign aid). For details concerning the economic evolution by branches, see ibid., pp. 392–437. On the same score, see also: Nguyen Van Hao, "Mot Sach Luoc Phat Trien Kinh Te Hoa Binh Cho Mien Nam Vietnam" (Part I), mimeographed (Saigon, 1975); Vu Quoc Thuc, "Hau Qua Kinh Te Cua Chinh Sach Cua My O Mien Nam Viet Nam" (Lecture delivered at the Institute of Social Sciences, Ho Chi Minh City, 1976); Vo Nhan Tri, "Vien Tro My Va Chien Tranh Viet Nam" (Vien Khoa Hoc Xa Hoi, Thanh Pho Ho Chi Minh, 1980); Nguyen Van Ngon, *Kinh Te Viet Nam* (Saigon: Tu Thu Dai Hoc Van Hanh, Tu Sach Giao Khoa, 1974); Douglas C. Dacy, *Foreign Aid, War, and Economic Development. South Vietnam, 1955–75* (Cambridge, London, New York: Cambridge University Press, 1986), Chapter I; and M. Beresford, *Vietnam. Politics, Economics and Society* (London and New York: Pinter Publishers, 1988), pp. 147–51.

    Concerning Hanoi's viewpoint on South Vietnam's economy, see Nguyen Quan, "Mot So Tu Lieu Ve Kinh Te Mien Nam Truoc Ngay Giai Phong", *Hoc Tap*, no. 3 (Hanoi, 1976), pp. 50–63; Nguyen Bich, "Mot So Y Kien Ve Luc Luong Cong Nghiep Nho Va Thu Cong Nghiep O Mien Nam", *Hoc Tap*, No. 8 (Hanoi 1976); Huy Nam, "Ve Nang Luc San Xuat Cua Cac Co So Cong

Nghiep Mien Nam", *Hoc Tap*, no. 2 (Hanoi, 1976); and Hoan Quoc Thinh, "Cai Tao Nen Thuong Nghiep Cu, Xay Dung Nen Thuong Nghiep Xa Hoi Chu Nghia O Mien Nam Nuoc Ta", *Hoc Tap*, no. 11 (Hanoi, 1976).

A more qualified assessment of South Vietnam's economy has appeared recently: Cao Van Luong, "Tim Hieu Chu Nghia Tu Ban O Mien Nam Viet Nam Duoi Thoi My-Nguy", *Nghien Cuu Lich Su*, no. 5 and 6 (1987).

3. Douglas C. Dacy, *Foreign Aid, War and Economic Development*, pp. 19–20.
4. Truong Nhu Tang (former Minister of Justice in the Provisional Revolutionary Government [PRG] of South Vietnam), *Journal of a Vietcong* (London: Jonathan Cape, 1986), p.283.

At Hanoi's instigation, the PRG had also advocated the establishment of a non-aligned state in South Vietnam, and a period of 12–14 years of transition was envisaged before national reunification could take place. See Huynh Kim Khanh, "Year One of Postcolonial Vietnam", *Southeast Asian Affairs 1977* (Singapore: Institute of Southeast Asian Studies, 1977), p. 299.

5. *50 Years of Activities of the Communist Party of Vietnam* (Hanoi: Foreign Languages Publishing House, 1980), pp. 255–57.
6. Ibid.
7. Nguyen Van Canh, *Vietnam under Communism, 1975–1982* (California: Hoover Institution Press, Stanford University, 1983), p. 19.
8. Truong Chinh, "Thuc Hien Thong Nhat Nuoc Nha Ve Mat Nha Nuoc", *Hoc Tap*, no. 11 (1975), pp. 22–23; and his *Selected Writings* (Hanoi:Foreign Languages Publishing House, 1977), pp. 803–4.
9. Ibid.
10. P.R. Feray, *Le Vietnam* (Paris: Presses Universitaires de France, 1984), p. 93. See also William J. Duiker, *Vietnam Since the Fall of Saigon*, Ohio University, Monographs in International Studies, Southeast Asia Series no. 56 (Athens, Ohio: Ohio University, 1985), p. 19.
11. Quoted in *Vietnam Courier*, October 1975, p. 3.
12 Truong Chinh, "Thuc Hien Thong Nhat ...", p. 26; and his *Selected Writings*, p. 811. See also, Che Viet Tan, "Phat Huy Suc Manh Tong Hop Cua Nen Kinh Te Thong Nhat", *Hoc Tap*, no. 12 (Hanoi, 1975).
13. *50 Years of Activities ...* , pp. 256–57.
14. See his Political Report in *Communist Party of Vietnam (CPV). 4th National Congress. Documents* (Hanoi: Foreign Languages Publishing House, 1977), p. 39. Truong Chinh, in his speech delivered in November 1975, also alluded to the role of Vietnam as an "outpost [of socialism] in Southeast Asia" (see his *Selected Writings*, p. 795). For other external factors such as continuing U.S. hostility and tension with Kampuchea and China, see Tan Teng Lang, *Economic Debates in Vietnam. Issues and Problems in Reconstruction and Development (1975–84)* (Singapore: Institute of Southeast Asian Studies, 1985), p. 13.
15. Suzy Paine, "Best Laid Plans of Rice and Hens ...", *New Statesman* (London), 31 January 1986, p. 20. Melanie Beresford also wrote: "... It would appear that the burden of sustaining the economy of the South in the immediate

aftermath of the war was placed squarely on the shoulders of the northern population" (in "Vietnam: Northernizing the South or Southernizing the North?", *Contemporary Southeast Asia* 8, no. 4 [March 1987]: 267).

These foreign observers repeated more or less the arguments of Hanoi's spokesmen, such as Nguyen Khac Vien ("Vietnam 1975-79", *Etudes Vietnamiennes*, no. 58, p.11) and Nguyen Xuan Lai (ibid., p. 37), concerning the sending of footstuff, raw materials, and spare parts, etc., from North to South in the immediate aftermath of the war. However, they did not realize that those shipments were destined particularly for North Vietnamese troops and cadres sent to the South (foodstuff), and for newly confiscated or nationalized factories in the South (raw materials, spare parts, etc.). Moreover, they were not aware of the fact that the North had swept up a massive amount of brand-new machines and equipment, high-grade imported raw materials and spare parts from the South and shipped them to the North. A high-ranking official in the Ministry of Light Industry told this writer in 1976 that some new Southern factories in the consumer industry were even dismantled and shipped to the North! On the whole, one can safely say that what the North swept up from the South was *much, much greater*—in value as well as in quantity—than what it sent to the South.

16. Vu Quoc Tuan, "Ve Dac Diem Kinh Te Xa Hoi Nuoc Ta...", *Nghien Cuu Kinh Te*, no. 2 (1984), p. 3.
17. Tran Ho, "Ve Su Lac Hau Ve Nhan Thuc Ly Luan Kinh Te", *Tap Chi Cong San*, no. 2 (1988), p. 20; and Nguyen Duc Binh's statement in *Tap Chi Cong San*, no. 9 (1988), p. 29. On the same subject, see also Hoang Van Hoan, *Giot Nuoc Trong Bien Ca (Hoi Ky Cach Mang)* (Nha Xuat Ban Tin Vietnam, 1986), p.433; M. Beresford, "Vietnam: Northernizing the South ...", pp. 261; 264; and A. Fforde, "After the Apocalypse", *Marxism Today* (London, October 1987), p. 38.
18. Le Duan, *Communist Party of Vietnam. 4th National Congress ...*, p. 35.
19. Le Duan, *Communist Party of Vietnam. 5th National Congress* (Hanoi: Foreign Languages Publishing House, 1982), p. 30.
20. *6th National Congress of the Communist Party of Vietnam. Documents* (Hanoi: Foreign Languages Publishing House, 1987), pp. 39,42,188.
21. See Le Duan, *Communist Party of Vietnam, 4th National Congress ...*, pp. 41, 43, 59. A Party philosopher wrote in 1984 that this transitional period would consist of three great phases: 1976-80 ("socialist transformation" of the South); 1981-2005 ("socialist industrialization"); and 2006-2010 ("perfecting" the transitional period). See Nguyen Van Nghia's article in the journal *Triet Hoc*, no.4 (Hanoi: Institute of Philosophy, December 1984), pp. 93-98.
22. *Tap Chi Cong San* (editorial), no. 9 (1986), p. 3.
23. *6th National Congress ...*, pp. 18, 32-33. For more details on the transitional period to socialism, see: *Thoi Ky Qua Do Len Chu Nghia Xa Hoi O Viet Nam. Mot So Van De Kinh Te—Xa Hoi Trong Chang Durong Dau Tien*, edited by Pham Nhu Cuong (Hanoi: NXB Khoa Hoc Xa Hoi, 1987); Vu Huu Ngoan, "Thoi Ky Qua Do Len Chu Nghia Xa Hoi—Tinh Chat Lau Dai Va Phuc Tap", *Tap Chi Cong San*, no. 6 (1987), pp. 26-30; Chu Van Lam, "Dai Hoi VI Dang Cong San

Viet Nam Va Nhung Van De Kinh Te Chinh Tri Hoc Trong Thoi Ki Qua Do", *Nghien Cuu Kinh Te*, no. 3 (1987), pp. 1–6; Nguyen Thanh Le, "The October Revolution — A Torch Lighting the Way of Vietnam and Eastern Peoples", *Far Eastern Affairs*, no. 3 (Moscow 1988), pp. 25–30.

It is worth noting that, contrary to what Chu Van Lam wrote (see "Dai Hoi VI ..., p.2), the concept of "initial stage" (or "stage ahead") of the transitional period (see also *Communist Party of Vietnam. 5th National Congress*, pp. 38 and 42) was not an original "contribution" of the Communist Party of Vietnam to the theory of "transitional period to socialism". For the Chinese Communist Party had already coined this term at its Sixth Central Committee Plenum (11th Congress) held in June 1981 when, for the first time, it clearly stated that "China's socialist system remains at its initial stage" (*Social Sciences in China* 9, no. 1 [March 1988]: 11–12).

24. Nguyen Van Linh, "Cach Mang Thang Muoi Va Cach Mang Viet Nam", *Tap Chi Cong San*, no. 11 (1987), p.7.
25. Le Duan, *Communist Party of Vietnam. 4th National Congress ...*, p. 38; and Truong Chinh, *Selected Writings*, p. 804.
26. *50 Years of Activities ...*, p. 256.
27. Nguyen Van Tran, "Tiep Tuc Dau Tranh Xoa Bo Giai Cap Tu San Mai Ban Va Nhung Ke Dau Co Tich Tru Lung Doan Thi Truong Hien Nay", *Hoc Tap*, no. 10 (1976), p. 7. The term, "compradore bourgeoisie" derives from Mao's concept which means "that section of the bourgeoisie which directly served the capitalists of imperialist countries and was nurtured by them". See Mao Tse Tung, "Analysis of Classes in Chinese Society", in *Selected Readings From the Works of Mao Tse Tung* (Peking: Foreign Languages Press, 1971), pp. 12; 19.
28. Nguyen Hoang, "South Vietnam: The Struggle Against Compradore Capitalists", *Vietnam Courier*, November 1975, p. 10.
29. Nguyen Van Linh, *Dau Tranh Giai Cap Trong Chang Dau Thoi Ky Qua Do* (NXB Thanh Pho Ho Chi Minh, 1984), p. 19.
30. Ibid., p. 20.
31. *Vietnam Courier*, November 1975, p. 10.
32. *50 Years of Activities ...*, p. 259.
33. See *Vietnam Courier*, November 1975, p. 10. Regarding the attack against the "compradore bourgeoisie", see *Bao Cao Tong Ket Danh Tu San Mai Ban O Cac Tinh Phia Nam Sau Ngay Giai Phong*, "Top Secret" Party Document (Hanoi: Ban Cai Tao Cong Thuong Nghiep Tu Doanh Trung Uong, Dang Cong San Viet Nam, undated); "Giap Cap Tu San Mai Ban O Nam Viet Nam", "Top Secret" Party Document; mimeographed (Hanoi: Ban Cai Tao Cong Thuong Nghiep Tu Doanh Trung Uong, Dang Cong San Viet Nam, 1977); Nguyen Van Linh, *Dau Tranh Giai Cap ...*, p. 20ff; Nguyen Van Tran, "Tiep Tuc Dau Tranh ..."; *A Pas Surs. Au Sud Vietnam depuis la Liberation 1975–85* (Hanoi: Editions en Langues Etrangeres, 1978), pp. 141–56; Tien Lam, "Peking's solicitude for *Hoa* capitalists", *Vietnam Courier*, November 1978, pp. 9–11; Nguyen Hoang, "South Vietnam ...", pp. 6–10; W. Burchett, "Cracking down on Saigon's Compradores", *Far Eastern Economic Review*, 17 October

1975, pp. 31–32; and Lewis M. Stern, "The *Hoa Kieu* under the Socialist Republic of Vietnam", *Issues and Studies* (Taipei, March 1987), pp. 120–34.
34. *Bao Cao Tong Ket* ....
35. *Saigon Giai Phong*, 20 September 1975. The revolutionary regime even encouraged the "non-compradore" capitalists and petty bourgeoisie to join in the anti-compradore campaign to disclose the "reactionary exploiters"— a classic tactic of "divide and rule".
36. Nguyen Van Tran, "Tiep Tuc Dau Tranh ...", p. 7.
37. For more details, see *The Hoa in Vietnam. Dossier* (Hanoi: Foreign Languages Publishing House, 1978), pp. 20–21.
38. Tien Lam, "Peking's solicitude ...", p. 9. For a non-communist viewpoint on the *Hoa* bourgeoisie, see: Tsai Maw Kuey, *Les Chinois au Vietnam* (Paris: Bibliotheque Nationale, 1968 [Deuxieme Partie]); Frederic T.C. Yu, "The Chinese Community in Vietnam", mimeographed (Columbia University, Simulnatics Corp., 1968); Luong Nhi Ky, "The Chinese in Vietnam: A Study of Vietnamese-Chinese Relations, With Special Attention to the Period 1862–1961" (Ph.D. thesis, University of Michigan, 1963); Nguyen Van Sang, *Nguoi Viet Goc Hoa Va Kinh Te Viet Nam* (Luan An Tot Nghiep Cao Hoc Kinh Te), Hoc Vien Quoc Gia Hanh Chinh, Saigon, 1970–72 (National Library, Ho Chi Minh City); Clifton G. Barton, "Credit and Commercial Control: Strategies and Methods of Chinese Businessmen in South Vietnam" (Ph.D. thesis, Cornell University, 1977); Lewis M. Stern, "Vietnamese Communist Policy toward the Overseas Chinese, 1920–82" (Ph.D. thesis, University of Pittsburgh, 1984), especially Chapter 7; and idem, "The Overseas Chinese in Vietnam, 1920–75: Demography, Social Structure, and Economic Power", *Humboldt Journal of Social Relations* (Spring/Summer 1985), pp. 12–14; 16–18 and 21; and E.S. Ungar, "The Struggle over the Chinese Community in Vietnam, 1946–86", *Pacific Affairs*, no. 4 (Winter 1987–88), pp. 606–7.
39. *The Hoa in Vietnam*, p. 81; and L.M. Stern, "The *Hoa Kieu* ...", pp. 121–23. Nguyen Van Hao, Vice-Premier in charge of economic affairs in the latest Saigon administration, also told this writer that before 1975 the *Hoa* compradore capitalists controlled 70 per cent of the south's economy, and more precisely 80 per cent of the processing industry, 100 per cent of the wholesale trade, more than 50 per cent of retail trade, and 90 per cent of the import-export trade. (Interview given in Ho Chi Minh City, June 1976.)
40. *A Pas Surs* ..., p. 155; *Vietnam Courier*, November 1975, pp. 8 and 10; and ibid., June 1977, pp. 24 and 30.
41. Tien Lam, "Peking's solicitude ...", p. 10.
42. Ibid., p. 11.
43. Ibid., p.9. See also Dao Van Tap, "La politique economique du Vietnam dans la lutte pour l'independance nationale et le socialisme", *Sciences Sociales*, no. 1 (Hanoi, 1984), p. 30.
44. Nguyen Van Tran, "Tiep Tuc Dau Tranh ...", p. 8.
45. Ibid., p.7.
46. *Far Eastern Economic Review*, 14 April 1978, p. 12.

47. Nguyen Tien Hung, *Economic Development* ..., pp. 166–70.
48. *Far Eastern Economic Review*, 26 May 1978, p. 81.
49. Nguyen Khac Vien, interview in *Rinascita*, 30 April 1976. By the same author, see *Sud Vietnam Au Fil des Annees 1975–85* (Hanoi: Editions en Langues Etrangeres, 1984), p. 364ff. See also Chien Thang's article in *Nhan Dan*, 1 December 1975. Regarding the revolutionary land reform campaign, see Lam Quang Huyen, *Cach Mang Ruong Dat O Mien Nam Vietnam* (Hanoi: NXB Khoa Hoc Xa Hoi 1985), pp. 61–171; 218–22. Concerning Thieu's land reform, see Lam Thanh Liem, *Collectivisation Des Terres. L'exemple du delta du Mekong* (Paris: Sedes, 1986), pp.61–72. For a critical point of view of this reform, see Nguyen Xuan Lai, "Questions of agrarian structures and agricultural development in Southern Vietnam", *Vietnamese Studies* (A new series), no. 5 (1984), pp. 30–36.
50. Nguyen Xuan Lai, "Questions of agrarian structures ...", pp. 44; 47–49.
51. Ibid.
52. Linh's speech at the Fifth Plenum of the Central Committee in June 1988 (*Nhan Dan*, 23 June 1988). See also his speech at the Conference of Chief Editors of the communist newspapers, held in Hanoi in March 1980 (*Vietnam Courier*, no. 6 [1988], p. 20).
53. Quoted by Alain Ruscio, *Vivre au Vietnam* (Paris: Editions Sociales, 1981), p. 59.
54. For a selective bibliography of the political economy of socialism, see Truong Dang Cao Cap Nguyen Ai Quoc, *Kinh Te Chinh Tri Mac — Le-Nin*, Tap II A: *Chu Nghia Xa Hoi-Giai Doan Dau Cua Phuong Thuc San Xuat Cong San Chu Nghia* (Hanoi: NXB Sach Giao Khoa Mac-Lenin, 1984); Vu Huu Ngoan, *Nhung Van De Kinh Te Xa Hoi Trong Chang Duong Dau Tien Cua Thoi Ky Qua Do Len Chu Nghia Xa Hoi O Nuoc Ta* (Hanoi: NXB Su That, 1984); Institute of Social Sciences, *Political Economy of Socialism* (Moscow: Progress Publishers, 1985); J. Wilczynski, *The Economics of Socialism*, 4th ed. (London: George Allen & Unwin, 1982); W. Brus, *The Economics and Politics of Socialism* and *The Market in a Socialist Economy* (London and Boston: Routledge and Kegan Paul, 1973 and 1972 respectively); W. Brus, "Political Systems and Economic Efficiency", *Journal of Comparative Economics*, no 4 (1980); J. Kornai, *Economics of Shortage* (Amsterdam-London: North-Holland Pub. Co., 1980); idem, *Growth, Shortage and Efficiency* (Oxford: Blackwell, 1982); idem, *Contradictions and Dilemmas. Studies on the Socialist Economy and Society* (Cambridge, Massachusetts, London: The MIT Press, 1986); A. Nove, *The Economics of Feasible Socialism* (London: George Allen and Unwin, 1983), pp. 176–230; R. Bideleux, *Communism and Development* (London-New York: Methuen, 1985).
55. CPV. *4th National Congress* ..., pp. 58–59.
56. Ibid.
57. *Tap Chi Cong San* (editorial), no. 9 (1986), pp. 3–4.
58. Contrary to what Nguyen Tien Hung wrote (see *Economic Development* ..., p. 174), this FYP was officially regarded as the *Second* FYP, the first FYP being already implemented in North Vietnam in 1961–65. This denomination

purposely implied that there would be a *continuation* of the Party's economic policy after reunification.

For a selective bibliography of Socialist Vietnam's economy during the 1976–85 period, see:

Books:

Vien Kinh Te Hoc, 35 *Nam Kinh Te Viet Nam* (1945–1980), edited by Dao Van Tap (Hanoi: Nha Xuat Ban Khoa Hoc Xa Hoi, 1980), pp. 98–113; 158–60; 246–61.

Nguyen Van Linh, *Thanh Pho Ho Chi Minh 10 Nam* (Hanoi: NXB Su That, 1985), pp. 101–79; 237–43; 291–339.

Vo Nhan Tri, "Party Policies and Economic Performance: The Second and Third Five-Year Plans Examined", in *Postwar Vietnam: Dilemmas in Socialist Development*, edited by David G. Marr and Christine P. White (Ithaca: Cornell University Press, 1988), pp. 77–89; and "Socialist Vietnam's Economy, 1975–85. An Assessment", mimeographed (Tokyo: Institute of Developing Economies, 1987).

Tetsusaburo Kimura, *The Vietnamese Economy 1975–86. Reforms and International Relations* (Tokyo: Institute of Developing Economies, 1989).

Tan Teng Lang, *Economic Debates in Vietnam: Issues and Problems in Reconstruction and Development 1975–84*, Research Notes and Discussion Paper No. 55 (Singapore: Institute of Southeast Asian Studies, 1985).

Melanie Beresford, *Vietnam. Politics ...*, pp. 146–76.

Christine P. White, "Recent Debates in Vietnamese Development Policy", in *Revolutionary Socialist Development in the Third World*, edited by G. White, R. Murray and C. White (University Press of Kentucky, 1983), pp. 234–70.

Francoise Direr, "Quelques Traits de l'economie Vietnamienne", in *Objectif Cooperation: Le dossier Franco-Vietnamien* (Paris: Ed. l' Harmattan, 1985), pp. 203–12.

Sotzyalistychyeskaya Respublika Vietnam: Sotzalno-Ekonomicheskye Problemy (Moskva: Nauka, 1982) (in Russian).

Sotzyalistychyeskaya Respublika Vietnam, edited by E.P. Glazunov et al. (Moskva: Nauka, 1985), Parts II & III (in Russian)

Articles:

Nguyen Van Quy, et al., "Ve Tinh Hinh Phat Trien Kinh Te Quoc Dan Nuoc Ta Giai Doan 1976–1985", *Tap Chi Thong Ke*, nos. 5–6 (Hanoi, 1987), pp. 36–41.

"Nhung Van De Kinh Te Co Ban Cap Bach Hien Nay", *Nghien Cuu Kinh Te* No. 2 (1986).

Le Can, "Tinh Hinh Va Nhiem Vu", *Tap Chi Cong San*, no. 8 (1986).

Nguyen Xuan Lai, "Economic Development 1976–85", *Vietnamese Studies* (A New Series), no. 1 (Hanoi, 1983).

Vo Nhan Tri, "Vietnam: Radioscopie de l'economie", *Sudestasie* (Paris), February–March 1986.

Le Thanh Khoi, "Modele Socialiste et Pays en Developpement. L'experience Vietnamienne", *Revue Tiers-Monde*, no. 91 (Paris: IEDES, July-September 1982).

C. Fourniau, "Vietnam: Necessité, Originalité et Ajustements du Socialisme", *Recherches Internationales*, no. 14, (Paris, October-December 1984); and "Vietnam: La Construction Du Socialisme A L'Heure de Verite", *Recherches Internationales*, no. 20 (April-June 1986)

M.A. Crosnier and E. Lhomel, "Vietnam: Les Mécomptes D'un Socialisme Asiatique", *Le Courrier Des Pays De L'Est*, La Documentation Francaise, no. 320 (Paris, July-August 1987).

Ton That Thien, "Vietnam's New Economic Policy", *Pacific Affairs*, no. 4 (Winter 1983-84).

T. Kimura, "Vietnam: Ten Years of Economic Struggle", *Asian Survey*, no. 10 (October 1986).

59. *CPV, 4th National Congress . . .*, pp. 63–64.
60. Ibid., p. 64. For more details, see Pham Van Dong's report on the objectives of the Second FYP, *Nhan Dan*, 18–19 December, 1976.
61. *6th National Congress . . .*, pp. 18–19
62. *Nhan Dan*, 23 June 1988. For an understanding of these "illnesses", see Le Huu Nghia, "Mot So Can Benh Trong Phuong Phap Tu Duy Cua Can Bo Ta", *Triet Hoc*, no. 2 (1988), pp. 21–26.
63. C.A. Thayer, "Building Socialism: South Vietnam Since the Fall of Saigon", in *Vietnam Since 1975 — Two Views From Australia*, CSAAR Research Paper no. 20 (Griffith University, 1982), pp. 22–24; *Asia 1979 Yearbook*, pp. 322–23; W. Duiker, *Vietnam Since The Fall of Saigon*, pp. 25–26; 32; 49; Nguyen Van Canh, *Vietnam under Communism*, pp. 29; 231–32; 236–38; 253–55.
64. Concerning the "Regulations on Foreign Investment in the Socialist Republic of Vietnam", see *Vietnam Courier*, July 1977, pp. 6–8; 28.
65. Resolution of the 5th session of the National Assembly, 28–30 May 1979, quoted in Nguyen Xuan Lai, "Problemes Economiques", pp. 61–62.
66. See the Resolution of the Second Plenum on agricultural development in *Vietnamese Studies*, no. 51 (1977), p. 11.
67. Nguyen Duy Trinh, "May Van De Co Ban Va Cap Bach Ve Kinh Te", *Tap Chi Cong San*, no. 7 (1980), p. 19.
68. *Nhan Dan*, 18–19 December 1976.
69. *Nien Giam Thong Ke 1982*, p. 230.
70. *Nhan Dan*, 5 and 6 December 1986.
71. *CPV. 4th National Congress . . .*, p. 95.
72. See *Vietnamese Studies*, no. 51 (1977), p. 32. For more details concerning the alleged rationale of collectivization in the South, see Hoang Tung, "Developing Agriculture and Creating a New Rural Environment in Vietnam", *Vietnam Courier*, April 1978, pp. 10–11.
73. See *Vietnamese Studies*, no. 51 (1977), p. 33.
74. The Dat, *Nen Nong Nghiep Viet Nam Tu Sau Cach Mang Thang Tam Nam 1945*, (Hanoi: NXB Nong Nghiep, 1981), p. 206. See also Vo Chi Cong, "Day Manh Cai Tao Xa Hoi Chu Nghia Doi Voi Nong Nghiep O Cac Tinh Mien Nam", *Tap Chi Cong San*, no. 2 (Hanoi, 1979), p. 5; Vu Oanh, *Hoan Thanh Dieu Chinh Ruong Dat, Day Manh Cai Tao Xa Hoi Chu Nghia Doi Voi Nong Nghiep Cac Tinh*

Nam Bo (Hanoi: NXB Su That, 1984), pp. 9–10. Lam Quang Huyen, *Cach Mang Ruong Dat* ..., p. 186ff; Quang Truong, *Agricultural Collectivization* ..., pp. 183; 187–88; 194; 217; D. Elliott, "Vietnam. Institutional Development in Crisis", *Southeast Asian Affairs 1979* (Singapore: Institute of Southeast Asian Studies, 1979), pp. 351; 353.

Hoang Tung even predicted in February 1978 that "in the South [cooperativization would] certainly go faster than in the North" (see his "Developing Agriculture and Creating a New Rural Environment..." p. 10).

75. Collectivization in the South also assumes three forms as in the North: (1) "Mutual-aid-teams" (or work-exchange teams) in which although their members work collectively, private ownership of the means of production was maintained; (2) "Production collectives" in which the fruits of collective labour, once production costs are deducted, are divided into two parts to pay respectively for the workdays and the material contributions of their members (land, draught animals and farm implements); (the "production collective" is the equivalent of elementary producers' co-operative in the North); (3) "Agricultural Cooperatives" in which land, draught animals, machines and farm implements are collectivized (the "agricultural co-operative" is the equivalent of an advanced producers' co-operative in the North). However, the first two forms of collectivization are actually the main ones found in the South (see *Vietnam Courier*, October 1978, pp. 25–28; and Vu Oanh, *Hoan Thanh* ..., pp.33–39).

76. *Nhan Dan* 9 November 1981.

77. *Nhan Dan*, 4 March 1983. Concerning the various coercive methods, see Quang Truong, *Agricultural Collectivization* ..., pp. 267; and Ngo Vinh Long, "View from the Village", *Indochina Issues*, no. 12 (Washington D.C., December 1980), p. 5.

78. Tran Duc, "Tim Hieu Viec...", *Tap Chi Cong San*, no. 3 (1988), p. 30; and idem, "Thu Phac Hoa Con Duong Hop Tac Hoa Cua Nuoc Ta", *Tap Chi Cong San*, no. 6 (1988), p. 47.

79. *History of the Communist Party of Vietnam* (Hanoi: Foreign Languages Publishing House, 1986), p. 279.

80. "Bai Noi Cua Dong Chi Truong Chinh...", *Tap Chi Cong San*, no. 8 (1986), pp. 8 and 10. Nguyen Thanh Binh, then Secretary of the Central Committee, stressed that when the Party asserts that "working people are the masters" in the revolutionary regime, it "should not carry out collectivization by giving orders" to the peasants (*Dai Doan Ket*, no. 22–23 [Hanoi, 6 November 1985], p. 6). He also criticized the fact that in some localities when people refused to be pushed into the co-operatives they were even forbidden to produce! (ibid).

81. Nguyen Xuan Lai, "Question of agrarian structures...", pp. 37–40.

82. Quang Truong, *Agricultural Collectivization* ..., pp. 261; 267–68; Ngo Vinh Long, "View from the Village", p. 5; Lam Thanh Liem,"Collectivisation des terres et crise de l'economie rurale dans le delta du Mekong", *Annales de Geographie*, no. 519 (Paris, 1984), pp. 552–62.

83. Vu Oanh, *Hoan Thanh* ... , p. 10. Another Vietnamese author wrote: "In 1976, ... the Socialist transformation of agriculture in *Nam Bo* began. Within a short time 70% of the households with 65% of the land joined the cooperatives. But those hastily set-up cooperatives soon fell apart" (*Vietnamese Studies* [A New Series], no. 12 [1986], p. 178)
84. Vu Oanh, *Hoan Thanh* ... ,p. 11.
85. Chu Van Lam, "Khoan San Pham . . .", p. 35. Concerning various "shortcomings" related to this collectivization drive, see Duong Phu Hiep, "Chu Nghia Xa Hoi Can Duoc Nhan Thuc Lai", *Triet Hoc*, no. 1 (1988), p. 15.
86. Nguyen Ngoc Long, "Chong Benh Kinh Nghiem ... ", p. 36. See also Tran Ho, "Su Lac Hau Ve . . .", p. 21.
87. Mao Zedong, *A Critique of Soviet Economics*, translated by Moss Roberts (New York: Monthly Review Press, 1977), p. 51.
88. Vien Kinh Te, *35 Nam Kinh Te Viet Nam* ... , p. 178.
89. Quoted in *Asia 1979 Yearbook* (Hong Kong, 1979), p. 322.
90. Huu Tho, "Reflection on the food problem", *Vietnam Courier*, no. 3 (1982), p. 21.
91. Quoted by Tran Dinh Thien, "Ve Moi Quan He Trao Doi Giua Nha Nuoc Va Nong Dan . . .", *Nghien Cuu Kinh Te*, no. 3 (1984), p. 19. Le Duan had more or less reversed his stand expressed at the Thai Binh Conference on agriculture in 1974; see his *Selected Writings*, pp. 480–81. The then Minister of Agriculture Nguyen Ngoc Triu also acknowledged that "some policies relating to the prices of agricultural products ... which were issued ... in the past have proved obsolete and no longer suit the new conditions. Yet, we have been late in modifying or correcting them", *Vietnam Courier*, no. 9 (1980), p. 12.
92. *Tap Chi Cong San*, no. 8 (1986), p. 10.
93. Nguyen Xuan Lai, "Question of agrarian structures ...", p. 54. See also ibid., p. 46.
94. Nguyen Khac Vien's statement, quoted in John Spragens, Jr., "Cautious Policy Reforms", *Indochina Issues*, no. 12 (December 1980), p. 3.
95. Le Duc Thuy, "Ve Co Che Van Dung Cac Quy Luat Kinh Te Cua Chu Nghia Xa Hoi O Nuoc Ta Hien Nay" *Nghien Cuu Kinh Te*, no. 1 (1986), pp. 28–29.
96. Melanie Beresford, *Vietnam* ... ,pp. 153–55; William J. Duiker, *Vietnam Since the Fall of Saigon*, p. 47.
97. Tran Bach Dang, "But Ky Kinh Te", *Tap Chi Cong San*, no. 7 (1988), p. 43.
98. *History of the Communist Party of Vietnam*, p. 306.
99. Ibid., p. 305.
100. See Resolution issued by the Sixth Plenum, *Nhan Dan*, 9 October 1979; and Nguyen Ngoc Triu, "Vietnam's Agriculture: Problems and Prospects", *Vietnam Courier*, no. 9 (1980), pp. 12–13. See also Nguyen Huu Dong, "6th Plenum: Adaptations conjoncturelles ou reformes durables? Essais sur la politique economique du socialisme", *Viet Nam*, no. 2 (Paris April 1981), p. 46.
101. A senior Party official recently acknowledged that the primary reason for the fall in the output of staples was the collectivization drive — which was one

of the "serious errors committed by the Party's [leadership] itself" — and not the natural calamities (see Tran Bach Dang, "But Ky Kinh Te", *Tap Chi Cong San*, no. 7 [1988], p. 42).
102. Nguyen Thanh Bang, "Thu Ban Ve Van De Luong Thuc O Nuoc Ta Trong May Nam Truoc Mat", *Tap Chi Cong San*, no.6 (1988), p. 20.
103. *Nien Giam Thong Ke 1982*, p. 86.
104. Tran Phuong, "*Chinh Sach Kinh Te* . . ." (Internal Document). A senior official of the Vietnamese Foreign Ministry also disclosed that "between 1976 and 1980 [Vietnam] had to import 1.7 million tonnes of food a year" (*Far Eastern Economic Review*, 15 November 1984, p. 128). However, *Nien Giam Thong Ke 1982* (p. 325) reported that Vietnam imported 633.6 thousand tons of food in 1976, 1,576.3 in 1979, and 890.6 in 1980.
105. *CPV 4th National Congress* . . . , p. 209.
106. See Resolution of the 2nd Plenum, *Vietnamese Studies*, no. 51 (1977), p. 33; and Vo Chi Cong, "Day Manh . . .", p. 11.
107. See Nguyen Thanh Bang, "Thu Ban Ve Van . . .", p. 20.
108. *Nien Giam Thong Ke 1982*, p. 136.
109. *CPV 4th National Congress*, pp. 199–200. Concerning the meaning of "*rational development of heavy industry*" see *Gop Phan Tim Hieu Duong Loi Kinh Te Cua Dang* (Hanoi: NXB Su That, 1981), pp. 17; 24.
110. Ibid.
111. *Nien Giam Thong Ke 1982*, p. 230.
112. *CPV 4th National Congress*, pp. 211–12.
113. Le Duc Thuy, "Ve Co Che . . .", p. 27.
114. Speech delivered at the 10th Congress of the Hanoi municipal party organization, *Nhan Dan*, 20 October 1986. For more details, see "Mot So Van De Thuoc Quan Diem Kinh Te", *Nhan Dan*, 5 and 6 November 1986.
115. *6th National Congress* . . . , pp. 18–19. On the same score, see Tran Ho, "Su Lac Hau . . .". p. 21; and particularly Duong Phu Hiep, "Chu Nghia Xa Hoi . . ." pp. 14–15.

V. Afanasyev, Chief-Editor of *Pravda* (4 April 1988) wrote in his newspaper that the Soviets must also share the responsibility in the erroneous policy of "comprehensive and rapid industrialization [with priority given to heavy industry]" advocated in Vietnam (in Russian).
116. Nguyen Van Linh's speech at the Fifth Central Committee's Plenum (June 1988), *Nhan Dan*, 23 June 1988.
117. Nguyen Ngoc Long, "Chong Benh Kinh Nghiem . . . ", p. 35.
118. *CPV. 4th National Congress*, p. 211.
119. Nguyen Xuan Lai, "L'economie artisanale dans la periode actuelle", *Etudes Vietnamiennes*, no. 62 (Hanoi, 1982), p. 68.
120. See Resolution of the Politburo No. 254 NG/TU, quoted in Do Muoi, "Day Manh Cai Tao Xa Hoi Chu Nghia Doi Voi Cong Thuong Nghiep Tu Ban Tu Doanh O Mien Nam", *Tap Chi Cong San*, no. 7 (1978), p. 55.
121. *CPV. 4th National Congress*, pp. 93–95; and Le Duan, *Cai Tao Xa Hoi Chu Nghia O Mien Nam* (Hanoi: NXB Su That, 1980), p. 24 ff.

122. Quoted in *Tap Chi Cong San*, no. 8 (1987), p. 44.
123. Nayan Chanda, *Brother Enemy. The War After the War* (San Diego, New York: Harcourt Brace Jovanovich Publishers, 1986), pp. 234–35; and also Nayan Chanda's article in *Far Eastern Economic Review*, 23 February 1979, p. 33.
124. This motto was conveyed to the writer by a Party member and Senior Research Fellow at the Institute of Economy in Hanoi in 1961.
125. The Nguyen, "The commercial network in the Southern Provinces: From capitalism to socialism", *Vietnam Courier*, May 1978, pp. 13–16. See also Nayan Chanda, *Brother Enemy* ... , pp. 231–33, and his articles in *Far Eastern Economic Review*, 14 April 1978, and 26 May 1978.
126. Do Muoi, "Day Manh Cai Tao ... ", p. 53.
127. The Nguyen, "The commercial network ...", p. 14.
128. See the "Government Decision on Transfer of the Capitalist Trade Sector to Production" (31 March 1978), *Vietnam Courier*, May 1978, pp. 14–15.
129. *Nhan Dan*, 4 January 1979.
130. "Communique on Private Trade", *Radio Ho Chi Minh City*, Domestic Service, 23 March 1978; *SWB* (BBC), 28 March 1978.
131. Quoted in Nayan Chanda, *Brother Enemy* ... , p. 234. It was estimated that more than half the money in circulation and most of the gold and U.S. dollar holdings in the South were in Cholon (R.P. Paringaux, *Le Monde* [Paris], 20 April 1978).
132. Cao Van Luong, "Tim Hieu Chu Nghia ... ", pp. 16–17.
133. Retrospectively in 1987, Mr Huynh Tan Phat, Chairman of the "Vietnam Fatherland Front" admitted in an interview with an Overseas Vietnamese that the *de facto* elimination of the private sector during the "socialist transformation" process in the South in the late 1970s was "an error which was harmful to the solidarity spirit of the Vietnam Fatherland Front". *Doan Ket*, no. 390 (Paris, April 1987), p. 24.
134. "Council of Ministers' Decree", and "State Bank Communique", Hanoi Radio (Domestic Service), 2 May 1978.
135. For an overview of the "socialist transformation in private industry and trade" in the South, see Nguyen Van Linh, *May Van De Cai Tao Xa Hoi Chu Nghia Doi Voi Cong Thuong Nghiep Tu Doanh*, NXB Thanh Pho Ho Chi Minh, 1985; and idem, *Dau Tranh Giai Cap* ... , p. 22ff; and idem, *Thanh Pho Ho Chi Minh 10 Nam*, pp. 151–54; 157–63; 298; 300–2; Vo Nhan Tri, "Transformation Socialiste de l'economie Vietnamienne", in *Le Viet Nam Post-Revolutionnaire. Population-Economie-Societé 1975–1985*, edited by Nguyen Duc Nhuan et al. (Editions l'Harmattan, 1987), pp. 44–66; Lam Thanh Liem, "Bilan de dix annees de reformes economiques (1975–85), *Reflets d'Asie* (Bulletin de l'Institut de l'Asie du Sud-Est), no. 2 (Paris, March-April 1987), and no. 3 (July–August 1987); Lewis M. Stern, "The *Hoa Kieu* ... ", pp. 134–43; and E.P. Glazunov, *Pryeobrazovanye Chastnoy Promishlyennosti I Torgovli Vo Vietnamye* (Moskva: Nauka, 1981), Chapters 5 and 6 (in Russian).
136. See Vo Van Kiet's articles in *Nhan Dan*, 23 August 1983, and 10–11 December 1984.

137. *Vietnam Courier*, December 1979, p. 11.
138. Resolution of the Sixth Plenum, *Nhan Dan*, 9 October 1979.
139. Nguyen Xuan Lai, "Economic Development...", p. 37. The beneficial role of material incentives was acknowledged by *Nhan Dan* (24 September 1979) in these terms: "Any tendency to regard attention to individual material incentives as inconducive to the working masses' revolutionary zeal is erroneous. On the contrary, completely ignoring the workers' economic interests while emptily calling for revolutionary zeal is nothing more than the manifestation of an extremely dangerous kind of voluntarism".
140. *Nhan Dan*, 20 October 1986. Before him, Nguyen Van Linh had already pointed out this "leftist error" in *Thanh Pho Ho Chi Minh*..., p. 328, and also in *Dau Tranh*..., p. 22.
141. *Tap Chi Cong San*, no. 8 (1986), p. 10. (See also Truong Chinh's speech in *Nhan Dan*, 20 October 1986). By this statement, Truong Chinh espoused Linh's thesis, expressed in *Dau Tranh Giai Cap*..., p. 22; and in *May Van De Cai Tao*..., pp. 29–30.
142. *6th National Congress of the Communist Party of Vietnam*, p. 21.
143. *Nhan Dan*, 23 June 1988.
144. *Vietnam News Agency*, 15 April 1987, quoted in the *Straits Times*, 17 April 1987. See also Tran Ho, "Su Lac Hau...", p. 20; Hong Chuong, "Ve Cuoc Van Dong Doi Moi", *Tap Chi Cong San*, no. 2 (1988), pp. 28–29; and Duong Phu Hiep, "Chu Nghia Xa Hoi...", p. 15.
145. *Nien Giam Thong Ke 1982*, p. 176.
146. In Ho Chi Minh City, for example, where the impact of "socialist transformation" was most conspicuous, it was acknowledged that "its industrial production has met with enormous difficulties" at that time (*Tap Chi Cong San*, no. 5 [1985], p. 27).
147. *Vietnam Courier*, January 1977, pp. 6–7.
148. *Nien Giam Thong Ke 1980*, p. 184; and *Nien Giam Thong Ke 1982*, p. 205.
149. Vo Van Kiet, *Ban Linh Va Sang Tao Trong Doi Moi Co Che Quan Ly O Co So*, (NXB Thanh Pho Ho Chi Minh, 1985), p. 25.
150. *Dai Doan Ket* (Hanoi, 1 March 1980).
151. As in other communist countries, Vietnam's National Income does not include income from the "non-material production sectors" such as public services, education, health, and so forth. Therefore, its growth rate is always higher than that calculated by the U.N. method. In Vietnam, one makes also a distinction between "Produced National Income" and "Used National Income". The latter includes foreign aid.
152. See *Vietnam Courier*, January 1977, pp. 6–7.
153. *Nien Giam Thong Ke 1982*, p. 69.
154. Quoted in *Asiaweek*, 21 September 1986, p. 20. Concerning Chinese aid, see "The Truth about Vietnam-China Relations...", pp. 58; 60–61.
155. Nayan Chanda, *Brother Enemy*..., p. 242.
156. Concerning the reasons for the cut in Chinese aid, see *Asia 1979 Yearbook*, p. 320. See also Nayan Chanda, *Brother Enemy*..., pp. 238ff. A Chinese official

revealed to Nayan Chanda that "already in early July 1978, the Chinese Politburo decided 'to teach Vietnam a lesson' for its 'ungrateful and arrogant' behaviour" (ibid., p. 261).

157. Hoang Van Hoan, *Giot Nuoc* . . . , pp. 373; 426.
158. For reasons and details on this score, see N. Chanda, *Brother Enemy* . . . , p. 245.
159. Tran Duc Luong, "Vietnam joined the Council of Mutual Economic Assistance Ten Years Ago", *Vietnam Courier*, no. 9 (1988), p. 21.
160. Ibid.
161. See V. Produkin's article in *Ekonomicheskoye Sotrudnichestvo Stran-Chlenov SEV*, no. 1 (Moskva, 1980), pp. 17–21 (in Russian).
162. M. Petrov, "Vietnam's Cooperation in the CMEA Framework", *Far Eastern Affairs*, no. 1 (Moscow, 1983), p. 176.
163. "Mot So Tu Lieu Ve Quan He Hop Tac Kinh Te Van Hoa Viet Nam — Lien Xo", *Tap Chi Cong San*, no. 11 (1985), p. 70; Le Khac, "Soviet-Vietnamese Treaty on Trade and Navigation: 25th Anniversary", *Foreign Trade*, no. 4 (Moscow, 1983), p. 7.
164. For details, see *Vietnam News Agency*, 4 November 1978.
165. *Vietnam Courier*, no. 11 (1983), p. 1. By "two-pronged threat" Vietnam meant that China "on the one hand wirepulled the Pol Pot-Ieng Sary clique to attack [it] in the Southwest, and on the other posed a military threat to the northern border". See *History of the Communist Party* . . . , pp. 288, 302; and also *The Truth about Vietnam-China Relations* . . . , pp. 55–56; 62–63; 81–82. Concerning the reasons leading to the signing of this Treaty, see *inter alia* Nayan Chanda, *Brother Enemy* . . . , pp. 256–58.
166. *Vietnam News Agency*, 4 November 1978. Regarding the military and political aspects of this Treaty, see *Asia 1979 Yearbook*, pp. 320–21; Lau Teik Soon, "The Soviet Vietnamese Treaty", *Southeast Asian Affairs 1980* (Singapore: Institute of Southeast Asian Studies, 1980), p. 59ff; and A. Lakshamana Chetty, "Soviet Stakes in Asia-Pacific", *Indochina Review* (Centre for Studies on Indochina, S.V. University, Tirupati, India, January-March 1987), p. 39.
167. In a recent interview with R. Leroy, a French communist official, Nguyen Van Linh explained the reason for the Vietnamese invasion of Kampuchea as follows: " . . . After the 1975 victory, the Pol Pot regime . . . . , supported by China, launched hostilities against Vietnam, systematically massacring civilians . . . . [In addition to this] Pol Pot perpetrated genocide against his own people. We therefore entered Cambodia because of the traditional solidarity between [the Vietnamese and Khmer] peoples and as a defensive measure" (*L'humanite* [Paris], 28 October 1988).
168. Nguyen Xuan Lai, "Economic Development . . . ", *Vietnamese Studies* (A New Series), no. 1 (1983), p. 33.
169. M. Petrov, "Vietnam's Cooperation in the CMEA . . . ", p. 169.
170. *Izvestia*, 1 November 1979 (in Russian).
171. *Pravda*, 4 July 1980 (in Russian).
172. E. Rybalko, "URSS-RSV: 30 ans de cooperation feconde", *Commerce Exterieur*,

no. 7 (Moscow, 1985), pp. 6–7. See also Le Khac, "Les perspectives du Commerce Exterieur du Vietnam et les Relations Commerciales et Economiques Sovieto-Vietnamiennes", *Commerce Exterieur*, no. 8 (Moscow, 1985), p. 11.
173. Quoted in *Far Eastern Economic Review*, 24 May 1984, p. 80.
174. See Nayan Chanda's article, *Far Eastern Economic Review*, 27 February 1981, p. 32. For an overview of economic relations between Vietnam and the USSR, see Vo Nhan Tri, "Soviet-Vietnamese Economic Cooperation Since 1975", in "Behind the Vladivostock Initiative. The Soviet Strategic Reach in Southeast Asia", *Indochina Report*, no. 8 (Singapore, October 1986), p. 39ff; and Douglas Pike, *Vietnam and the Soviet Union, Anatomy of An Alliance* (Boulder and London: Westview Press, 1987), pp . 115–16; 127–61.
175. According to another Vietnamese source "besides grant aid, the USSR loaned Vietnam 1.5 billion rubles (including 800 million rubles in interest-free loans); see *Nong Nghiep*, 5 November 1987.
176. *Far East and Australasia*, 1982–83 (London: Europe Publications, 1983). T. Hayter and C. Watson wrote that "probably the most blatant recent example of open political US intervention in the operations of the Bank is in Vietnam". See *Aid, Rhetoric and Reality* (London: Pluto Press,1985), p. 17.
177. Nayan Chanda, "Vietnam's Economy: Bad but not worse", *Indochina Issues*, no. 41 (Washington, D.C., October 1983), p. 4.
178. *Nien Giam Thong Ke 1982*, p. 317.
179. Ibid., p. 324.
180. Ibid., p. 315.
181. Ibid., p. 321.
182. M. Morrow, "Vietnam's Embargoed Economy: In the US Interest?, *Indochina Issues*, no. 3 (August 1979), pp. 2; 8.
183. IMF, *Socialist Republic of Vietnam, Recent Economic Developments*, 19 December 1980, pp. 37, 46.
184. Ibid., p. iv.
185. For details, see ibid., pp. 13–15.
186. Huynh Van Cang's (Director of War Invalids and Social Affairs Service in Ho Chi Minh City) interview with *Vietnam News Agency*, 21 August 1988. He also reminded that at that time, the Party's policy implemented in Ho Chi Minh City "brought the situation to near disaster"! (ibid). Concerning the drastic fall of the living standard of the Southern people, see *Far Eastern Economic Review*, 8 November 1984, p. 29 and 22 May 1985, p. 22; and *Southeast Asian Affairs 1981* (Singapore: Institute of Southeast Asian Studies, 1981, p. 343).
187. Vo Van Kiet, *Ban Linh Va . . .* , pp. 33–34.
188. *Nien Giam Thong Ke 1982*, p. 374.
189. Quoted in *Far Eastern Economic Review*, 27 February 1981, p. 28.
190. See J.P. Gallois, "Interview with Hoang Tung", *Agence France Presse* (AFP), 19 April 1980. The then Minister of Agriculture admitted that there were "hardships in the life of workers and civil servants, and flagging enthusiasm among the peasants" (*Vietnam Courier*, no. 7 [1980], p. 19).

191. See Murray Hiebert, "The Food Weapon: Can Vietnam Be Broken?", *Indochina Issues*, no. 15 (April 1981), p. 2.
192. Quoted in *Far Eastern Economic Review*, 8 January 1981, p. 42.
193. Quoted in Nayan Chanda, "Vietnam's Economy ... ", p. 5.
194. *Asia 1981 Yearbook*, pp. 10, 41. Note that the "people's army" is composed of the regular Armed Forces (1.029 million) and the paramilitary forces (70,000 Frontier and Coast Security Forces, and about 1.5 million Armed Militia).
195. Nguyen Manh Tuan, *Dung Truoc Bien* (NXB Van Nghe, Thanh Pho Ho Chi Minh, 1982), pp. 15; 105; 141; 163; 204.
196. *CPV. 4th National Congress* ... , p. 86. See also pp. 219–20.
197. *CPV 5th National Congress* ... , p. 23. See also Vu Quoc Tuan, "Xay Dung Tung Buoc Mot Co Cau Kinh Te Moi", *Nghien Cuu Kinh Te*, no. 1 (1984), pp. 1–2.
198. Tran Bach Dang, "But Ky Kinh Te", p. 42. See also p. 47.
199. *6th National Congress* ... , p. 26.

Chapter 3

The Third Five-Year Plan, 1981-85

Since the Sixth Plenum of the Fourth National Congress held in September 1979, "heated discussions on many [economic] topics" have taken place within the Party leadership of which the most revealing was the Tenth Plenum (Fourth National Congress) which lasted from 9 October to 3 November 1981, one of the longest sessions of the Central Committee in recent years.[1] According to a knowledgeable Vietnam watcher, "the pragmatists won the day" at this Plenum which adopted the draft politico-economic report to be presented to the Fifth Party Congress.[2] This draft report was, however, challenged by many grass-roots Party chapters during the months preceding the Party Congress, and ultimately some important amendments were made to it.

In March 1982, the Fifth Party Congress, initially scheduled for the last quarter of 1981, was at last convened. The economic policies advocated at this Congress confirmed and expanded the decisions taken since the Sixth Plenum in September 1979. In his political report to this Congress, Le Duan emphasized that following the Chinese attack, Vietnam "must strive to carry out two strategic tasks: first, to build socialism . . . ; second, to stand ready to defend the homeland".[3] Although these two tasks "are closely related", the Party should "give priority to the task of building socialism".[4]

In the same report, after acknowledging that during the previous five-year plan the Party leadership had made serious "mistakes" because of "failure to really grasp the laws governing the transition from small-[scale] production to large-scale socialist production..., to fully grasp the reality [of the country], and ... lack of economic knowledge", mistakes which were "the main causes leading to, or aggravating, the economic and social difficulties of the past [five] years",[5] Le Duan mapped out the following "socio-economic strategy for the *first stage* of socialist industrialization" which began with the Third Five-Year Plan (FYP) and stretched up to 1990:

1. "To meet the most pressing and essential requirements of everyday life, gradually stabilizing, and eventually improving to some extent the people's material and cultural livelihood. First of all, we must end the grain and foodstuffs shortage, and make efforts to meet the requirements of clothing, [education], medical care, housing, transportation, child care, and other essential consumption needs.
2. To continue building the material and technological [basis] of socialism, with emphasis on boosting agriculture, consumer goods [industry], and exports while at the same time improving the technical basis of other economic branches, and making preparations for a more vigorous development of heavy industry in the next stage.
3. To complete the socialist transformation in the Southern provinces; to continue perfecting the socialist relations of production in the North ...
4. To meet the requirements of national defence, and to maintain [internal] security and order".[6]

For the first time the Party perceived — but still very vaguely — the necessity to divide the whole transitional period towards socialism into various stages, each one having its specific character.[7] During the "first stage" or "initial stage", Le Duan said, the Party should "in particular concentrate [the country's] forces on the development of agriculture, taking it a step further towards large-scale socialist production in a rational agro-industrial structure combining right from the outset agriculture, consumer goods [industry], and heavy industry".[8]

To this end, the Party advocated ten major socio-economic policies to be implemented during the 1980s:
— a "correct combination" of industry with agriculture,
— a combination of a centrally-run economy with the "vigorous development" of local economies;
— a "good correspondence between productive forces and relations of production";
— a combination of economic construction with national defence;
— a combination of internal economic development with expansion of foreign economic relations;
— a redistribution of the labour force on a national scale;
— a boost to scientific and technological work;
— a "correct" allotment between accumulation and consumption in the National Income;
— a "new socialist order" in the distribution and circulation of commodities;
— and lastly, a replacement of existing centralized bureaucratic economic management and planning by an efficient managerial and planning system.[9]

The specific tasks of the Third Five-Year Plan (1981-85) which were also mentioned in Le Duan's report, consisted of "stabilizing and improving to some extent" the people's living conditions which represented "the most pressing problem"; developing while reorganizing the production; reorganizing the sector of capital construction (building industry); improving the circulation and distribution of goods; basically completing the "socialist transformation" in the South; developing economic co-operation with the COMECON countries, Laos and Kampuchea; practising thrift, particularly in capital construction and production; applying scientific and technological progress to production; renovating the macro-economic management system; stepping up cultural and public health activities; and lastly, consolidating national defence and internal security.[10]

Agriculture
In the Third FYP, the paramount importance of agriculture was

clearly stated, at least in theory. "In the five years 1981-85 (and in the eighties as a whole) *it is necessary to concentrate on a vigorous development of agriculture, to regard it as a [top] priority, to take it a step further to large-scale socialist production . . .*", said Le Duan in his report at the Fifth Party Congress.[11] It is interesting to note that it took the Party twenty-seven years (since it regained power in 1955) to unequivocally give [top] priority to agriculture in its strategy for economic development, a strategy needed for the initial stage of development in an economically backward country like Vietnam.

It should also be noted that the emphasis laid upon agriculture in the Third FYP did not mean that the Party intended to develop agriculture in isolation and neglect the development of industry in general, and heavy industry in particular. For Le Duan also stressed in his report that it was necessary "to combine agriculture, consumer goods industry, and heavy industry in a rational agro-industrial structure". In this "agro-industrial structure" — which was perceived by the Party as a dialectical unity — agriculture constituted a basis for the development of industry, whereas industry represented a driving force in the modernization of agriculture.[12] Moreover, in the Party's view, agricultural development was part and parcel of the "socialist industrialization" process, and it was proclaimed that such was "a new and creative concept of industrialization".[13]

As said earlier in Chapter 1, Le Duan's viewpoint bore a great resemblance to Mao Zedong's idea of balanced growth of the main sectors of the economy in the late 1950s[14] which, in turn, was reminiscent of Nicolai Bukharin's argument during the Soviet industrialization debate of the 1920s,[15] as all of them envisaged a balanced relationship between agriculture and industry, and viewed agriculture and light industry as the foundation for the development of heavy industry. However, there was an important difference between Mao Zedong's and Le Duan's models on the one hand, and Bukharin's model on the other. The latter was based on:

1. a *balanced* socialist economic growth which must be coupled with a maintenance of the state, co-operative and private sectors;

2. an unqualified acceptance of Lenin's NEP (New Economic Policy) in which a private agricultural sector would continue for a long time to co-exist with a socialist industrial sector, the relationship between them being mediated by the market. As Stephen Cohen stressed, "the linchpin of his program was the encouragement of private peasant accumulation . . .".[16]

In contrast, the agricultural base of Mao Zedong's and Le Duan's models rested not on the private peasant farm but on collectivized agriculture which should exist parallel to a socialist industrial sector.[17]

To give priority to agriculture also means gradually shifting from an autarkical, small-scale production to a large-scale socialist production in the 1980s. In the Party's view, it means: (a) an integration of agricultural production and distribution of agricultural produce into an overall economic plan whose objective is to ensure food supply for the whole country, supply agricultural raw materials for the consumer goods industry, and create a source of export goods; (b) a stepping up of the scientific and technological revolution in agriculture, particularly in the field of water conservancy, application of the achievements of biology to farming, increase of fertilizers, gradual mechanization, and development of the processing industry, and so forth; (c) a completion of the "socialist transformation" of agriculture in the South; and (d) a building up of the district into a viable economic structure by combining agriculture with small-scale industry and handicrafts (or forestry, fishery, agriculture and industry depending on the specific conditions of each district).[18]

Concerning the "socialist transformation" of agriculture, it should be recalled that the redistribution of 384,689 hectares of land regained from the landlords and rich peasants to 403,052 landless and poor peasant households in the South[19] was carried out simultaneously with the reorganization of the latter into "solidarity production teams", that is, the first form of co-operativization in every village [20]

In the collectivization drive during this FYP, besides Directive No. 93, the Central Committee Secretariat also issued two communiqués, Nos. 14 and 138, in April and November 1981 respectively, in which the Party criticized members for their hesitation and indecision after the previous failure to accelerate collectivization, and urged the stepping up of agricultural co-operativization.[21] This stance was confirmed by Le Duan at the Fifth Party Congress when he emphasized that the Party should "continue the movement of agricultural co-operativization in the Mekong delta provinces ... overcome ... hesitation, inaction in directing the co-operativization movement.... Along with setting up production collectives and cooperative farms, develop marketing and credit cooperatives". And he insisted that by the end of 1985, the Party should "complete in the main agricultural co-operativization in the Mekong Delta ... with production collectives as the most common ... form".[22]

In March 1983, the Central Committee Secretariat issued new directives concerning the tasks of collectivization for the 1983-85 period.[23] Consequently, from mid-1984 onwards the Southern provinces were under strong pressure to complete the collectivization programme before the target date of December 1985.[24] At the end of the Third FYP, there were reportedly 39,380 "production collectives" (or elementary agricultural producers' co-operatives) and more than 2,292 "agricultural cooperatives" (or advanced agricultural producers' co-operatives) which accounted for 54.4 per cent and 28.5 per cent respectively of the peasant households in the South.[25]

The Party's newspaper acknowledged, however, that "on the whole, the quality of production collectives and [agricultural] cooperatives was still low ... , their management was still weak".[26] Later on, the Party even admitted that most of these "production collectives" and "agricultural cooperatives" were "generally weak and their existence was, for the most part, merely nominal. Their production increased slowly and their debts to the State was substantial".[27]

As for the whole country, it was reported that in 1985 there existed altogether 16,334 agricultural producers' co-operatives (of which 13,735 were advanced ones) which accounted for 67.4 per cent of the peasant households.[28]

***

The Party's view of the "household economy" of the members of the co-operatives has changed markedly since its Sixth Central

Committee Plenum (Fourth Congress) in 1979, and particularly since its Fifth Congress in 1982. Before 1979, the Party had dogmatically regarded the "household economy" as a vestige of the system of individual ownership which would inexorably lead to a "spontaneous development of capitalism" if not stopped,[29] and should therefore be "temporarily tolerated so long as the State and [cooperative] economies are unable to meet the ... needs of the Society".[30] This "erroneous" stance, this Vietnamese writer acknowledged, "led to restrictive measures which naturally harmed the national economy". Moreover, the "household economy" was considered to be an "auxiliary" economy, that is, an adjunct to the co-operative economy. But at the Sixth Plenum in 1979, which affirmed the key importance of small-scale production at the present stage of Vietnam's economic development, the door was opened for the "household economy" to make use of all its dispersed potential to produce much needed food and handicraft consumer goods.[31] At that time, the Party newspaper even stigmatized "a number of weak-spirited comrades [who] are obsessed with the spectre of the spontaneous development of capitalism inherent in any productive or exchange activity which is not organized",[32] that is, not performed by the socialist sector. (In fact, the position ascribed to the "weak-spirited" comrades in 1979 was precisely the view expressed by Secretary-General Le Duan himself in 1974).[33]

Following the Sixth Plenum (Fourth Congress), the Resolution of the Fifth Party Congress and Directive No. 35 of the Party Secretariat dropped the term "auxiliary" and asserted that the "household economy" should henceforth be considered as "an integral part of the socialist economy,"[34] and be encouraged to develop, but "in the right direction"[35] (that is, in accordance with both the plans of the co-operative and the locality) and in close association with the collective and state sectors, thus forming a dialectical unity of the three economic sectors.[36]

In 1983, the "household economy", which represented only 5 per cent of land alloted by the co-operatives, supplied some 50-60 per cent of the total income of the members of the co-operatives, 30-50 per cent of the foodstuffs and more than 90 per cent of the pork and chicken, vegetables and fruits consumed by them.[37] Le

Duc Tho disclosed in a 1982 report that, thanks to intensive farming, the private plot of the co-operative members "yielded twice as much as the cooperative".[38]

* * *

In connection with the "household economy" one should also mention the expansion of the "end-product contract" system (*Khoan San Pham*) to the peasant team or individual peasant with the issuance of the Party Secretariat's Directive No. 100 CT/TU, in January 1981,[39] following the Ninth Plenum's decision (December 1980) on "expanding and perfecting the product-based contract system in agriculture".[40]

This Directive, which represented one of the most important changes in the Party's agricultural policy during this FYP, consists of the peasant team or individual peasant signing a contract directly with the co-operative for farming on its land, linking remuneration directly to the quality of work.[41] The responsibility for fulfilling the contract lies with the household, which allocates work based on relations within the household. The responsibility for production, therefore, shifts down from the level of the co-operative to the production team, and from the team to the peasant family which, in principle, takes over the last three tasks formerly performed by the co-operative, namely, transplanting of rice seedlings, tending the crop and harvesting, whereas the other five tasks such as ploughing, water irrigation, seed preparation, fertilizer preparation, and pest control are still performed by the co-operative using collective labour. However, the co-operative must see to the efficient execution of all these eight tasks. In theory, it must not let its members do as they think fit, or contract everything to the household (*Khoan Trang*) provided that the latter deliver all the production quota it had contracted for. This "end-product contract" system provides incentives for increased output, by setting a production quota for the co-operative, a quota which is determined on the basis of the productivity of the land during the previous three years. If production falls short, the producers must make up the deficit in the following year, except in the case of natural disaster or exceptional circumstances. If there is a

The Third Five-Year Plan, 1981-85

surplus, they can keep it, sell it on the free market, or to the State-trading agencies at "negotiated prices". (These prices are theoretically calculated to allow an attractive profit margin and to take account of local supply and demand conditions in order to promote such above-quota sales to the state; however they are usually slightly lower than the free market prices which fluctuate according to supply and demand.) For agricultural products, free market prices and "negotiated prices" are considerably higher than state-fixed procurement prices, so that with the new "end-product contract" system peasants have the opportunity to increase their income.

The new "end-product contract" system is different from the "three-point contract" system which existed before. The fundamental flaw of the latter was that it was based on the number of work-days irrespective of the quality of work; moreover, it was the production brigade who disposed of the crop, and this led to the peasants working carelessly.[42] But in the new "end-product contract" system, the members of the co-operatives can draw benefits from their work-days and at the same time derive a profit from their above-quota sales; and their remuneration is directly linked to their quality of work.[43] After two years of enforcement, the Council of Ministers issued a Resolution on 4 December 1983 adding some amendments to the Party's Directive No. 100 CT/TU.[44]

Nearly two years later, the Party Politburo issued Directive No. 67/CT/TU (on 22 June 1985), on "perfecting the (end) product contract system" in the light of the Eighth Plenum's Central Committee Resolution (10-17 June 1985). This Directive emphasized, *inter alia*, the necessity for the co-operatives to: (1) "abolish the system of management that is plagued with bureaucratic centralism and subsidization", (2) "improve and expand the application of the (end) product contract system in all branches (cultivation, animal husbandry, afforestation, raising of marine products, and small-scale industry and handicrafts); stabilize contracted quotas in order to encourage everybody to engage confidently in productive work; apply a remuneration system for management cadres based on the extent to which the co-operatives and production units fulfill their plan"; (3) "improve economic management and perfect the (end) product contract system in conjunction with efforts to strengthen the material and technical base of the co-operatives"; (4) "consolidate agricultural co-operatives in terms of organization, and closely co-ordinate the activities of production, marketing and credit co-operatives in the countryside".[45]

From the preceding pages, it is clear that the "end-product contract" system is not a return to capitalism in agriculture as some Western observers have suggested, but rather a "recuperation" by the Party from the peasants' initiative — which started with the successful experience in Haiphong province[46] — with a view to "further consolidating and strengthening the socialist relations of production in the countryside".[47] Vietnamese officials said that this new contract system prompted the peasants to work harder and to use industrial inputs more efficiently than the old "three-point contract" system; that it helped boost yield and agricultural production in the North, and speeded up collectivization in the South.[48] Even Truong Chinh, who fiercely condemned this household contract system in 1968 (see Chapter 1), acknowledged in 1986 that "the nationwide implementation of the [end-product contract] system . . . , though still defective, has played a major role in boosting agricultural production, and has given a correct orientation for strengthening the collective economic relations in the countryside."[49] Had Truong Chinh and with him, the whole Party leadership, not dogmatically condemned this beneficial contract system in the late 1960s, the Party would not have waited until 1981 to popularize it in the whole country and consequently Vietnamese agriculture would not have stagnated for so long!

However, from 1983, the co-operative members lost their zeal to work on the basis of the "end-product contract" system, and returned part of the land operated under this contract system to the co-operatives because, due to various reasons, they had incurred losses.[50] They preferred to concentrate their efforts on their private plot instead, which was much more profitable. After fulfilling all their numerous obligations, they finally got only 16-17 per cent[51] — or even 13 per cent in some places[52] — of the contract output which far from compensated them for their production expenses.

Let us examine now how the above-mentioned agricultural policy was implemented.

To give top priority to agriculture implied that first of all the State should concentrate significant investments on this branch of the economy, but in reality this was not the case at all. The data in Table 3.1 bear witness to this:

TABLE 3.1
Structure of State Investments by Branches, 1981–85
(In per cent)

	1981	1984	1985
Gross fixed investment in the *"productive sector"* only (in constant 1982 prices) of which:	100.0	100.0	100.0
Industry	51.6	40.6	40.0
Capital construction (building industry)	3.9	2.8	2.7
Agriculture	22.8	22.9	23.8
Forestry, etc...	2.4	3.6	4.1

SOURCE: *Nien Giam Thong Ke 1985* (Hanoi: Tong Cuc Thong Ke, 1987), p. 186.

From the table it can be seen that, in spite of the official rhetoric, it was industry and not agriculture which got the lion's share of state investments during the Third FYP. In 1985, for instance, agriculture accounted for only 23.8 per cent whereas industry had 40 per cent of the total gross investment in the "material production sector", compared with 22.8 and 51.6 per cent respectively in 1981. The Party acknowledged that it was a "shortcoming" for "not concentrating enough [state investments] on the foremost battlefront which is agriculture".[53] Moreover, these scarce investments were neither judiciously allocated to the most important links in the agricultural sector nor well coordinated. Intensive investments were neglected, and many projects dragged out. Hence, there was great waste and low economic efficiency.[54]

It should be noted, however, that compared with 1980, state investments allocated to agriculture increased by 51.7 per cent whereas those to industry were augmented by only 19.3 per cent.[55]

To regard agriculture as "the foremost battlefront" also implied that the State should advocate a policy which favoured the peasants' interests, but in fact this was not so. Agricultural tax, for instance, usually amounted to 12–14 per cent of the actual crop[56] (and not 10 per cent as officially fixed) which was "twice as high as the industrial-commercial tax rate".[57] Apart from agricultural tax, co-operative members were liable to the corvée (fifty working days for each of them) and had to make all kinds of contributions[58] which were, in fact, taxes in disguise.

Concerning the unequal urban-rural terms of trade, suffice it to mention that state-fixed quota procurement prices in the "two-way contract" system were so low, in spite of their increase, that they did not cover all the production expenses, whereas the prices of industrial inputs, many times more than those of agricultural goods, were too high. Moreover, the prices of industrial inputs actually sold to the end-users were much higher than those fixed by the central government. "While prices of industrial commodities increased 5–10 fold, farm prices remained the same", complained a peasant at a collectivized farmers' congress in Ha Bac province. And he added "We [the peasants] do not demand much, only hope there is fairness in all this". When co-operative members sold their products to the State, they "had to transport them to its storehouses ..., were subject to arbitrary grading and pricing of their products, and still were not paid cash right away". Moreover, the state-trading agencies "paid the peasants only after three months, and in the meantime the *Dong* lost its purchasing power every day, every month".[59]

The abovementioned facts show that, despite the Party's rhetoric, "agriculture has not been regarded — as Truong Chinh admitted in his political report at the Sixth Party Congress — as a branch of prime importance; conditions necessary for its development have not been ensured, especially with regard to [industrial inputs], capital [that is, investment], and incentive policies".[60]

The Third Five-Year Plan, 1981-85

What was the impact of the described policy on the evolution of agricultural production? Table 3.2 contains some official data on this score. The table shows that total staples output, that is, paddy and subsidiary crops converted into paddy equivalent, increased significantly from 1981 to 1983 but began to slow down in 1984 and 1985. This sizeable increase during the first three years of the FYP was due particularly to the generalization of the "end-product contract" system, the favourable climatic conditions and the application of scientific and technical research to production in a more effective way. The slowing down of staples production during the last two years of the FYP can be explained by the lack of zeal of the co-operative members to work under the "end-product contract" system, the irrational prices and other disincentive policies *vis-à-vis* the farmers, the increased shortage of industrial inputs, and the unfavourable weather conditions.

From 1981 to 1985, paddy production alone increased by 27.8 per cent whereas the subsidiary crops (measured in paddy equivalent) declined by 10.3 per cent. In 1985, the output of subsidiary crops reached 2.32 million tons, far below the target set by the Third FYP at 3.5 million tons. According to the Party newspaper, the fall in subsidiary crops production "stemmed from a number of ... shortcomings: .... Many provinces still do not pay enough attention to the importance of subsidiary crops ...; adequate policies have not yet been formulated to encourage the development of such crops, etc. ....."[61]

On the whole, however, total staples output increased by 21.3 per cent whereas the population grew by 9 per cent from 1981 to 1985; the average increases were 4.9 and 2.7 per cent respectively. Compared to the crisis of food production in the previous FYP, the augmentation of staples output in this FYP was a noteworthy achievement. However, the target of 19–20 million tons set by the Third FYP was not reached.[62] In 1985 only 18.2 million tons of food staples were recorded.

The per capita staples production evolved as follows: 273 kg in 1981; 299 kg in 1982; 298 kg in 1983;[63] 303 kg in 1984; and 304 kg in 1985.[64] According to a Vietnamese writer, the 304 kg per capita staples output reached in 1985 "testifi[ed] to great efforts, yet it [was] a very low figure, which [was] a bare minimum and

TABLE 3.2
Agricultural Production, 1981–85

	1981	1982	1983	1984	1985
	(In millions of new dong)				
Gross value of agricultural output	7,096.3[a]	8,729.2[a]	85,001.8[b]	89,471.8[b]	91,044.6[b]
of which: Crop cultivation	6,139.3[a]	82,253.7[b] 6,838.8[a] 63,920.9[b]	64,766.0[b]	68,360.6[b]	69,615.0[b]
Animal husbandry	1,767.0[a]	1,890.4[a] 18,332.8[b]	20,225.0[b]	21,111.2[b]	21,429.6[b]
	(In thousands of tons)				
Total staples output (paddy and subsidiary crops converted into paddy equivalent)	15,005.2	16,828.8	16,985.8	17,800.0	18,200.0
of which: Paddy	12,415.2	14,390.2	14,743.3	15,505.6	15,874.8
Subsidiary crops	2,590.0	2,438.6	2,242.5	2,294.4	2,325.2
Average yield per annum (quintal/ha)					
by product: Paddy	22.0	25.2	26.3	27.3	27.8
Subsidiary crops (paddy equivalent)	19.4	19.4	19.3	20.1	20.6

[a] At 1970 constant prices
[b] At 1982 constant prices

SOURCE: *Nien Giam Thong Ke 1985*, pp. 36, 40, 44, 68.

approach[ed] the limits of hunger".[65] As a matter of fact, "every year there were nearly 3 million peasants who experienced food shortage during the gap between the harvests".[66] According to a Vietnamese expert, the necessary per capita food staples output should amount to 300 kg for current consumption, and at least 50 kg for reserves.[67] Consequently, with a population of 59,872.0 thousand inhabitants, Vietnam's food production should have been at least 21 million tons but in fact it produced only 18.2 million tons in 1985.

The fact remains that in 1983, the Party's mass media already sounded the big drum to celebrate "food self-sufficiency".[68] Again in 1985, according to the Party's journal, Vietnam "solemnly declared to the world that for the first time it completely achieved food sufficiency. But immediately a few months later, in order to bridge the gap between the harvests, [it] had to silently import some hundred thousand tons of food".[69] At the end of 1985, the then Minister of Agriculture admitted in an interview that Vietnam "has not yet ... solved the food [staples] problem".[70]

It should be noted that significant losses of food staples occurred between the harvest and consumption. "Due to inadequacies in drying, storage, packing, and transport facilities, the rate of loss averaged 7–8% [of the total output] and in many cases even higher".[71] "In some localities, it [reached] even 20%".[72] Concretely, these losses amounted to "approximately 2–3 million tons of food crops every year, a quantity sufficient to feed 10 million people".[73] A senior official in the Service of Agriculture in Ho Chi Minh City told this writer in 1984 that losses usually accounted for about 30 per cent of the total staples output.

The annual average paddy yield, despite its increase from 22 quintal per hectare in 1981 to 27.8 quintal per hectare in 1985, remained "one of the lowest in the world".[74] During the last two years of the Third FYP, it began to level off.

Animal husbandry, on the other hand, has developed in many respects during the period under review, compared with the previous crisis period. In particular, by putting an end to compulsory deliveries, increasing the purchasing prices, and introducing new breeding techniques, pig raising in Vietnam has developed significantly. However, the number of pigs reached only 11.8 million in 1985,[75] whereas the target set by the Third FYP was 13 million.

Industry and Handicrafts

As mentioned earlier, the Party's emphasis on agriculture "does not mean in any way developing agriculture in isolation, but as part of a structure which closely and correctly combines agriculture with industry".[76] Le Duan stressed in his political report at the Fifth Party Congress that "the development of agriculture must be combined with that of consumer goods industry in both extent and scope, from food-processing and light industries to small industry and handicrafts ... (in order) to meet the material and cultural needs of society ..., (and) create an important source of exports".[77] A few years later, the Party's newspaper emphasized again that "the development of consumer goods industry ... is a strategic socio-economic objective".[78]

As for small-scale industry and handicrafts, which "have great potential in Vietnam", and hold "an important position in the national economy over a long period, especially in this first stage [of the transitional period]", the Party's policy consisted of transforming them "into a component of the socialist economy" while "paying due attention to increasing supplies of equipment, ... raw materials, [and] using economic incentives" in order to boost their production.[79]

The emphasis laid by the Fifth Party Congress on boosting light industry was not, however, seriously implemented. In his political report at the Sixth Party Congress, Truong Chinh admitted that the "consumer goods industry, including handicrafts, [were] still neglected in terms of organization, investment and policy" during the Third FYP.[80] In the present stage of the transitional period, "to develop agriculture and the consumer goods industry is, in the Party's view, to lay the foundation for the development of heavy industry". And, reciprocally, the primary purpose of "build[ing] in a rational way the essential heavy industries" (such as "electric power, coal, petrol, fertilizers, insecticides, basic chemicals, [farm implements], building materials, etc.") was to "boost agriculture and the consumer goods industry".[81]

The emphasis upon the boosting of agriculture and light industry as the foundation for the development of heavy industry recalls somewhat the stance adopted by Nicolai Bukharin in the 1920s and Mao Zedong in the mid-1950s, which has been discussed earlier. In spite of the Party's rhetoric, in fact, as Truong Chinh acknowledged, "heavy industry fail[ed] to serve agriculture and light industry in good time" during the period under review.[82]

It should be noted that Le Duan had already stressed in the Third FYP that

> while developing heavy industry — primarily with the purpose of boosting agriculture and the consumer goods industry, we should make preparations ... so that ... we can start the construction of a number of key heavy industrial projects, especially in engineering and metallurgy. For we must not lose sight of the fact that the material-technological basis of socialism remains mechanized heavy industry capable of ... providing new technical equipment to the whole economy.[83]

Thus, contrary to what a foreign observer wrote, there was no "rupture with the dogma of the priority of heavy industry" in the Party's stance.[84] On the contrary, the Resolution of the Fourth Central Committee Plenum in June 1983 emphasized that:

> It is a mistake not to regard agriculture as the foremost battlefront. But it is also a mistake not to give serious attention to the central task of the whole transitional period to socialism, that is, socialist industrialization, the contents of which is the combination of agriculture with industry ..., and the [top] priority given to a rational development of heavy industry.[85]

At the Sixth Central Committee Plenum a year later (July 1984) Le Duan stressed again that: "In order to take agriculture to large-scale socialist production and to develop ... the consumer goods industry, we must ... give priority to a rational development of heavy industry ...".[86]

Concerning the "socialist transformation" of private industry and trade, the Party continued to advocate the reconversion of capitalist industrial enterprises into "joint State-private enterprises" or other forms of "state capitalism".[87] (However, the capitalist commerce "is to be radically eliminated".)[88] Since the issuance of the Politburo's Directive No. 1 on the tasks of Ho Chi Minh City in 1982, the Party did not advocate any longer the "restriction" of private industry but emphasized instead its "transformation for better use; and use for better transformation".[89]

With regard to small-scale industry and handicrafts, the Party advocated either "collective forms of operation or [preservation] of individual ownership, depending on the particular features of each trade".[90] Like collectivization, this transformation of private industry and handicrafts was to be "completed in the main" by 1985.[91]

However, in retrospect, Truong Chinh has acknowledged that, regarding "socialist transformation" generally,

> there have been manifestations of hastiness: we [the Party leadership] wanted to do away at once with non-socialist economic sectors, to rapidly turn the private capitalist sector into a State-run sector. We laid stress on changing the ownership of the means of production, but overlooked the settlement of problems relating to management, organization, and the system of [income] distribution. We often resorted to campaigns — like, coercive measures .... Thus, many so-called joint State-private enterprises ... were established only for form's sake ....[92]

Nguyen Van Linh put it more clearly in a speech delivered at the Fifth Central Committee Plenum (June 1988):

> Concerning socialist transformation, [in the late 1970s] we have ... implemented it in a rush ... with the aim of promptly nationalizing and collectivizing the property without recognizing the reality of a multi-sector economy. Although Vietnam is a backward agricultural country advancing to socialism ..., we have not attached importance to tapping various economic sectors to push ahead the productive forces, and failed to regard the development of the latter as our most important task. These mistakes ... stemmed mainly from voluntarism and subjectivism ..., [and] from errors in theoretical thinking ... about the transitional period [to socialism] .... It is because we failed to pay adequate attention to our country's most important characteristic, namely, the prevalence of small-scale production ... that we have subjectively advocated advancing directly to socialism, bypassing all necessary intermediary steps.[93]

Concerning the state-run industry, suffice it to recall that, following the important Resolution of the Sixth Central Committee Plenum in July 1984 devoted to the "renovation of economic management",[94] the Council of Ministers issued Directive No. 156/HDBT on 30 November 1984 which dealt with the improvement of its management. This Directive consisted of five parts. The first part dealt with the reorganization of industrial production on a national scale in accordance with each economic-technical characteristic (including centrally as well as locally-run enterprises, and production units in various sectors of the national economy). Secondly, it dealt with the renovation of overall planning concerning industrial complexes, amalgamated enterprises and corporations. Thirdly, it addressed issues concerning "economic accounting" which remained a very weak link for many years and failed to correctly reflect the economic results.[95] Fourthly, it dealt with economic and financial policies; it specified that the Finance Ministry should create conditions for state-run enterprises to fully implement their financial autonomy, and to secure sufficient capital for their production. Lastly, it called for improvement in the management mechanism and the training of management and technical cadres.[96]

The Council of Ministers decided that this Directive, which went into effect from 1 November 1985, superseded Decree No. 25/CP, which dealt with the encouragement of initiative in production and financial autonomy of state-run enterprises, and Decree No. 26/CP, dealing with the system of contract quotas payment, piece-rate and bonus systems in state-run enterprises which had been promulgated in January 1981.[97] However, Directive No. 156/HDBT could not be fully implemented as long as the old system of subsidized prices and wages was still in force.[98]

At its Eighth Central Committee Plenum in June 1985, the Party pointed out the "necessity to do away with bureaucratic centralism and subsidy-based management [in prices and wages]" and regarded their abolition "as the decisive breakthrough which would lead to a change over to economic accounting and socialist [business]."[99] At this Plenum, the Party emphasized again that, at least in theory, "all economic establishments must be accountable for their own profits and losses, and all subsidies for irrational losses in production ... paid from the State (central as well as local) budgets must be terminated. Subsidies for losses may be paid only on a case-by-case, and temporary basis ...."[100] Following the Eighth Plenum's decision, the Council of Ministers issued on 23 December 1985 a Directive which required that the management of all public industrial enterprises should be based on actual prices and be profitable.[101]

How was the above-described policy put into practice? Despite the fact that light industry was proclaimed to have precedence over heavy industry, the lion's share of investment in gross fixed investment (including both the material and non-material production sectors) was still allocated to heavy industry and not to light industry. The data in Table 3.3 demonstrate this.

TABLE 3.3
State Investments, 1981–85
(In per cent)

	1981	1982	1983	1984	1985
Gross fixed investment (in "productive" as well as "unproductive" sectors) of which:	100	100	100	100	100
Industry:	41.7	53.2	40.4	33.8	31.2
— Heavy industry	(35.0)	(45.3)	(32.3)	(25.1)	(22.2)
— Light industry	(6.7)	(7.9)	(8.0)	(8.7)	(7.3)

SOURCES: Data provided by the Vietnamese authorities, quoted in IMF, *Vietnam — Recent Economic Developments*, 30 June 1986, p. 35 (for the 1981–82 period); and ibid., 15 May 1987, p. 40 (for the 1983–85 period).

Table 3.3 shows that during the Third FYP the share of heavy industry in total gross fixed investment rapidly increased during the first two years, then decreased significantly during the last three years, whereas the share of light industry gradually increased during the first four years, but decreased in the last year. In 1985, the share of heavy industry amounted to 22.2 per cent of total gross fixed investment, compared to 35 per cent in 1981, whereas that of light industry represented only 7.3 and 6.7 per cent respectively.

However, according to the Party journal, the share of light industry in total industrial investment decreased gradually: 21.4 per cent in 1984, compared to 27.4 per cent in 1980 (and 32.9 per cent in 1976).[102] This "insufficient" investment was "one of the main causes" of the "slow development of the consumer goods industry".

Despite the Party's rhetoric, in fact, as in the previous FYP, "consumer goods industries, including handicrafts [were] still neglected in terms of ... investment and policy"[103] in favour of heavy industry because, as Truong Chinh admitted, of the Party leadership's "fondness for developing heavy industry on a large scale", which was one of the "errors of leftist infantilism".[104] Because of the large allocation of state investment to heavy industry at the expense of agriculture and light industry the shortage of food staples and essential consumer goods continued to occur.[105] The lopsided economic structure characterized by great imbalances at the macro-level, already evident in the previous FYP, thus continued to exert its negative impact over the whole national economy.

As for the result of "socialist transformation" in private industry, suffice it to quote some statements made by the then Chairman of the State Planning Committee, Vo Van Kiet:

> The final result of socialist transformation should be the development of production, the increase of productivity, and the profitability of enterprises .... . But our management was clearly so bad that the [reconverted enterprises] had an extremely low productivity, and were in deficit .... . In practice, after the socialist transformation had taken place, the reconverted enterprises fell into stagnation; their production decreased, the quality of their products diminished, [and] their cost of production increased ....[106]

Regarding the state-run enterprises — which were supposed to play a "leading role" in the industrial sector — Kiet complained that: "[they] were managed worse than the collective enterprises; and [in turn] the latter were managed worse than the individual [private] enterprises as far as productivity as well as quality were concerned".[107]

In a speech delivered at the Fifth Plenum in December 1983, Le

Duan singled out the state-run sector for its failings in these terms: "We are not satisfied with the present situation in the state-run sector, especially the central-level industry, which has been growing slowly in productivity as well as in quality and efficiency".[108] He also noted that state-run enterprises operated at "only 50% of its capacity because of the shortage of energy and materials" although "some of these materials [were] produced in the country itself"[109]

Following the Eighth Plenum's decision to implement "economic accounting" in state-run enterprises, it was reported that in Ho Chi Minh City, for instance, 130 of them were commended or rewarded for fulfilling their physical and financial targets. But after a close examination of their performance, it was revealed that most of them "were, in fact, operating at a loss ...".[110]

The gross industrial output (industry and handicrafts output) are shown in Table 3.4. From the table, it can be seen that gross industrial output of industry and handicrafts, reckoned in 1982 constant prices (which were manifestly overpriced), increased by 57.4 per cent in 1985, compared with 1980; it rose to an average annual rate of 9.5 per cent, a noteworthy achievement compared with the previous crisis period. The share of small-scale industry and handicrafts represented 41 per cent and 43.5 per cent, respectively, in 1981 and 1985, of the total gross industrial output;[111] their output, according to a Vietnamese official, was, however, generally overpriced.[112]

Compared with 1980, the output of heavy industry increased by 36.2 per cent in 1985, whereas that of light industry was augmented by 70.3 per cent. As for their specific weight in total gross industrial output, the share of heavy industry gradually decreased (32.7 per cent in 1985, compared with 37.8 per cent in 1980) whereas that of light industry increased correlatively (67.3 per cent in 1985, as against 62.2 per cent in 1980). [113]

A comparison of the targets of this FYP and the actual performance of some essential industrial products is shown in Table 3.5. The table shows that, except for sugar and molasses, and cigarettes, other planned targets of the essential industrial products were not met at the end of the Third FYP.

Despite the dramatic increase in gross industrial production during the period under review, the per capita output of some

TABLE 3.5
Performance of Essential Industrial Products

	(1976)[b]	1981[b]	1985 Targets[a]	1985 Performance[b]
Heavy Industry				
— Coal (million tons)	(5.7)	6.0	8–9	5.7
— Electricity (billion kWh)	(3.06)	3.83	5.5–6	5.22
— Rolled Steel (thousand tons)	(63.8)	36.1	72.2	61.6
— Phosphate Fertilizer (thousand tons)	(282.2)	173.2	350–400	322.0
— Cement (million tons)	(0.743)	0.554	2.0	1.50
Light Industry				
— Cloth and Silk (million metres)	(218.0)	167.0	380–400	374.3
— Sugar and Molasses (thousand tons)	(72.8)	201.7	350–400	401.7
— Cigarettes (million packets)	(404.2)	545.3	1,000.0	1,050.6
— Paper & cardboard (thousand tons)	(75.0)	45.2	90–100	78.5

SOURCES: [a] Targets for 1981–85: *Vietnam Courier*, no. 5 (1982), p. 10.
[b] *Nien Giam Thong Ke 1985*, pp. 152–57.

essential industrial products was still very low. Moreover, the per capita output of some products in 1985 was even below that of 1976, as shown by the figures in Table 3.6.

Furthermore, the quality of the consumer goods, especially such items as electric bulbs, thermos-flasks and matches, was, according to the then Deputy Premier Do Muoi, "mediocre".[114] Premier Pham Van Dong complained that in the industrial sector, "labour productivity [was] low ..., production costs [were] high, and the quality of goods — which [had been] already bad — was getting worse everyday as far as a certain number of products [was] concerned".[115] Finally, during this FYP, the specific

TABLE 3.4
Industrial Production, 1980–85
(In million dong, at 1982 constant prices)

	1980	1981	1983	1984	1985
Gross Industrial Production (Industry and Handicrafts)	66,925.1	67,594.3	83,033.5	93,952.5	105,340.1
By group:					
Group A (heavy industry)	25,297.7	24,333.9	28,302.9	30,935.1	34,463.0
Group B (light industry)	41,627.4	43,260.4	54,730.6	63,017.4	70,877.1
By type of management:					
Central management	24,427.7	25,010.0	29,105.5	32,607.1	35,618.3
Local management	42,497.4	42,584.3	53,928.0	61,345.4	69,721.8
of which:					
(a) Public and "joint private-state enterprises"	15,861.2	14,870.7	17,141.9	20,234.4	23,946.1
(b) Small-scale industry and handicrafts	26,636.2	27,713.6	36,786.1	41,111.0	45,775.7

SOURCE: *Nien Giam Thong Ke* 1985, pp. 136, 139, 142.

importance of industry in the Produced National Income, reckoned in 1982 constant prices, was still relatively weak: in 1985 it represented only 28.2 per cent of the total, compared to 25.6 per cent in 1981, whereas that of agriculture constituted 50.8 per cent and 52.1 per cent respectively.[116]

TABLE 3.6
Per Capita Output of Some Essential Industrial Products, 1976–85

	1976	1981	1985
Electricity (kWh)	62.8	69.9	87.2
Clean coal (kg)	115.9	108.7	93.9
Steel of all kinds (kg)	1.26	0.66	1.03
Bicycles (units/per thousand people)	1.9	2.9	3.3
Chemical fertilizers (kg)	8.8	4.9	8.9
Laundry soap (kg)	0.48	0.53	0.85
Bicycle tyres	0.11	0.11	0.19
Cement (kg)	15.1	10.0	25.1
Bricks (units)	75.3	39.3	49.0
Sawn wood (cubic metres)	0.031	0.025	0.024
Paper & cardboard (kg)	1.53	0.82	1.31
Matches (boxes)	8.0	3.4	2.6
Sleeping mats (units)	0.16	0.19	0.22
Porcelain (pieces)	1.61	1.97	2.78
Salt (kg)	11.9	8.5	11.2
Sea fish (kg)	12.3	7.5	10.5
Fish sauce (litres)	2.01	1.7	2.4
Sugar and molasses (kg)	1.5	3.7	6.7
Cigarettes (packets)	8.2	9.9	17.5
Cloth and silk (metres)	4.5	3.0	6.2

SOURCE: *Nien Giam Thong Ke 1985*, p. 158.

Foreign Economic Relations

The progress obtained in the domains of agriculture and industry described earlier was due not only to endogenous efforts but also to important economic aid from the CMEA countries, particularly the USSR. Unlike the 1960s and the beginning of the 1970s, during which the Party, following the Maoist slogan, repeated *ad nauseam* the motto of "self-reliance" (while Vietnam was blatantly dependent upon foreign aid), in the late 1970s, it vowed fidelity to the CMEA countries, and in particular to the USSR, the very country which it had violently criticized in 1963 for its "revisionism".

Indeed, at that time, in a speech delivered at the Ninth Central Committee Plenum (Third Congress, December 1963), Le Duan had attacked the Soviet Union in these words:

> Our Party ... must vigorously criticize modern revisionism [that is, Khruschev's "revisionism"] ... which [was] a terrible evil in the revolutionary movement (and which) became in fact an ally of imperialism. The more we loathe imperialism, the more we hate revisionism. Modern revisionism must be opposed in order to defend ... our party's and people's revolutionary cause ....[117]

Nearly twenty years later, however, contrary to what he had said before, the same Le Duan extolled the Soviet Union at the Fifth Party Congress in March 1982 in these terms:

> Solidarity and all-round cooperation with the Soviet Union is the corner-stone of the foreign policy of our Party and State.... Close links and all-round cooperation with the Soviet Union are a matter of principle, strategy and revolutionary sentiment.[118]

After making such a volte-face, Le Duan wrote in the Soviet Party's newspaper in 1985 that: "Solidarity with the Soviet Union, from generation to generation is the unswerving (*sic!*) feeling, political platform, principle and strategy of our Party and people"![119]

As for the relations with the CMEA (or COMECON) countries, Le Duan said in his speech at the Fifth Party Congress that

> ... the solidarity and cooperation between [Vietnam] and other countries in the socialist community, has undergone a new qualitative development since our country became a full member of COMECON. In the forthcoming period, we shall do our utmost together with the socialist countries to achieve good cooperation in the framework of bilateral treaties and agreements, and promote the development of cooperation in planning and policy coordination among the member countries of COMECON".[120]

How was this economic co-operation implemented in practice? In this connection, suffice it to mention the Summit Conference of the CMEA held in Moscow in June 1984 during which the leaders of the socialist countries reportedly agreed to, *inter alia*,

> speed up the process of gradual evening out of the levels of economic development of the CMEA countries, and first of all to bring the levels of economic development of the Socialist Republic of Vietnam, the Republic of Cuba, and the Mongolian People's Republic to those of the European CMEA countries.[121]

In accordance with the resolution of this Summit Conference and the agreements signed earlier, the CMEA countries granted Vietnam long-term development loans at low interest rates; scientific and technological assistance, chiefly in the form of grants; assistance in elaborating long-term socio-economic development plans, and in working out overall schemes for the redeployment of "productive forces"; and assistance in extensive geological surveys to explore new deposits of ores, etc.[122]

Worth noting is the fact that concessional terms were also extended to the prices of a series of export commodities from the CMEA to the advantage of Vietnam, and low interest credit given by the International Investment Bank and the International Economic Cooperation Bank (of which Vietnam became an official member in 1977). In 1984, for example, the average interest rate of credit granted to Vietnam by the latter was four times lower than the one reserved for Eastern European countries.[123]

According to a joint agreement on multilateral co-operation signed in 1981 and aimed at accelerating the scientific and technical development of Vietnam up to 1990,[124] the CMEA countries joined efforts in studying eight problems of great importance to Vietnam's economy, and in building and equipping 35 projects of which eleven was scheduled to be carried out in the 1981–85 period.[125] During this period, Vietnam received 17.5 million rubles in grant, and 8.2 million rubles as low-interest credit from the CMEA countries for the implementation of scientific-technical projects. Vietnam also sent about 5,000 scientists and technicians to other CMEA countries for further studies, and admitted some 1,500 specialists from those countries for joint research and mutual assistance during the same period.[126]

Regarding the co-ordination of various national economic plans — which characterizes the process of "socialist economic integration" — it was reported that "it has prompted Vietnam to constantly improve and upgrade its planning" in order to tap all the possibilities in terms of investment and technology from other CMEA countries.[127]

As in the earlier period, the basic efforts of the CMEA countries were aimed at accelerating "socialist industrialization", particularly the development of heavy industry. The CMEA countries have helped Vietnam to build a number of power plants, power lines and transformer stations, develop oil and gas exploitation on the continental shelf of Southern Vietnam, non-ferrous and ferrous metallurgy, mechanical engineering and the electronics industry, the chemical industry, transport and communications and the infrastructure of postal services.[128] As for light industry, the CMEA countries have particularly helped Vietnam to develop its textile industry. They have also supplied Vietnam's agriculture with fertilizers, insecticides, tractors, means of transport and other important materials, including fuels and lubricants.[129]

For its part, Vietnam has pledged to export to the CMEA countries the produce of its agriculture — especially tropical industrial crops (natural rubber, coffee beans, tea, jute, and so forth), tropical fruit and vegetables — and that of its processing and mining industries.

Assessing the co-operation with the CMEA countries, the journal *Ngoai Thuong* (Foreign Trade), recently acknowledged that

> various special measures designed to help Vietnam during the 1981-85 period have not brought about concrete results.... Various CMEA decisions on uniformly upgrading the capabilities of Vietnam, Cuba and Mongolia to the level of Eastern European countries are but general guidelines, and there is nothing concrete yet. ... Vietnam has not been able to fully tap the superiority of multilateral cooperation to meet its demand in some kinds of goods, and obtain material and financial sources for its economic development.[130]

Overall, it pointed out, Vietnam's participation in the CMEA "has so far brought about some results which are by no means fundamental".

Some Soviet specialists were also reportedly critical of aid provided to Vietnam by the CMEA countries. Donor countries, they said, think only "in terms of total numbers of aid projects, while forgetting that Vietnam could not supply matching funds, or guarantee supplies of fuel, raw materials or electricity. At the same time, the potential of export-oriented industries was in the past largely ignored".[131]

Regarding the dispatching of young Vietnamese workers and trainees to the CMEA countries, mostly to the USSR, East Germany, Czechoslovakia and Bulgaria, the army newspaper reported that their average monthly wage was equivalent to only "1/5 of that in the Middle-East". Moreover, they were paid in non-convertible rubles, given arduous work in dangerous or toxic areas, and sometimes "have to work alongside convicts under a system of forced labour".[132]

As for Vietnamese-Soviet economic co-operation specifically, suffice it to recall the signing of the "USSR-Vietnam Long–Term Programme for Economic, Scientific and Technological Cooperation" in Hanoi on 31 October 1983. In this Programme, both countries agreed:

1. To step up co-operation in the key sectors of the Vietnamese economy, primarily in agriculture and in the energy industry, including geological survey, and extracting and processing of oil, and in the development of the transport and communications and postal sectors.
2. To continue co-operation in building up the machinery and metallurgical industry, the chemical industry, and the building materials industry.
3. To promote the training of Vietnamese cadres in the areas of culture, education and medicine.
4. To create the necessary conditions for quickly advancing Vietnamese science and technology.
5. To step up co-operation on joint research projects of mutual concern.
6. To increase the manufacture of export goods in Vietnam with Soviet aid, taking into consideration the needs of the Soviet economy.

7. To establish joint ventures as a new mode of co-operation in order to develop the Vietnamese economy and facilitate the training of Vietnamese personnel with advanced qualifications.
8. To expand co-operation on a mutually advantageous barter basis.
9. To promote co-operation in the manufacture of goods in Vietnam with Soviet-supplied raw materials.
10. To expand commodities exchange through marketing co-operatives and home trade organizations on the one hand, and through foreign trade corporations on the other hand.
11. To seek ways to expand commodities exchange on a long-term basis in keeping with the export capacities and import needs of both countries, and to improve the existing forms of reciprocal trade.
12. To co-ordinate between both countries' planning commissions and economic organizations in order to organize the process of examining and resolving various issues concerned with the implementation of programmes for development and co-operation on a systematic basis.
13. And finally, to take necessary steps aimed at the fuller utilization of the production potential already established in Vietnam, and to concentrate the existing means and resources on the building of key projects in the major sectors of the Vietnamese economy.[133]

According to one Vietnamese source, the amount of Soviet economic aid given to Vietnam amounted to 3.223 billion rubles (2.5 billion rubles in loans to compensate for the trade deficit, 600 million rubles in interest-free loans, and 223 million rubles in grant to complete projects left unfinished by the People's Republic of China, as well as for new projects for scientific development, education and public health),[134] equivalent to approximately US$4.866 billion. (Once again, it should be noted that Soviet economic aid reckoned in U.S. dollars is overestimated because rubles are over-valued in relation to the U.S. dollar at the official exchange rate).

During the Third FYP, the Soviet Union helped Vietnam to design, build, and upgrade about 150 construction projects. Nearly

40 projects were put into operation, among them the Pha Lai thermo-electric power plant, with a capacity of 330 megawatt; the 5.5 kilometre-long Thang Long bridge; the Lam Thao superphosphate plant, with an annual output of 330,000 metric tons of superphosphate and 180,000 metric tons of sulfuric acid; the Cao Son open-cast coal mine, with an annual output of 2.2 million metric tons; and the Bim Son cement plant, with an annual output of 1.2 million metric tons. During the period under review, large-scale projects such as the Hoa Binh and Tri An hydroelectric power plants were also in the process of being built.

In 1981, the Vietsovpetro joint venture for exploration and production of oil and natural gas in the continental shelf of the southern part of the country was set up (by late June 1986, the exploitation of oil had begun).[135] The USSR also helped Vietnam to re-equip and enlarge coal mines in the Quang Ninh basin, and to build various construction materials factories. In 1985, it was reported that the share of the more than 200 Soviet assisted projects in total industrial production came to 35 per cent for the generation of electric power; 95.2 per cent for coal mining; 50.5 per cent for cement, and 100 per cent for apatite, superphosphate, sulphuric acid and metal-cutting tools.[136] During the 1981-85 period, with Soviet aid, Vietnam also expanded the cultivation of rubber by 50,000 hectares.

Apart from economic and technical aid, the Soviet Union also paid much attention to scientific and technological assistance. The most important result of this aid was the training of a large contingent of scientific-technical cadres, skilled workers, engineers and scientists who have been playing an important role in economic, scientific, cultural and other fields. Vietnamese-Soviet co-operation in science and technology has reportedly "brought about many concrete results in terms of development and consolidation of [Vietnam's] socio-economic potentials". However, these results were "still limited and did not match with the efforts made". The main reason for this was that "the scope of cooperation projects was too wide".[137]

Soviet-Vietnamese two-way trade has also increased rapidly since 1976 as the major part of economic co-operation between the two countries was through the medium of bilateral trade.

TABLE 3.7
Soviet-Vietnamese Trade
(In million rubles)

	1976	1981	1982	1983	1984	1985
Soviet exports	232.5	724.6	804.2	904.1	1,004.0	1,165.3
Soviet imports	63.6	167.2	206.5	234.9	257.9	280.8
Surplus	168.9	557.4	597.7	669.2	746.1	884.5

SOURCES: *Vnechniaia Torgovlia SSSR* (for the 1977–83 period) (in Russian); and *Foreign Trade* (monthly journal), No. 3 (Supplement) (Moscow, 1985 and 1986).

Table 3.7 shows that Soviet exports to and imports from Vietnam multiplied by more than 5 and 4.4 times respectively during the 1976–85 period. By the mid-1980s, the Soviet Union accounted for "about two-thirds of Vietnamese total foreign trade",[138] but the share of Vietnam in the overall amount of Soviet foreign trade was negligible: only 0.9 per cent in 1983.[139]

The USSR supplied Vietnam most of its domestic needs for various kinds of raw materials, fuels, and important materials and equipment. It helped to create a substantial productive capacity in key economic sectors such as fuel, energy, engineering, chemical, building materials industries, and communications and transport. Despite the "economic blockade" set by "hostile forces", Vietnam did not collapse, and this was due chiefly to the "generous and whole-hearted aid of the Soviet people", wrote the Party's journal recently.[140]

However, in a mood of self-criticism, the same journal acknowledged that Vietnam had a strong tendency "to rely too much on Soviet aid, to expect to get it in a unilateral way", and "did not pay attention to the principle of mutual benefit". Furthermore, it admitted that Vietnam used Soviet economic aid "wastefully and in an inefficient way".[141] This latter point had already been acknowledged by Truong Chinh in 1986 when he disclosed to the world that

> due to [Vietnam's] system of management marked by bureaucratic centralism and state subsidization, we have not

turned this aid to good account. Instead, we have spent each year a few hundred million rubles on social consumption, (State) subsidies and loss compensation [for unprofitable state-owned enterprises]. Several other hundred millions of rubles have been scattered on so many construction projects. This has been our great mistake.[142]

In another speech, he confessed that "the great assistance of the Soviet Union and other fraternal socialist countries ... has been seriously wasted ...."[143]

Regarding Western aid, it should be mentioned that because of its military involvement in Kampuchea, no Western bilateral aid of any significance has reached Vietnam since 1979, with the exception of Swedish aid (US$45-50 million annually). Vietnam has not received any multilateral financial assistance (World Bank, IMF, ADB) either.[144] However, it may not be correct to assert that "much of Vietnam's ... economic predicament is of course the result of its almost total international isolation".[145] The root cause of Vietnam's faltering economy was rather the Party's self-defeating internal economic policy. Its relative international isolation contributed only to exacerbate the already deteriorating endogenous economic situation.

It is worth noting that, despite the loss of Western aid, the share of external revenues resulting from foreign aid in the total budgetary revenue was still sizeable: 30.7 per cent in 1982.[146]

* * *

Regarding foreign trade, Le Duan emphasized in his report at the Fifth Party Congress that:

> A task of strategic importance for our Party ... [was] to strive to increase exports for the purpose of imports. We must promote exports to import technology, equipment, machinery, spare parts, and materials for the scientific-technological revolution and industrialization.[147]

The figures in Table 3.8 show the evolution of Vietnam's foreign trade during the Third FYP. From 1981 to 1985 exports reckoned "in rubles-US dollars" increased by 74.1 per cent, whereas that calculated in U.S. dollars grew by 86.9 per cent.

TABLE 3.8
Vietnam's Foreign Trade, 1981–85

	1981 A	1981 B	1982 A	1982 B	1983 A	1983 B	1984 A	1984 B	1985 A	1985 B
Trade Balance (Deficit)	981.0	721	945.6	710	910.2	722	1,095.4	895	1,158.9	844
Convertible area		161		125		106		192		123
Non-convertible area (CMEA) countries		560		585		616		703		721
Exports	401.2	399	526.6	475	616.5	588	649.6	665	698.5	746
Convertible area		149		210		224		276		336
Non-convertible area	235	250		265		364		389		410
Imports	1,382.2	1,120	1,472.2	1,185	1,526.7	1,310	1,745.0	1,560	1,857.4	1,590
Convertible area		310		335		330		468		459
Non-convertible area		810		850		980		1,092		1,137

Notes: A: In million rubles–US dollars (Vietnamese source)
B: In million US$ (IMF source).

SOURCES: *Nien Giam Thong Ke 1985*, pp. 253, 257; data provided by the Vietnamese authorities, and IMF staff estimates quoted from IMF Document, *Vietnam — Recent Economic Developments* (SM/87/108), 15 May 1987, p. 25; and my own calculations concerning the trade balance in Column A.

Imports increased by 34.3 per cent if reckoned in "rubles-US dollars", and by 42 per cent if calculated in U.S. dollars, during the same period. Despite efforts to increase exports, the trade deficit remained large: 1,158.9 million "rubles-US dollar" in 1985, compared with 981 million in 1981, that is, an increase of 18.1 per cent; or US$844 million in 1985, compared with US$721 million in 1981, that is, an increase of 17 per cent.

In the last year of the Third FYP (1985), exports came to only 37.6 per cent of imports if reckoned in "rubles-US dollars", or 46.9 per cent if calculated in U.S. dollars.

Concerning the structure of exports, reckoned in "rubles-US dollars", it was reported that in 1985, the heavy industrial and mining products represented 9 per cent, while small-scale industry and handicraft products accounted for 33.7 per cent, the processed and unprocessed agricultural products 39.3 per cent, the forestry products 5.8 per cent, and the sea food products 11.8 per cent, compared with 17.1 per cent; 40.2 per cent; 30.6 per cent; 4.9 per cent, and 7.2 per cent respectively in 1981.[148]

As regards the structure of imports calculated in "rubles-US dollars", the share of "the means of production" (that is, capital and intermediate goods) represented 85.4 per cent of the total, whereas that of consumer goods was only 14.6 per cent in 1985, compared with 82.7 per cent and 17.3 per cent respectively in 1981.[149]

The greatest part of Vietnam's exports, reckoned "in rubles-US dollars" was, as usual, oriented towards the CMEA countries, particularly the Soviet Union: 71.6 per cent of the total in 1985, compared with 64.3 per cent in 1981. As for exports destined for the Western industrialized and Third World countries, they represented 9 per cent and 18.6 per cent respectively in 1985, compared with 13.4 per cent and 18.7 per cent in 1981. "On-the-spot exports", that is, sales to foreigners within Vietnam which were paid in foreign exchange, amounted to 0.8 per cent in 1985, compared with 3.6 per cent in 1981.[150]

Vietnam's imports, also reckoned in "rubles-US dollars", were reported in 1985 to consist of 81.1 per cent from the CMEA countries, 12.1 per cent from Western industrialized countries, 4.1 per cent from Third World countries, and 2.7 per cent from international organizations, compared with 71.4 per cent; 20.4 per cent; 2.2 per cent; and 6 per cent respectively in 1981.[151]

The total outstanding of Vietnam's external debt reportedly amounted to US$ 6,640.7 million at the end of 1985, with outstanding debt to the convertible and non-convertible areas reaching US$1,713.6 million and US$4,716 million respectively. Interest in arrears and imputed interest on arrears amounted to US$211.1 million.[152] Vietnam's external indebtedness represented an extremely heavy burden on the balance of payments, but since 1980 the proportion of scheduled debt service that has been paid has decreased sharply.

Living Standard

In the preceding pages, it has been shown that since the economic crisis of the previous FYP, the economic situation has significantly improved during the Third FYP. This was reflected in the growth of the "Produced National Income" (PNI). Table 3.9 shows that, compared with 1980, the PNI increased by 36.6 per cent in 1985. Its annual average increase reached 6.4 per cent whereas the population grew by an average of 2.2 per cent during the same period.

Calculated according to U.N. methods, Vietnam's per capita National Income had been US$101 in 1976, US$94 in 1981, and US$101 in 1983.[153] Unfortunately since then, the Vietnamese General Office of Statistics has not disclosed any data concerning the per capita National Income reckoned in U.S. dollars. However, in 1985, the then Premier Pham Van Dong acknowledged that per capita National Income had not increased much compared with that of 1976.[154] In an interview with a French correspondent, he admitted that the Vietnamese were "very poor".[155] According to a knowledgeable Soviet scholar, "Vietnam's per capita National Income [was] less than US$100" in 1985.[156] Compared with other socialist countries, Vietnam's per capita Produced National Income in 1985 was only 7 per cent of that of the Eastern European countries (on average), 40 per cent of that of Mongolia, and 60 per cent of that of Cuba.[157]

TABLE 3.9
Produced National Income, 1980–85
(In million dong, at 1982 constant prices)

	1980	1981	1982	1983	1984	1985
Produced National Income	120,130	122,930	133,790	143,360	155,280	164,110

SOURCE: *Nien Giam Thong Ke 1985*, p. 26.

Did the abovementioned increase in the National Income bring about an amelioration of the living standard of the working people during the Third FYP?

The Party had proclaimed that the foremost objective of the Third FYP, among twelve others, was the "stabilization and improvement" of the people's living standard which had fallen dramatically during the previous FYP. It had also promised to "guarantee the real wages of the workers and [civil] servants".[158]

However, during the period in question, there was no "stabilization", and no improvement whatsoever in the living standard of the fixed-income earners such as workers, civil servants, intellectuals, and pensioners. In spite of the fact that, until the Eighth Central Committee Plenum (June 1985) they had twice received some compensation for the rising cost of living, in June 1981 and September 1984 respectively, their real wages kept falling. This was because after each increase of allowance, the prices of foodstuffs, clothes, etc., multiplied many times in the free market (where people bought most of their basic needs, in addition to a few rationed items of mediocre quality sold in the state-run shops at subsidized prices) as well as in the socialist market.[159] All things considered, the working people were worse off after each increase in the so-called allowance to compensate for the rising cost of living.

This writer can testify that by 1984, the overall monthly salary of a thrifty fixed-income earner, including that of a high-ranking official or a Senior Research Fellow, hardly covered a quarter of his/her stringent monthly budget.[160] The remainder was assured by raising poultry or pigs, selling gifts received from family members living abroad, ... or by engaging in illegal trading. (Unfortunately, one cannot refer to any official data to substantiate the continuing fall in the people's living standard during the period in question for the simple reason that in the *Nien Giam Thong Ke 1985*, the latest available statistical yearbook, the usually detailed section dealing with "Living Standard" was entirely deleted!)

Owing to the steep rise in prices since 1981, Dao Thien Thi, then Minister of Labour, stated that "the real wages of workers and civil servants — in kind as well as in money — have been continuously falling, and cannot even secure the reproduction of their [own] labour force in a normal way"[161] to say nothing of their family.

The peasants' living conditions had significantly improved during the first three to four crops following the generalization of the "end-product contract" system. After that, however, many localities began to raise the assigned contract quota — "because they were afraid that farmers would become rich"[162] — and consequently reduced the marketable agricultural surplus. In addition to this, the peasants had to pay all kinds of contributions, besides the already high agricultural tax, and ultimately they got only, according to the Party-controlled trade union's newspaper, "13 or 15% of the crop"[163] which hardly compensated them for their production expenses. In other words, in Socialist Vietnam, the peasants, who are supposed to be the close allies of the ruling "working class", were, in fact, more exploited than under the previous "semi-feudal and colonial" regime, during which, after paying the land rent to the landlord "they still eventually got about 20% of the crop". [164]

It is worth noting also that during this FYP, about 3 million peasants in the North experienced food shortage every year during the interval of some months between the two harvests.[165]

To have a general idea of the peasants' living conditions in Vietnam, it would be preferable to listen to the following testimony of a chairman of an agricultural cooperative:

> ... I have served as a cooperative chairman for 13 years, and have never seen the agricultural situation as difficult as it is today [1986].... Agriculture is called the main front, ... the number-one goal, but most of the peasants do not earn enough to eat and only want to abandon the agricultural front. They would lead a much better life as merchants ....[166]

On the level of malnutrition in Vietnam, a knowledgeable special correspondent of *Le Monde* wrote:

> Malnutrition ... looms large today [1984] as one of Vietnam's most serious problems. Altogether, each Vietnamese only takes in on average 1,850 calories a day, while the required minimum is estimated at 2,300.... These figures are the lowest we have ever

met, much lower than the figures (already very low) given by Madagascar or Uganda, asserts M. Marcel Autret, one of the world's outstanding specialists in the subject.[167]

According to the Party's journal, malnourished children represented "a fairly high percentage" of the total number of children. Besides, "their height and weight were far behind those of other children all over the world. Particularly since 1980, the percentage of new-born babies whose weights were below 2.5 kg have been increasing every day. In some localities, this percentage amounted to 20-30% of the total of new-born babies".[168] A Western aid official was reported to have said that "one out of every ten children die[d] of gastro-enteritis brought on by malnourishment".[169]

Concerning public health, Dang Hoi Xuan, then Minister of Health, admitted in 1986 that

> the health situation of [Vietnamese] people is presently declining in a concerning manner. The average weight of new born infants as well as the weight, height and physique of students and youths have all declined. The percentage of cadres and workers who stop work [due to poor health] is higher .... Many mothers lack sufficient milk to nurse their children .... The difficult economic situation has ... adversely affected the health of the people, and the quality of public health service .... Foreign exchange for importing medicines and raw materials for making medicines ... are annually only equal to one-fourth of the level 10 years ago, while the population ... has increased by an additional 10 million people .... The shortage of drugs ... has thus become severe .... (State) investment in public health service is too little, amounting to less than 4 per cent [of total budget expenditure] .... The serious shortage of drugs ..., of hospital funds [which] is sufficient for only 40 per cent of essential [expenditures], and the deteriorating condition of hospitals ..., sanitation stations .... have directly and adversely affected the quality of public health service.[170]

This was generally the situation until mid-1985 when the Party convened the Eighth Central Committee Plenum in June 1985 to deal with the "prices, wages and currency" issues. One of the proclaimed goals of this Plenum was "to stabilise the livelihood of the working people, mainly workers, civil servants and soldiers ..., control the distribution-circulation sector, the market and prices ...".[171] Implementing this Plenum's Resolution, the Council of Ministers promulgated on 13 September 1985 two decrees on the exchange of banknotes (No. 01/HDBT and No. 2/HDBT). This was the third monetary reform since the reunification of the country as a result of a galloping inflation which lasted for many years.[172] According to the above-mentioned decrees, a new dong was equivalent to 10 old dong.[173] Parallel to the exchange of banknotes there was also an official devaluation of the dong. On 5 September 1985 the dong was devalued by 92 per cent, from 12.06 old dong to 150 old dong, or 15 new dong per U.S. dollar. The new official rate of exchange was, however, well below that in the free market.

Following the exchange of banknotes, the government promulgated a few days later a decree (No. 235/HDCT, 18 September 1985) concerning the renovation of the wage system. Its proclaimed goal was

> to ensure the regeneration of labour force of workers and civil servants (by "resetting the minimum wage in order to meet the basic needs of wage earners") ..., to guarantee better distribution according to labour, and gradually eliminate egalitarianism, ... [and] encourage efforts to increase labour productivity.[174]

During the fall of 1985, a far-reaching price reform which aimed at reducing price distortions and state subsidies at all levels of the economy was introduced, substantially increasing official prices of intermediate and consumer goods.

Agricultural quota procurement prices were raised almost tenfold in the North and six to sevenfold in the South by the government, which took into account the state of hyper-inflation since 1981. A new element in the price structure was that agricultural quota procurement prices might be determined according to local demand and supply conditions.[175]

The prices of industrial products were also increased by factors ranging from 5–26 so as to better reflect production costs. At the same time, the decision-making authority of each production unit to determine output prices was enhanced.[176]

The system of differentiated official consumer prices established before this price reform was abolished in September 1985, when official prices posted in state-run shops for all consumer goods were set at levels close to those prevailing in the free market. Civil servants and workers were theoretically compensated for the loss in subsidies with higher cash salaries.[177] Consumer prices in the free market, which accounted for a substantial share of total retail sales, also increased sharply in 1985, chiefly as a result of rapid monetary expansion.[178]

Presiding over a conference on "Market and Price Management" in October 1985, Vo Van Kiet, then chairman of the State Planning Committee, explained: "If market prices cannot be maintained firmly, the stabilization efficiency of the new price system [would] be lost, lowering the value of wages and diminishing the purchasing power of the new currency".[179] Effectively, this prediction came totally true. Recently, the Party's journal disclosed that the index number of retail prices evolved as follows: 1976:100; 1980:189; 1985:2,890. It also revealed that the purchasing power of the dong fell drastically: 1976:100; 1980:52.9; 1985:3.8.[180]

In 1986, the then Deputy Premier To Huu admitted in one of his speeches that after the "price-wage-currency" reform, "there have been great price fluctuations [read, steep increase], and our currency is quickly losing its value.... In their material and cultural life, the working people, especially cadres, workers, civil servants, soldiers, and the rural population in a number of areas are suffering many privations".[181]

Pham The Duyet, then Chairman of the Party-controlled trade union, also acknowledged at the Sixth Party Congress that "the wages earned by our workers and civil servants are not enough to regenerate their strength for continued labour (...) they cannot make both ends meet; their grown children are unemployed, and prices of goods are skyrocketting .... This has negatively affected production, diminished the diligence and creativity of our workers, damaged their ... morale, and lessened their confidence in the Party leadership."[182] At the same Party Congress, Duong Quang Dong, a Veteran Party member, also voiced this cry of alarm: "There is a severe loss of faith among the people as regards the

Party and State. They are complaining about their sordid poverty and the rising of prices, as well as about their precarious and unsecure fate ...".[183]

As one can see, by 1985 Vietnam was very far from the target set by Secretary-General Le Duan when he promised the Vietnamese working people on the occasion of the Lunar New Year celebrations in early 1976 "a better life in five or ten years", even going so far as to predict "a radio set, a refrigerator, and a television set for each family in ten years' time".[184] In 1985, such goods were still far from realization for the vast majority of Vietnamese families.

The living standard of the working people, which was already deteriorating significantly from 1981 to mid-1985, experienced another sharp decline after the ill-conceived "price-wage-currency" reform in September 1985 which brought about, as said earlier, a severe and widespread crisis of confidence among the people — including Party members and cadres — as regards the Party leadership. This prompted it to acknowledge that

> since the third quarter [of 1985] following the hectic undertaking of three tasks at the same time — exchange of banknotes first, followed by the general big readjustment of prices and wages — the socio-economic situation has evolved on a very complex [read, chaotic] manner with prices abruptly skyrocketting, the market plunging into a mess, production, circulation [of goods], and the people's life encountering more difficulties ... . The responsibility for the above situation first of all rests with various Party and State leadership at the central level. Various relevant sectors and localities have also to share responsibility for this.[185]

It was the first time that the Party leadership *per se* unequivocally took on the responsibility for this matter whereas, until then, it had shifted the blame for mistakes onto cadres who did not "correctly implement" the Party's policy (which was supposed to be *a priori* always correct).

At the Sixth Party Congress (December 1986) Truong Chinh once again admitted in his Political Report: "We [the Party leadership] have made mistakes in tackling the price, wage and money problems. The specific solutions to such problems ... did not suit the actual situation, as they were carried out without good preparations, without concerted and effective measures .... The[se] errors ....were very serious [ones] in terms of economic leadership and management ...."[186]

Nguyen Van Linh also lamented that "this blunder [referring to the reform on price, wages and currency in 1985] could be compared to a man who falls and breaks his backbone".[187]

It should be emphasized that the abovementioned drastic fall in the living standard affected only the working people but not the ruling stratum of the Party and State — the "politocracy" — whose privileges in kind and services, besides the nominal salary, strongly contrasted with general destitution.[188] Paraphrasing George Orwell's *Animal Farm* it could be asserted that all Party members and cadres were equal, but some were (and are) more equal than others.

For an overall assessment of the Vietnamese economy at the end of the Third FYP, the following passage in Truong Chinh's political report at the Sixth Party Congress in December 1986 is illuminating:

> ... We [the Party leadership] see that our country is facing many socio-economic difficulties.
> — Though there has been some outgrowth in production, it is slow in comparison with the capabilities available and labour spent, with the people's demand for a rapid stabilization of their life, and with the need to accumulate funds for industrialization and strengthening our national defence. Failure to fulfil a number of major targets of the third five-year plan such as production of grain, coal, cement, wood, textiles, and items for export has affected all aspects of economic activity and the working people's life.
> — Production and investment efficiency has been low. In general, only half of the designed capacity of enterprises has been utilized with reduced labour productivity and low product quality.
> — Our country's natural resources have not been satisfactorily exploited and have been wasted in their use, especially farmland and forest resources; the ecological environment is being destroyed.
> — Clogged-up circulation, chaotic distribution of commodities, and skyrocketting prices are exerting a negative impact on production, the people's life, and society.

The Third Five-Year Plan, 1981-85

— Far from being reduced, the great imbalances in the economy between supply and demand in grain, foodstuffs, consumer goods, energy, raw materials, and transportation; between (budget) revenue and expenditure; and between export and import have, in some respects, become even more acute.
— Socialist production relations have been slowly consolidated. The leading role of the state economic sector is weak. Non-socialist economic sectors have not been made good use of.
— The life of the people, especially workers and civil servants, is beset with many difficulties. A great number of working people are unemployed or under-employed. Many basic legitimate material and cultural necessities of life of the people are not met. There is a shortage of common consumer goods and medicines in the rural areas. Housing, hygienic conditions, and cultural life in some areas are still poor.
— Negative phenomena in society have increased. Social justice has been violated ....

The aforementioned state of affairs has lessened the confidence of the masses in the party's leadership and the functioning of state organs. On the whole, we have not yet achieved the objective set by the Fifth Party Congress, namely stabilizing in the main the socio-economic situation and the people's life.[189]

Such was the socio-economic situation at the end of the Third FYP. It was against this background that the Party Politburo decided to convene an important meeting in August 1986 to overhaul the strategy of economic development advocated since the reunification, and made a strategic shift in the overall economic policy for the following period.

NOTES

1. Nguyen Khac Vien, "The Economic Options of the 5th Congress", *Vietnam Courier*, no. 6 (1982), p. 14.
2. Nayan Chanda, "Cracks in the edifice", *Far Eastern Economic Review*, 4 December 1981, p. 84.

5. *Communist Party of Vietnam. 5th National Congress*, pp. 24, 26.
6. Ibid., pp. 42–43.
7. This division into various stages was claimed to be in accordance with Lenin's precepts. See Chu Van Lam, "Dai Hoi VI Dang . . . ", *Nghien Cuu Kinh Te*, no. 3 (1987), p. 2.
8. *Communist Party of Vietnam. 5th National Congress*, p. 40. For more details on the readjustment of the national "economic structure", see, in particular, Vien Kinh Te Hoc, *Xay Dung Co Cau Kinh Te Trong Thoi Ky Qua Do O Nuoc Ta* (Hanoi: NXB Khoa Hoc Xa Hoi, 1986).
9. Ibid., pp. 44–74.
10. Ibid., pp. 75–80.
11. Ibid., p. 52. See also *Tai Lieu Huong Dan Hoc Tap Nghi Quyet Dai Hoi Lan Thu 5 Cua Dang* (Ban Tuyen Huan Trung Uong) (Hanoi: NXB Sach Giao Khoa Mac-Lenin, 1981), pp. 123–49; Dao Duy Tung's article in *Vietnam Courier*, no. 9 (1983), pp. 15–18.
12. Nguyen Anh Bac, "Quan He Cong-Nong Nghiep Trong Chang Dau Cua Thoi Ky Qua Do O Nuoc Ta", *Nghien Cuu Kinh Te*, no. 6 (1984), p. 24; Vu Huu Ngoan, *Nhung Van De Kinh Te Xa Hoi Trong Chang Duong Dau Tien Cua Thoi Ky Qua Do Len Chu Nghia Xa Hoi O Nuoc Ta* (Hanoi, 1984), pp. 33–45; Tran Duc, *Tim Hieu Mot So Van De Muc Tieu Kinh Te Xa Hoi Cua Nuoc Ta* (Hanoi: NXB Khoa Hoc Xa Hoi, 1984), pp. 145–46; Le Hong Tam, "Vietnam: Building Industrial-Agricultural Complexes", in *Unreal Growth. Critical Studies on Asian Development*, edited by Ngo Manh Lan (New Delhi: Hindustan Publishing Corporation, 1984), p. 527ff.
13. *Sciences Sociales*, no. 1 (Hanoi, 1984), p. 59.
14. See his *On The Ten Great Relationships*, Speech delivered in 1956 (Peking: Foreign Languages Press, 1977); and his critique of two Soviet books, "Political Economy: A Textbook", and J. Stalin's "Economic Problems of Socialism in the USSR", in *A Critique of Soviet Economics* (New York: Monthly Review Press, 1977). It is worth noting, however, that Mao Zedong's "Bukharinism" ended in 1958 with the "Great Leap Forward".
15. N. Bukharin, "Notes of an Economist", reprinted in *Economy and Society* 8, no. 4 (November 1979): 481, 492. See also Stephen Cohen, *Bukharin and the Bolshevik Revolution* (Oxford University Press, 1977), pp. 179–80; and A. Erlich, *The Soviet Industrialization Debate, 1924–28* (Cambridge, Mass.: Harvard University Press, 1960), p. 82; and R. Bideleux, *Communism and Development* (London, New York: Methuen, 1985), pp. 86–88.
16. Stephen Cohen, *Bukharin and the Bolshevik Revolution*, p. 177. He told *all strata* of the peasantry: "Enrich yourselves, accumulate, develop your economy".
17. For more details on the similarity and difference between Mao's and Bukharin's models, see R. Kalain, "Mao Tse Tung's Bukharinist Phase", *Journal of Contemporary Asia*, no. 2 (1984), pp. 150–52.
18. For more details, see *Communist Party of Vietnam. 5th National Congress*, pp. 45–49; and also Tran Van Doan, *Nhu The Nao La (Dua) Nong Nghiep Mot Buoc Len San Xuat Lon Xa Hoi Chu Nghia* (Hanoi: NXB Nong Nghiep, 1986); Hong

Giao, *Dua Nong Nghiep Mot Buoc Len San Xuat Lon Xa Hoi Chu Nghia* (Hanoi: NXB Su That, 1984); Nguyen Huy, *Dua Nong Nghiep Tu San Xuat Nho Len San Xuat Lon Xa Hoi Chu Nghia* (Hanoi: NXB Khoa Hoc Xa Hoi, 1983). By the same author, see also, "Dua Nong Nghiep Mot Buoc Len San Xuat Lon Xa Hoi Chu Nghia", in *Nghien Cuu Kinh Te*, nos. 4 and 5 (1983), pp. 17–28, and pp. 20–31 respectively.

Concerning the important problem of building up the *district*, see, in particular, Le Binh's article in *Nhan Dan*, 23 December 1986; Vu Oanh, *Mat Tran Nong Nghiep. Thanh Tuu Va Kinh Nghiem Moi* (Hanoi: NXB Su That, 1986), pp. 38–41; Nguyen Dinh Nam, "Hoan Thien Co Cau Kinh Te Huyen Trong Chang Dau Cua Thoi Ky Qua Do O Nuoc Ta", *Nghien Cuu Knh Te*, no. 2 (1986), pp. 10–17; 50; "Hoi Nghi Tong Ket Chuong Trinh Huyen", ibid., no. 3 (1986), pp. 69–73; and Tran Duc, *Xay Dung Huyen Nong Cong Nghiep Trong Thoi Ky Qua Do* (Hanoi: NXB Nong Nghiep, 1983).

19. Interview with Nguyen Ngoc Triu (then Minister of Agriculture) in *Vietnam Courier*, no. 2 (1986), p. 12.
20. Vu Oanh, *Hoan Thanh Dieu Chinh Ruong Dat, Day Manh Cai Tao Xa Hoi Chu Nghia Doi Voi Nong Nghiep Cac Tinh Nam Bo* (Hanoi: NXB Su That, 1984), p. 29.
21. Ibid., p. 11.
22. See *Communist Party of Vietnam. 5th National Congress*, pp. 55–56.
23. *Nhan Dan*, 4 March 1983.
24. See Vu Quoc Tuan's article in *Nghien Cuu Kinh Te*, no. 1 (1985), p. 4.
25. *Nien Giam Thong Ke 1985* (Hanoi: Tong Cuc Thong Ke, 1987), pp. 129; 132. Concerning the change from "production collectives" to "agricultural cooperatives", see *inter alia*, Vu Trong Khai, "Mot So Hinh Thuc Va Bien Phap Kinh Te Chuyen Tap Doan San Xuat Len HTX Nong Nghiep O Nam Bo", *Nghien Cuu Kinh Te*, no. 3 (1987), pp. 35–44, 69; and Dao Duy Huan, "Lien Tap Doan San Xuat . . . ", *Nghien Cuu Kinh Te*, nos. 1 and 2 (1988), pp. 60–64.

For an overview of the collectivization in the South, see Lam Thanh Liem, "Collectivisation des terres et crise de l'economie rurale dans le delta du Mekong", *Annales de Geographie*, no. 519 (Paris, 1984), pp. 21–39, and M. Beresford's field report, "Revolution in the Countryside: Report on a Visit to Vietnam: October-November 1985", *Journal of Contemporary Asia*, no. 3 (1986), pp. 391–424.

26. *Nhan Dan*, 20 August 1986.
27. Ibid., 17 March 1987. This acknowledgement regarding the co-operativization of Ho Chi Minh City was also valid for the collectivization process in the South in general.
28. See *Nien Giam Thong Ke 1985*, p. 129. Concerning the theoretical and practical aspects of the Vietnamese collectivization process in general, see Nguyen Huy, *May Van De Ly Luan Va Thuc Tien Cua Cach Mang Quan He San Xuat Trong Nong Nghiep Nuoc Ta* (Hanoi: NXB Khoa Hoc Xa Hoi, 1983).
29. Following Lenin, Le Duan always emphasized: "Small[scale] production by itself begets capitalism daily and hourly". See his *Selected Writings* (Hanoi: Foreign Languages Publishing House, 1977), p. 522.

30. Tran Van Ha, "The Family Economy of the Vietnamese Peasants", *Vietnam Courier*, no. 2 (1986), p. 14.
31. *Nhan Dan* (editorial), 22 October 1979. On the same score, see also Nguyen Huu Dong, "6th Plenum: Adaptations conjoncturelles on reformes durables? Essais sur la politique economique du socialisme", *Viet Nam*, no. 2 (Paris, April 1981), pp. 41–60; Christine P. White, "Recent Debates in Vietnamese Development Policy", in *Revolutionary Socialist Development in the Third World*, edited by G. White, R. Murrary and C. White (University Press of Kentucky, 1983), pp. 258–59.
32. *Nhan Dan*, 22 October 1979.
33. See his *Selected Writings*, p. 522.
34. See Tran Van Ha, "The Family Economy . . . ", p. 16.
35. See *Communist Party of Vietnam. 5th National Congress*, p. 47.
36. Vu Oanh, *Mat Tran Nong Nghiep* . . . , p. 43; and Truong Son, "Encouraging the Family Economy", *Vietnam Courier*, no. 10 (1982), p. 7.
37. Nguyen Huy, "Ve Moi Lien He Giua Kinh Te Tap The Va Kinh Te Gia Dinh Xa Vien", *Nghien Cuu Kinh Te*, no. 3 (1983), p. 20; and *Nhan Dan*, 23 August 1982.
38. *Nhan Dan*, 4 September 1982. The same phenomenon happened also in Eastern Europe. For more details on the "household economy", see Truong Son, "Kinh Te Gia Dinh", *Tap Chi Cong San*, no. 7 (1983); Thanh Toan, "Kinh Te Phu Gia Dinh Duoi Chu Nghia Xa Hoi", *Nghien Cuu Kinh Te*, no. 3 (1983). (According to this writer, since 1971 Soviet economists had already regarded "household economy" as an integral part of the socialist relations of production.) Tran Van Ha, "L'economie familiale et le systeme ecologique VAC", *Courrier du Vietnam*, no. 12 (Hanoi, 1983); Melanie Beresford, "Household and Collective in Vietnamese Agriculture", *Journal of Contemporary Asia*, no. 1 (1985), pp. 12–18, 30; and Jayne Werner, "Socialist Development: The Political Economy of Agrarian Reform in Vietnam", *Bulletin of Concerned Asian Scholars*, no. 2 (April-June 1984), pp. 49–51.
39. Full text in English in BBC, *Summary of World Broadcasts* (FE/W1120/A/22), 11 February 1981. See also *Hoi Dap Ve Khoan San Pham Trong HTX Nong Nghiep* (Hanoi: NXB Nong Nghiep, 1985).
40. *History of the Communist Party of Vietnam* (Hanoi: Foreign Languages Publishing House, 1986), p. 311.
41. Incidentally, the "end-product" contract system is not synonymous with the "two-way" contract system (which is signed between a state-trading agency and an agricultural co-operative relating to the quota procurement), as mentioned by a Vietnam-watcher. See Lam Thanh Liem, *Collectivisation des terres* . . . , p. 22.
42. For more details, see Chapter I, and *Vietnamese Studies*, no. 51 (1977), pp. 133–62.
43. For more details on the difference between these two contract systems, see Nguyen Huy, "Van Dung Quy Luat Phan Phoi . . . ", *Tap Chi Cong San*, no. 9 (1987), pp. 61ff; Le Trong, "Thuc Chat Cua Khoan Moi . . . ", ibid., pp. 65ff;

and Nguyen Yem, "Contracted Work and Contracted Produce in Agricultural Cooperatives", *Vietnam Courier*, no. 3 (1981), pp. 14–15.
44. *Nhan Dan*, 26 December 1983.
45. *Nhan Dan*, 1 July 1985.
46. Dao Duy Thanh, "A Major Step to Improve Agricultural Management", *Vietnam Courier*, no. 3 (1981), pp. 16–19. See also *Nhan Dan*, 16 March 1984.
47. *Nhan Dan*, 13 September 1985; and 18 September 1986 (editorial). See also Le Thanh Khoi, "Le modele socialiste et Pays en developpement: l'experience Vietnamienne, *Revue Tiers Monde*, no. 91 (Paris, July 1982), p. 641.
48. *Nhan Dan*, 1 December 1986 (Nguyen Duc Binh's article); ibid., 19 January 1987 (editorial); and Nguyen Thanh Binh, *Cai Tao Va Hoan Thien Quan He San Xuat, Doi Moi Co Che Quan Ly Nong Nghiep* (Hanoi: NSB Su That, 1986), pp. 7–10. Concerning the North specifically, Hanoi Radio (Home Service, 18 November 1986) acknowledged that "faced with sluggishness and inertia in agricultural production in 1979 and 1980, if we had not resorted to the end-product contract system we would not have been able to score many important achievements during the past five years".
49. *6th National Congress of the Communist Party of Vietnam*, p. 12. For a detailed discussion on the "end-product contract" system see a series of important articles published in *Tap Chi Cong San*, no. 7–10 (1987), and a summary of this discussion ("Ve Khoan San Pham Trong Nong Nghiep") in ibid., no. 12 (1987), pp. 53–58; Chu Van Lam, "Khoan San Pham Va Che Do Kinh Te Hop Tac Xa Trong Nong Nghiep", *Nghien Cuu Kinh Te*, nos. 1 and 2 (1988), pp. 33–37; Le Thanh Khoi, "Modele Socialiste et Pays en Developpement. L'experience Vietnamienne", *Revue Tiers-Monde* (Paris: IEDES, July-September 1982), pp. 639–41; and Murray Hiebert, "Contracts in Vietnam: More Rice, New Problems", *Indochina Issues*, no. 48 (July 1984).
50. For more details, see *Nhan Dan*, 6 October 1986; ibid., 2 and 3 December 1986 (Nguyen Duc Binh's article); and particularly *Tap Chi Cong San*, no. 12 (1987), p. 56.
51. *Nhan Dan*, 20 July 1987 (Nguyen Duc Binh's article).
52. Ibid., 5 November 1987.
53. Ho Te, "Bo Tri Co Cau Dau Tu Hop Ly Nham Thuc Hien Ba Chuong Trinh . . .", *Tap Chi Cong San*, no. 6 (1987), p. 18; *Nhan Dan*, 1 August 1986; 5 and 6 November 1986; and 15 January 1987.
54. Nguyen Ngoc Triu, "Vietnamese Agriculture in the New Stage of Development", *Vietnam Courier*, no. 3 (1987), pp. 13–14; and "Nong Nghiep-Mat Tran Hang Dau", *Tap Chi Cong San*, no. 4 (1986), p. 63.
55. *Nien Giam Thong Ke 1985* (Hanoi: Tong Cuc Thong Ke, 1987), p. 186.
56. Huy Hung, "Tu Nan Doi Giap Hat Ma Tim Bien Phap Khac Phuc Nan Doi", *Tap Chi Cong San*, no. 9 (1988), p. 37. In certain co-operatives, the tax rate amounted to even 18 per cent of the crop (ibid.).
57. See Lien Huong's article in *Saigon Giai Phong*, 3 July 1987. The peasants proposed that the current 13–14 per cent rate should be lowered by 40 per cent (ibid.).

58. See Le Dien's article in *Dai Doan Ket*, 1 September 1987.
59. Le Ngoc, "Trong Cac Quan He Kinh Te Nong Dan Da Duoc Doi Xu Song Phang Chua", *Thong Ke*, no. 9 (Hanoi, 1987), p. 25. For more details concerning the "price scissors", see ibid., pp. 24–25; Vu Oanh, "Giai Cap Nong Dan Tap The Tren Mat Tran Nong Nghiep", *Tap Chi Cong San*, no. 5 (1987), p. 41; and Xuan Kieu, "Ve Chinh Sach Cung Ung Vat Tu Cua Nha Nuoc Doi Voi Nong Nghiep", *Tap Chi Cong San*, no. 6 (1987), pp. 54–55; and Duy Hung, "May Van De Ve Loi Ich Kinh Te Trong Nong Nghiep . . . ", *Nghien Cuu Kinh Te*, nos. 1 and 2 (1988), p. 59. See also Le Dien's article in *Dai Doan Ket*, 1 September 1987.
60. *6th National Congress* . . . , pp. 19–20. Nguyen Ngoc Triu, then Minister of Agriculture, acknowledged that "agriculture [was] not yet truly encouraged" (see *Vietnam Courier*, no. 2 [1986], p. 13).
61. *Nhan Dan*, 25 December 1984 (editorial).
62. *Vietnam Courier*, no. 5 (1982), p. 10.
63. *Nghien Cuu Kinh Te*, no. 1 (1985), p. 7.
64. *Nien Giam Thong Ke 1985*, p. 35.
65. Viet An, "Some major problems in food problem", *Vietnam Courier*, no. 2 (1987), p. 19. Note that the threshold of 300 kg is the minimum for human consumption only, to say nothing of seed, and livestock-breeding, and so forth.
66. See Le Ngoc, "Trong Cac Quan He . . . ", p. 21. See also Huy Hung, "Tu Nan Doi Giap . . . " p. 34. (In the North "usually 5-10 per cent of the peasant households experienced a food shortage every year during the gap between the harvests").
67. Nguyen Thanh Bang, "Thu Ban Ve Van De Luong Thuc . . .", p. 22.
68. See *inter alia* Nguyen Xuan Lai, who wrote: "In 1983, for the first time in forty years, Vietnam in the main achieved self-sufficiency in food [crops]". *Vietnamese Studies* (a new series), no. 5 (1984), p. 59. On the same score, see also *History of the Communist Party* . . . , p. 322.
69. See Huy Hung, "Tu Nan Doi Giap . . .", p. 35. In fact, Vietnam imported 357.9 and 422.2 thousand tons of food respectively in 1984 and 1985 (*Nien Giam Thong Ke 1985*, p. 259).
70. *Vietnam News Agency*, 6 December 1985.
71. See Viet An, "Some major problems . . . ", p. 19.
72. *Nhan Dan*, 23 July 1986.
73. See Nguyen Thanh Bang, "Thu Ban Ve Van De Luong Thuc . . .", p. 23.
74. See Viet An, "Some major problems . . .", and Bui Van Nhon's article in *Nghien Cuu Kinh Te*, nos. 5 and 6 (1987), p. 45.
75. *Nien Giam Thong Ke 1985*, p. 114. For more details on animal husbandry, see Quang Bien, "The Prospects for Animal Husbandry in Vietnam", *Vietnam Courier*, no. 2 (1987), pp. 20–21.
76. *CPV. 5th National Congress* . . . , pp. 49–50.
77. Ibid.
78. *Nhan Dan*, 3 June 1985.
79. See *CPV. 5th National Congress* . . . , p. 50. For more details, see Nguyen Van

Linh, *May Van De San Xuat Va Doi Song* (NXB Thanh Pho Ho Chi Minh, 1985), pp. 41–52; Nghiem Phu Ninh, *Cong Duong Phat Trien Thu Cong Nghiep, Tieu Cong Nghiep Viet Nam* (Hanoi: NXB Thong Tin Ly Luan, 1986); Nguyen Vinh Long, "Vietnamese Small-Scale Industries and Handicrafts: New Prospects", *Vietnam Courier*, no. 11 (1986), pp. 11–13; and Nguyen Khac Vien, "Creative Handicrafts in Vietnam", ibid., pp. 14–17.

80. *6th National Congress* . . . , p. 20. For more details, see Le Xuan Tung, "Cong Nghiep Hoa XHCN Trong Chang Dau Cua Thoi Ky Qua Do . . .", *Nghien Cuu Kinh Te*, no. 1 (1987), pp. 26–27; and Vu Quoc Tuan, "Ve Van De Bo Tri Mot Co Cau Kinh Te Hop Ly", ibid., pp. 33; 38.
81. See *CPV. 5th National Congress* . . . , p. 51.
82. See *6th National Congress* . . . , p. 20.
83. See *CPV. 5th National Congress* . . . , p. 51.
84. C. Fourniau, "Vietnam: Necessité, Originalité et Ajustements du Socialisme", *Recherches Internationales*, no. 14 (Paris, October-December 1984), p. 57; see also David Jenkins' article in *Far Eastern Economic Review*, 15 November 1984, p. 128.
85. Quoted by Nguyen Van Linh, *May Van De Ve San Xuat* . . . , p. 5.
86. *Nghien Cuu Kinh Te*, no. 6 (1984), p. 6.
87. For more details on various forms of "state capitalism", see Trinh Huy Hoa, "Buoc Di, Hinh Thuc Cua Cai Tao Cong Nghiep Tu Doanh", *Nghien Cuu Kinh Te*, no. 3 (1986), pp. 18–26.
88. See *CPV. 5th National Congress* . . . , p. 56.
89. See Vo Tran Chi's article in *Nhan Dan*, 17 December 1986.
90. See *CPV. 5th National Congress*, pp. 56–57.
91. Ibid., p. 78.
92. See *6th National Congress* . . . , p. 21.
93. *Nhan Dan*, 23 June 1988.
94. *Vietnam Courier*, no. 9 (1984), pp. 3–4; and Le Duan's speech at this Plenum: see ibid., no. 10 (1984), pp. 3–4.
95. It might be useful to recall here that in the language of the political economy of socialism, "economic (or cost) accounting" is a concept reflecting "the production relations between the state and individual enterprises, and those between individual enterprises" under socialism. This implies (1) an economic and operational autonomy of state-run enterprises *within* the framework of the state plan; and (2) their self-sufficiency and profitability in the production process (see Institute of Social Sciences, *Political Economy of Socialism* [Moscow: Progress Publications, 1985], pp. 143–45). In a socialist economy it is somewhat analogous — but not identical — to "managerial economics" in a market economy.

    In the Vietnamese context, the "economic accounting" (*Hach Toan Kinh Te*) system should take into account not only "profitability" but also the mode of "socialist business" (*Kinh Doanh Xa Hoi Chu Nghia*). The latter, apart from the fact that it must fundamentally conform with the state plan, should also take into consideration the relationship between production and demand, and the

judicious combination of "the three benefits", that is, the benefits of the society, the enterprise, and the worker. See Le Duan's speech at the Fifth Central Committee Plenum (December 1983), *Vietnam Courier*, no. 2 (1984), p. 2. Note that Le Duan had urged for the implementation of "economic accounting" in North Vietnam since 1970; see his *Selected Writings*, p. 271, 275.
96. *Nhan Dan*, 17 December 1984. See also Do Muoi, "Reorganization of Production and Continued Renovation of Industrial Management", *Vietnam Courier*, no. 2 (1985), pp. 18–21; and Vu Huy Tu, "May Kien Ve Chien Luoc Phat Trien Va Quan Ly Cong Nghiep Trong Thoi Ky Qua Do O Nuoc Ta", *Nghien Cuu Kinh Te*, no. 6 (1985), pp. 8–9.
97. For more details on these decrees, see Vu Huy Hoang, "Renovation of State-run Enterprises", *Vietnam Courier*, no. 6 (1982), pp. 18–21; and their amendments, ibid., no. 11 (1982), p. 12.
98. Vu Huy Tu, "May Kien Ve Chien Luoc . . . ", p. 9.
99. *Vietnam Courier*, no. 11 (1985), p. 4; and Le Xuan Dong, "A Resolution of Historic Import", ibid., p. 11. For more details on the characteristics of the "bureaucratic mechanism of management" in Vietnam, see ibid., pp. 11–12.
100. *Nhan Dan*, 22 June 1985.
101. Radio Hanoi, Home Service, 27 December 1985.
102. Ho Te, "Bo Tri Co Cau Dau Tu Hop Ly . . . ", *Tap Chi Cong San*, no. 6 (1987), p. 17. For more details on the structure of state investment in various sectors of the national economy, see Bach Hong Viet, "May Van De Su Dung Von Dau Tu Co Ban Trong Chang Dau Cua Thoi Ky Qua Do", *Nghien Cuu Kinh Te*, nos. 5 and 6 (1987), pp. 31–35.
103. See *6th National Congress . . .*, p. 20.
104. *Nhan Dan*, 20 October 1986.
105. Ibid., 5 November 1986.
106. Ibid., 10 December 1984.
107. Ibid., 23 August 1983.
108. Quoted by Nayan Chanda in *Far Eastern Economic Review*, 12 January 1984, p. 32.
109. Quoted in *Vietnam Courier*, no. 2 (1984), p. 2. However, according to another Vietnamese source, state-run enterprises "run only about 30–50 per cent their capacity, or even much lower in a series of grass-roots units" (Vu Huy Tu, "May Kien Ve Chien Luoc . . . ", p. 10). Note also that Vietnam "had to import 80–90 per cent of materials for its industry" (ibid., p. 8, footnote 1).
110. *Quan Doi Nhan Dan*, 22 October 1985.
111. *Nien Giam Thong Ke 1985*, p. 135.
112. See Vu Quoc Tuan's article in *Nghien Cuu Kinh Te*, no. 1 (1986), p. 6.
113. See *Nien Giam Thong Ke 1985*, p. 138.
114. *Nhan Dan*, 15 March 1986. See also ibid., 22 August 1986.
115. Ibid., 20 September 1985.
116. See *Nien Giam Thong Ke 1985*, p. 27.
117. Le Duan, *On Some Present International Problems*, 2nd edition (Hanoi: Foreign Languages Publishing House, 1964), pp. 179–81. It is worth noting that at that

time Vietnam's stance against Soviet "revisionism" was identical to Maoist China's standpoint (see *On the Vietnamese Foreign Ministry White Book* ..., p. 27; and Hoang Van Hoan, *Giot Nuoc Trong Bien Ca* (*Hoi Ky Cach Mang*) (Nha Xuat Ban Tin Vietnam, 1986), pp. 379–81; 385–86; 389.
118. See *CPV. 5th National Congress* ..., pp. 136–37.
119. *Pravda*, 2 September 1985. See also the article by former Deputy Premier Tran Quynh, one of the most vocal critics of the USSR in 1963, in *Nhan Dan*, 18 July 1985.
120. See *CPV. 5th National Congress* ..., pp. 139–40.
121. See "Statement on the Main Directions of the Further Development and Deepening of the Economic, Scientific and Technological Cooperation of the CMEA Countries", *New Times*, no. 26 (Moscow, 1984), p. 42.
122. M.E. To-ri-gu-ben-ko, "Tuong Tro Va Hop Tac Quoc Te Cua Cac Nuoc Thuoc HDTTKT ... ", *Nghien Cuu Kinh Te*, no. 6 (1985), pp. 43–45.
123. *Ekonomicheskaya Gazeta*, no. 11 (March 1985), p. 22 (in Russian).
124. Ibid., no. 49 (1983), p. 21.
125. *Ekonomicheskoye Sotrudnichestvo Stran Chlenov SEV*, no. 5 (1984), p. 22 (in Russian).
126. See Dang Huu's article in *Nhan Dan*, 28 June 1988.
127. Dao Van Tap, "Ban Ve Chien Luoc Kinh Te Doi Ngoai Cua Nuoc Ta", *Nghien Cuu Kinh Te*, no. 4 (1986), p. 10.
128. For more details, see Tran Duc Luong, "Vietnam joined the Council for Mutual Economic Assistance Ten Years Ago", *Vietnam Courier*, no. 9 (1988), pp. 21–22.
129. Ibid.
130. Quoted by Hanoi Radio, Domestic Service, 4 July 1988.
131. See Sophie Quinn-Judge and Murray Hiebert's article in *Far Eastern Economic Review*, 10 November 1988, p. 23. Regarding the "matching funds", it is generally known that 3 dong of foreign aid requires 1–2 dong of additional internal investment; see Nguyen Van Ky, "Quan He Tich Luy Va Tieu Dung Trong Chinh Sach Tai Chinh Quoc Gia O Nuoc Ta Hien Nay", *Nghien Cuu Kinh Te*, no. 4 (1988), p. 17.
132. *Quan Doi Nhan Dan*, 28 November 1988. This newspaper also mentioned that in spite of their low wages, they have to "contribute 10–20 per cent" of this salary to the Vietnamese government for the partial payment of its external debt. However, the newspaper complained that "the amount of foreign currency we earned was too small compared with the amount obtained by countries which have exported their labour". On labour co-operation with the CMEA countries, see also Hong Long, "Van De Hop Tac Lao Dong Voi Nuoc Ngoai", *Tap Chi Cong San*, no. 6 (1988), pp. 53–56.
133. *Vietnam News Agency*, 4 November 1983.
134. *Nong Nghiep*, 5 November 1987.
135. Hanoi Radio, Domestic Service, 2 August 1988.
136. *Tap Chi Cong San*, no. 11 (1985), pp. 71–72.
137. See Le Quy An's article in *Nhan Dan*, 4 November 1988.

138. See A. Glazunov's article in *International Affairs*, no. 9 (Moscow, 1986), p. 148.
139. Y. Rybalko, "USSR-SRV: 30 Years of Beneficial Cooperation", *Foreign Trade*, no. 7 (1985), p. 8.
140. "Quan He Viet Nam-Lien Xo. Tinh Hinh Moi, Tam Cao Moi", *Tap Chi Cong San*, no. 11 (1988), p. 3.
141. Ibid., p. 4.
142. *Tap Chi Cong San*, no. 8 (1986), pp. 9–10; and *Vietnam Courier*, no. 9 (1986), p. 5.
143. *Nhan Dan*, 20 October 1986.
144. See *Wall Street Journal*, 9 June 1987.
145. M. Williams, "Vietnam: The Slow Road to Reform", *Journal of Communist Studies* 3, no. 4 (London, December 1987): 104.
146. See *Nien Giam Thong Ke 1982*, p. 77. For an overview of Soviet-Vietnamese economic co-operation, see M.E. Trigubenko, "Hop Tac Kinh Te Xo-Viet. Kinh Nghiem Va Van De", *Nghien Cuu Kinh Te*, no. 2 (1987), pp. 30–40; O. Petrov, "USSR-Vietnam: Fraternal Cooperation", *Far Eastern Affairs*, no. 2 (Moscow, 1986), pp. 128–35; *Su Hop Tac Quoc Te Giua Dang Cong San Lien Xo Va Dang Cong San Viet Nam. Lich Su Va Hien Tai*, edited by Nguyen Vinh and A.G. E-go-rop (Hanoi: NXB Su That, 1987), pp. 391–403; 427–35 (for the 1975–85 period); *Thang Loi Cua Tinh Huu Nghi Va Su Hop Tac Toan Dien Vietnam-Lien Xo* (Hanoi: NSB Su That, 1983); Vo Nhan Tri, "Soviet Vietnamese Economic Cooperation . . . ", pp. 40–71; see also idem, "Soviet-Vietnamese Economic Cooperation 1975–87", in *Indoshina O Meguru Kokusai Kankai-Taiketsu To Taiwa*, edited by Tadashi Mio (Tokyo: Japan Institute of International Affairs, 1988), pp. 173–85 (in Japanese).
147. See *CPV. 5th National Congress* . . . , p. 59.
148. *Nien Giam Thong Ke 1985*, p. 255. Note that there was a *new* structural classification of export goods in this FYP which was different from the previous one.
149. Ibid., p. 258.
150. Ibid., p. 254.
151. Ibid., p. 257.
152. IMF, *Vietnam — Recent Economic Developments* (SM/87/108), 15 May 1987, p. 34.
153. *So Lieu Thong Ke 1983* (Hanoi, 1985), p. 20.
154. *Nhan Dan*, 20 September 1985.
155. *Le Monde* (Paris), 10 November 1984.
156. M. Trigubenko, "Cooperation between CMEA and Vietnam", *Far Eastern Affairs*, no. 4 (Moscow, 1988), p. 23. *Time* magazine (15 April 1985), wrote that "the per capita (National) Income [was] about US$125, less than a fifth of that in neighbouring Thailand". (This estimate was still too optimistic in my opinion).
157. *Argumenty I Fakty*, no. 39 (1987), p. 2 (in Russian).
158. See *CPV, 5th National Congress* . . . , pp. 75, 77.
159. Regarding the steep increase in prices due to spiralling inflation, see *Tap Chi*

Cong San, no. 6 (1985), pp. 60, 62–63, 70; and ibid., no. 1 (1985), p. 14; *Nghien Cuu Kinh Te*, no. 3 (1985), pp. 48–49; and ibid., no. 4 (1985), pp. 26, 33; and *Nhan Dan*, 10 December 1984 (see Vo Van Kiet's article); ibid., 9 April 1985 and 23 August 1985.

160. This fact was confirmed by a French correspondent of the Catholic newspaper *Temoignage Chretien* (Paris), 29 April–5 May 1985, p. 17.
161. Dao Thien Thi, "Cai Tien Tien Luong", *Tap Chi Cong San*, no. 7 (1985), p. 34; see also ibid., no. 8 (1985), p. 19 (Nguyen Duc Nhuan's article); and *Nghien Cuu Kinh Te*, no. 4 (1985), p. 26.
162. See Le Dien's article in *Dai Doan Ket* (Hanoi), 1 September 1987.
163. Thai Duy, "Nong Dan Phai Duoc Lam Chu Nong Thon", *Lao Dong* (Hanoi), 24 March 1988.
164. Ibid. This statement implies that the land rent amounted to approximately 80 per cent. However, according to Tran Bach Dang, a veteran Party member, the land rent paid to the landlord at that time "represented at utmost 30–40 per cent of the crop" only (see his article in *Tap Chi Cong San*, no. 7 [1988], p. 46). In other words, after paying the land rent to the landlord, the peasants still finally got 60–70 per cent of the crop in the previous semi-feudal and colonial regime.
165. Le Ngoc, "Trong Cac Quan He . . .", p. 21.
166. Quoted from Le Ngoc's article in *Thong Ke* (Hanoi), December 1986. This writer also remarked, " . . . . From other specific phenomena in many areas, it is possible to reach the conclusion that the life and interests of the peasants have not yet received adequate attention. . . . In some places, the peasants have boldly posed the question: 'Have the Party and State forgotten about the peasants?' The people want the answer to be real action. As Uncle Ho [Chi Minh] said: 'The people can understand the value of freedom and independence only when they are well-fed and well-clothed'" (ibid.).
167. *Le Monde* (Paris), 9 November 1984. For more details, see also M. Autret, "La situation alimentaire et nutritionnelle au Vietnam, 1984", in *Le Vietnam Post-Revolutionnaire . . .* , pp. 89–125. Apart from that, a 1986 UNICEF study estimated that the general Vietnamese population received an "average daily ration of 1,800 to 1,900 calories, about 400 calories short of the minimum daily requirement", *Far Eastern Economic Review* (M. Hiebert's article), 28 April 1988, p. 76. These statements were confirmed by the Vietnamese Nutrition Institution which acknowledged that "the average energy generated [by eating "458 grams of food staples a day"] does not exceed 1,940 calories, that is, 16–23 per cent less than required . . . . " (*Vietnam News Agency* [in English], 26 June 1985).
168. Dieu Huong, "Vi Loi Ich Tram Nam Phai Trong Nguoi", *Tap Chi Cong San*, no. 4 (1987), p. 17.
169. *Newsweek*, 15 April 1985, p. 35.
170. *Nhan Dan*, 22 December 1986. For more details, see also Hoang Dinh Cau's article in *Tap Chi Cong San*, no. 4 (1987), pp. 20–22.
171. *Tap Chi Cong San*, no. 7 (1985), p. 2; and *Vietnam Courier*, no. 8 (1985), p. 4.

172. *Nhan Dan* (14 September 1985) confessed that during the past years the "government had continually to issue a very large number of banknotes". See also ibid., 19 September 1985 (Nguyen Duy Gia's article).
173. Hanoi Radio, Home Service, 13 September 1985.
174. *Nhan Dan*, 23 September 1985.
175. IMF, *Vietnam — Recent Economic Developments*, 30 June 1986, pp. 10–11.
176. Ibid.
177. Ibid., p. 11. See *Nhan Dan*, 1 March 1986, and 10 October 1986.
178. See IMF, *Vietnam — Recent Economic Developments*, 30 June 1986, p. 11. See also *Nhan Dan* (editorial), 1 March 1986; and Vu Quoc Tuan's article in *Nghien Cuu Kinh Te*, no. 1 (1986), p. 5.
179. Hanoi Radio, Home Service, 6 October 1985. M. Beresford has drawn an interesting lesson from the Vietnamese price reform. See *Vietnam. Politics* ..., p. 169.
180. Huy Minh's article, *Tap Chi Cong San*, no. 11 (1988), p. 25.
181. *Vietnam Courier*, no. 6 (1986), p. 6.
182. *Nhan Dan*, 17 December 1986.
183. *Saigon Giai Phong*, 8 January 1987.
184. *Nhan Dan*, 2 February 1976.
185. Ibid. (editorial), 1 March 1986.
186. See *6th National Congress* ..., p. 25. For more details on the specific errors of the monetary reform carried out in September 1985, see Vu Ngoc Nhung's article in *Tap Chi Cong San*, no. 10 (1988), pp. 46–47.
187. See his speech delivered at the Nguyen Ai Quoc Institute on 22 October 1987, *Tap Chi Nghien Cuu* (Hoc Vien Nguyen Ai Quoc), (Internal Document), no. 5 (Hanoi, 1987), p. 3.
188. According to the *International Herald Tribune* (27 May 1988), Foreign Minister Nguyen Co Thach had said in 1985 that in Vietnam "poverty is well distributed". From experience, this writer can testify that this so-called well distributed poverty was simply an untruth.

Concerning the difference in income between a top-ranking official and an ordinary cadre in Ho Chi Minh City, for example, see Lam Thanh Liem, "Collectivisation des terres et crise de l'economie rurale dans le delta du Mekong", *Annales de Geographie*, no. 519 (1984), p. 564 (footnote).

For an interesting discussion on communist "politocracies", see P. Kende and Z. Strmiska, *Egalités et Inégalites en Europe de l'Est* (Paris: Presses de la Fondation Nationale des Sciences Politiques, 1984), Chapter 9.
189. *Nhan Dan*, 16 December 1986; and *6th National Congress* ..., pp. 16–17.

Chapter 4

Economic "Renovation", 1986–90

After living with the millstone of Stalinist-Maoist ideology around its neck for more than thirty years (including the 1979–85 period during which some piecemeal reforms were introduced), the Party leadership finally decided at the important Politburo meeting on 25–30 August 1986 to throw away that millstone, and began to initiate a major shift in its strategy of economic development. This strategic shift — based on the experience and lessons gained since the reunification of the country — was reflected in the important speech delivered by Truong Chinh — who, by a strange irony of fate, became one of the champions of the economic reform after being a staunch pro-Maoist and hard-liner for several decades — at the Tenth Congress of the Hanoi Party branch held in October 1986. In this speech he admitted that, since reunification, the Party leadership had

> committed serious shortcomings and errors in economic leadership .... The socio-economic situation in our country is facing a great many difficulties which require clear-sighted and cool-headed search for a correct solution ...
> ... In the past years, we committed errors springing from left infantilism and voluntarism and from acting against the objective [economic] laws. These errors have manifested themselves in

the fact that we have built an economic structure over-emphasizing large-scale heavy industry that exceeded our real possibilities; that we have maintained for too long a bureaucratic subsidy-based system of [macro-economic] management ... leading to a great deal of dependence on foreign aid; that we have been hasty in seeking to complete socialist transformation by quickly abolishing non-socialist economic sectors . . . .
These shortcomings and mistakes have resulted in the productive forces being inhibited; [macro-]imbalances becoming aggravated; productivity, quality and economic efficacy being steadily reduced; commodities becoming scarce, and their circulation being choked. The country's potentials as well as the great assistance of the Soviet Union and other fraternal socialist countries, far from being brought into full play, have been seriously wasted and face the danger of gradually becoming exhausted.

Land, labour, material and technical infrastructure, capital, capability, experience, intelligence and skills of the entire country, of the various sectors, and of every region, as well as the working people's potentials, have not been tapped and put into full use. Meanwhile, unemployment tends to rise; prices fluctuate [read, increase] wildly; and life is precarious. Negative phenomena [that is, corruption, theft of public property, etc.] have developed... Socio-economic activities are thrown into prolonged chaos. All this has led to general scepticism concerning the future and lack of confidence in the Party leadership.

And he concluded:

For the community of socialist countries, renovation is the way to surge forward....

For our country, renovation is all the more necessary: *it is a matter of life and death* .... Only by renovating our way of thinking and acting — renovating our thinking, especially economic thinking, renovating our style of work, our organization and our cadres — will we be able to extricate ourselves from the current very difficult situation (emphasis added)[1].

The abovementioned Politburo meeting in August 1986 was the second great turning point in the Party's strategy of economic development since reunification, the first having been carried out at the time of the Sixth Central Committee Plenum in 1979.

Following Truong Chinh's speech there was a series of important articles in the Party newspaper elaborating on this strategic shift of economic line.[2]

A few months after the Politburo meeting, the Sixth Party Congress was convened (December 1986). The latter not only endorsed the Politburo's abovementioned strategic change, but also elected a new Secretary-General, the reformist Nguyen Van Linh. This election — which could be construed as a *relative* triumph of the pragmatist-reformist branch of the old guard — has brought about a wind of "renovation" (*doi moi*) which has been slowly penetrating the labyrinth of the Vietnamese polity.

The Sixth Party Congress, after acknowledging the errors committed in the past years, pointed out that

> the comprehensive tasks and general objectives of the remaining years of the initial stage [of transition to socialism, that is, up to 1990] are to *stabilize all aspects of the economic and social situation*, [and] continue to build the premises necessary for the acceleration of socialist industrialization in the following stage.[3]

By stabilization of the socio-economic situation, the Party means "stabilization and development of production, ... [income] distribution, and circulation of goods; stabilization and gradual improvement of the material and cultural life of the people; enhancing the efficiency of organization and management; establishment of order and discipline; and realization of social justice".[4]

Proceeding from the abovementioned general tasks, the Sixth Party Congress set forth five concrete socio-economic objectives for the 1986–90 period, namely:

1. to produce enough for consumption and accumulation;
2. to readjust the national economic structure, and consequently, the investment structure;
3. to build and perfect "new relations of production in accordance with the character and level of productive forces"; and develop *all* the economic sectors (that is, socialist as well as non-socialist sectors);
4. to bring about significant social changes (particularly in the

domains of employment, and income distribution, and so forth);
5. and lastly, to strengthen national defence and internal security.[5]

Then, in December 1987, the Party Central Committee convened its Fourth Plenum (Sixth Congress) to review one year of economic "renovation", and finalize the tasks and targets of the Fourth Five-Year Plan (FYP) (1986-90). This Plenum emphasized that during the remaining years of the current FYP (1988–90), the Party

> must strive to achieve at all costs the target of substantially stabilizing the socio-economic situation, and prepare favourable conditions for socio-economic development for the ensuing years. To realize these objectives, it is imperative to vigorously develop commodity production, and improve productivity, quality and efficiency. Our priorities must be in the implementation of the three major economic programmes [food staples, consumer goods and export programmes] particularly the food staples programme.[6]

Finally, taking into account both the five socio-economic objectives set forth by the Sixth Party Congress and the tasks laid down by the Fourth Plenum, Deputy Premier Vo Van Kiet pointed out in his economic report delivered at the National Assembly in December 1987 the following tasks for the 1986–90 period.

> *First*, ... satisfy the basic needs concerning food staples, essential consumer goods and other pressing needs of the working people; quickly increase exports . . . , and expand economic relations with the USSR and other socialist countries as well as [non-socialist] countries. At the same time, one must also continue developing a number of important heavy industrial sectors and the communications and transport in order to support the aforementioned tasks effectively.
>
> *Second*, resolutely switch all economic activities to socialist economic accounting . . . to increase production and business efficiency, and strictly practice thrift; rationally distribute National Income; stabilize step by step the situation of [income] distribution and circulation [of goods], and ensure that all imperative needs of the working people in their daily life are met; and limit inflation.

Third, strengthen the state and collective sectors . . . , while developing all the potentials of other economic sectors in production and other activities along with reorganizing and satisfactorily managing the economy, continuing socialist transformation of trade in accordance with the new standpoint of the Sixth Party Congress . . .

Fourth, . . . create more jobs for labourers; . . . ameliorate social relations, . . . overcome negative phenomena . . . ;

Fifth, . . . consolidate national defence and [internal] security;

Sixth, . . . make preparations for the 1991–95 socio-economic development plan.[7]

In his report, Kiet emphasized that, during the initial stage of the socialist industrialization process, the implementation of the abovementioned three major economic programmes "cannot be separated from the building of various branches of heavy industry, communications and transport". He also disclosed the following targets for the current FYP (1986–90):

1. The Gross Social Product and Produced National Income will achieve an average annual increase of over 7%.
2. Food staples production will achieve an average annual increase of over 1 million metric tons. [In another passage of his report, he stressed: "We must achieve at all costs . . . 22 million metric tons in 1990"]
3. Industrial production will achieve an average annual increase of 11%, with group B (consumer goods industry) increasing by 13–15%. Electricity generating and construction materials will score fair development. The supply of ordinary consumer goods will be guaranteed.
4. Export revenue will increase by around 70% compared to that of the previous FYP.
5. Construction of various important projects will be completed, thus making it possible for the capacity of electric power to increase by 910 megawatts, and that of the coal sector to augment by 1.5 million metric tons. The extraction of a significant volume of oil and natural gas [will be achieved].
6. The rate of utilization capacity in light industrial enterprises will increase from the current level of 50% to 80-85% in 1990, while that in heavy industrial enterprises will increase from the current level of 40-50% to 60-65%.[8]

These tasks naturally reflect the Party's renovation policy, which is, in fact, a dialectical unity of continuity *and* change. Some of the reformist measures had already been implemented before Linh's accession to power (for example, the encouragement of household economy in 1979 and 1982, and the generalization of the "end-product contract" system in 1981 in the domain of agriculture; the stimulation of non-socialist economic sectors with a view to boosting the production of consumer goods in 1979; and the proclaimed switch to "economic accounting" for all state-run industrial enterprises in 1985, etc. . . .). However, these piecemeal measures did not yield expected results.

In his political report at the Sixth Party Congress, Truong Chinh admitted that during the past years

> about half of the equipment capacity . . . has not been utilized; the land with great possibility of intensive cultivation, the forests, the seas and other natural resources have not been properly exploited; the abundant labour force, [and] the contingent of scientific and technical cadres [have been] under-utilized . . . .

And he continued:

> These productive forces have been handicapped by [the Party leadership's] mistakes and shortcomings in [devising] the [macro] economic structure, the socialist transformation, and the [macro-economic] management mechanism.[9]

The Party's "renovation" policy should therefore aim at liberating all the potential of the country's "productive forces" with a view to increasing national production, *while remaining within the orbit of socialism*. In Truong Chinh's words:

> Economic plans and policies [from 1987 onward] must be governed by the following guiding principle: all existing production capabilities must be liberated, all potentialities of the country [tapped], [and] international assistance put to effective use with a view to vigorously developing the productive forces along with building and strengthening the socialist relations of production.

Echoing Truong Chinh's standpoint, Nguyen Van Linh, in a speech delivered at the First Peasants' Congress, two years later, harped on the same theme, nearly verbatim.[10] He also made a point of insisting, in an interview with an Italian communist newspaper in 1987 that the "renovation" should remain "within the realm of socialism, and aim at its better attainment in Vietnam".[11]

One should always bear in mind this key idea in order to correctly understand the present economic "renovation" policy of the Party and its limits.[12]

Agriculture

As said earlier, in the Fourth FYP, the Party aims "to really concentrate the country's human energy and material wealth on ... implementing the three major comprehensive programmes",[13] of which the food staples programme is the most important one. Consequently, agriculture — which continues to occupy "the foremost position" in the national economy — "should be given [high] priority in acquiring investment (for the building of its material and technical basis), ... materials [that is, industrial inputs], and skilled labour".[14]

To implement the Food Staples Programme, five important measures have been envisaged:

1. Correct determination of areas reserved for the cultivation of food crops.
2. Strengthening of the material and technical basis of agriculture.
3. Large-scale application of technological innovation in agriculture.
4. Switching towards economic accounting in state-run food agencies.
5. Comprehensive renovation of policies towards agriculture and peasants.[15]

Regarding the first measure, it was decided to allocate more industrial inputs and investment to the Mekong River delta (the country's largest paddy-growing area), the Red River delta, and other high-yield paddy-growing areas throughout the country.

To strengthen the material-technical basis of agriculture, it was decided to increase the efficiency of existing water conservancy projects, and to allocate more investment in this respect; supply adequate fuel and electricity for irrigation and drainage on the one hand, and chemical fertilizers and insecticides on the other.

As regards the application of technological advances, it was decided to use widely newly developed rice strains, corn and potato varieties that give high yield, and to set up a seed system to ensure the availability of good quality seed.

The state-run food staples agencies on their part should strive to economize, reduce losses, eliminate state subsidization, and shift to economic accounting.

Regarding the policy towards agriculture and the farmers it was decided "to renovate it in a comprehensive and synchronized way with a view to releasing rural productive forces", particularly in the area of state-peasant relationship. Besides agricultural tax,"which is the only obligation", all exchanges between the state and the peasants should be, at least in theory, in the form of commercial deals based on mutual agreement between the buyer (state agencies) and the seller (farmers) "with true equality being upheld". The imposition of numerous "supplementary taxes" on peasants (by various echelons which adversely affected their legitimate income) as it was done till the end of 1987 must be in principle eliminated. It was also decided to revise the rates of taxation to be imposed on food crops (and "stabilize it until 1990 so as to enable peasants to be at ease to step up production") and on perennial industrial crops and fruit orchards.

Concerning the management of agricultural co-operatives, Kiet emphasized the necessity to improve the "end-product contract" system, improve accounting work, and eliminate subsidies in the distribution of income in order to arouse the peasants' enthusiasm for work.

There were three important measures taken during the first three years of the current FYP to implement the abovementioned guidelines, namely, the Law on Land, the Politburo's Resolution on the renovation of economic policy in agriculture, or Resolution No. 10/NQTU, and the Politburo's Directive No. 47 on Land Disputes.

The Law on Land passed by the National Assembly on 29 December 1987, which consisted of six chapters, stipulated that "land is owned by all the people [the state] and put under ... state management". The State allots land to land users comprising both organizations and individuals for long-term as well as short-term use. The rights and obligations of land users are also clearly defined. Land users who are foreign firms and individuals, international organizations, and joint ventures must abide by this law unless provided otherwise. Generally, this law reflects the Party's policy to encourage *all* economic sectors to invest labour and capital in the development of agriculture, forestry, and fishery.[16]

The Politburo's Resolution on the "Renovation of economic management in agriculture" (Resolution No. 10/NQTU) issued in April 1988, "aims at creating a new driving force to strongly develop agriculture", particularly the "socialist commodity production" in agriculture.[17] In past years, for various reasons (such as insufficient and inefficient investment; forced collectivization and overhastiness in eliminating the individual and private sectors, unequal urban-rural terms of trade, lack of material incentives, etc.) "agricultural production, particularly food staples output, has slowed down, thus causing the socio-economic situation to change from bad to worse".[18] After acknowledging this situation, the Politburo's Resolution stressed the necessity to: consolidate the state and collective sectors while "creating favourable conditions for individual and private sectors to develop production, processing, services, and other trades in agriculture"; step up the application of technological progress and strengthen the agricultural material and technical base; and seriously take into consideration all the "three interests", that is, those of the State, the co-operative and the farmer (with, at least in theory, greater attention paid to the last) in order to boost the peasants' enthusiasm for work, release by all means the "productive forces", and ultimately increase the "socialist commodity production".[19]

Concerning the agricultural producers' co-operatives and production collectives, this Resolution stipulated that the size of very large co-operatives in a number of lowland and midland provinces in the North, the central coastal area and the Central

Highlands, which showed signs of stagnation in production and mismanagement, could be reduced, if so requested by the co-operative members. In the highlands, only those co-operatives which were operating profitably should be retained, while the rest should be reconverted into mutual-aid or work-exchange teams, or private holdings.

The Resolution also stressed that the "end-product contract" system, which had lost its appeal to the peasants after 1983, as mentioned previously, should be greatly improved. Thus, a new system of contract came into force and was applied in many localities from the 1988 winter-spring crop. Based on the scope of contract and on the contracted rate of remuneration for specific work already agreed upon at the co-operative members' congress, the management board of the co-operative or production collective compiles its overall plan estimate, including a remuneration plan — both in cash and in kind — which is *directly linked* to the production plan. This remuneration plan, which is announced right from the beginning of the crop for all members, should ensure that farmers ultimately receive approximately 40 per cent (not only 15 per cent as previously) of the total contract output.

Formerly, the co-operative member may have known the number of work-points he had earned but not the quantity of paddy he would actually receive after the harvest. With the new contract system, he would know at the very beginning of the crop what the total output and the share to be distributed would be; hence its name: *"Khoan Gon"* or "net product contract" system.[20] Furthermore, the co-operative should also stabilize the contracted quota for five years, and set the contracted acreage for a duration of fifteen years.

The Politburo's Resolution also pointed out the necessity to modify a number of major policies such as those concerning investment in agriculture, the supply of industrial inputs, agricultural tax and prices. Concerning the procurement prices, the Resolution emphasized that it should be done in such a way as to enable the peasants to still make a profit after covering all necessary expenses.

Lastly, this Resolution advocated the necessity "to combine the development of socialist commodity-producing agriculture with the building of a new socialist countryside".[21] This Resolution represents a significant tactical step backward in the hitherto dogmatic "socialist transformation" policy of the Party in agriculture. If seriously implemented, it would undoubtedly contribute to boost agricultural production, in particular the food staples programme. Had the Party advocated such a realistic policy since reunification instead of blindly copying the Stalinist-Maoist collectivization model, Vietnam's agriculture would now be in a much better shape!

After the issuance of Resolution No. 10, in some rural areas, especially in the Mekong delta, peasants demanded a return of those plots of land they had formerly owned because this Resolution encouraged them to farm as much land as they could. This was a sharp contrast to the situation a few years earlier, when peasants were not eager to farm at all for lack of material incentives. Their demands were made in various forms, including public protests in district and provincial capitals since July 1988, particularly the first known demonstration in Socialist Vietnam of 300 farmers from Cuu Long province — including former revolutionary fighters wearing their medals — who marched through the streets of Ho Chi Minh City on 12 August 1988.[22] They carried banners demanding the return of collectivized farmland, an "end to injustice", and the sanction on "local despots" who abused their power to appropriate more land than their due and often the best plots during the so-called land readjustment process.

Faced with this situation, the Politburo issued Directive No. 47 on "Solving a number of urgent land-related problems" (not on the land issue in general) on 31 August 1988.[23] The Directive stressed that local authorities should "settle cases of land disputes one by one" in a careful manner by holding open debates with the peasants at the grass-roots level "in a spirit of compromise". The settlement of these disputes should be based on the Party's policies, particularly on the Law on Land and the Politburo's Resolution No. 10.

In an interview with a *Nhan Dan* correspondent, Nguyen Van Linh stressed that "in our land policies, there are correct aspects which should be defended". He also warned that "if ["bad elements"] still insist on ["inciting people by persuading them to go to the city to disturb social order and security"], then they must be dealt with by the law". However, he also pointed out that "cooperatives and production collectives should expand their contracts with peasants who have made legitimate demands for land because they can cultivate more". Regarding collectivization, contrary to the assertions of some Western journalists,[24] he emphasized that:

> Agricultural cooperativization is an essential task, but it must be carried out with appropriate forms and steps .... In the past, we have committed mistakes by forcing the peasants [into cooperatives] .... Many cadres .. maintained an authoritarian and bureaucratic manner, and were involved in embezzlement. For these reasons, at some localities, production developed slowly, and many people suspected our cadres. Now, we must overcome this shortcoming, but it does not mean that we are going to dissolve cooperatives and production collectives as the rumours have it. Instead we must consolidate [them] .... We must make our country rich, our cooperatives strong ....[25]

It is worth noting, however, that since the end of 1988, peasant households have been encouraged to play a *chief role* in agricultural production, whereas the role of agricultural co-operatives is limited to economic planning and organizing technical services for peasant households.[26] (This evolution is somewhat similar to the Chinese agricultural reform.)

* * *

How was the new agricultural policy implemented during the first three years of the Fourth FYP?

Despite the official rhetoric which proclaimed agriculture as the "primary [economic] battle front", the share of agriculture and forestry in gross state investment represented only 24.5 per cent in 1986 (the latest available data at this writing) whereas that of industry amounted to 35.7 per cent (compared with 21.7 per cent and 31.2 per cent respectively in 1985). However, the share of agriculture *per se* (that is, excluding forestry) represented only 19.7 per cent of gross state investment in 1986.[27] Manifestly, state investment in agriculture was insufficient compared with its proclaimed importance. Moreover, this relatively small investment was not allocated rationally, and generally yielded poor economic results.[28] Although a high percentage of total investment outlays in agriculture had been allocated to irrigation, "the amount of land benefiting from active irrigation and drainage account[ed] for just over 10 per cent of the cultivated area" at the beginning of 1988.[29]

Concerning the impact of heavy industry on agriculture, Premier Do Muoi admitted that it "is still minimal and cannot meet the requirements of agriculture and light industry".[30] Nguyen Van Linh pointed out that "farmers' demand for many means of production and consumer goods — which are essential to them and can be domestically manufactured — is still unfulfilled, not to mention their quality".[31] And he continued: "What do peasants think, when they have to use poor quality industrial goods, and when they have no spare parts to repair their equipment?"

Regarding the state–farmer relationship, it is worth noting firstly that farmers unanimously complained about the excruciating burden of taxes (official agricultural tax *plus* various disguised taxes in the countryside). A manager of the Tan Xuan Co-operative No. 1 (in the South) said, for instance: "The agricultural tax is seriously askew compared with other types of taxes. After being readjusted according to the [quality] of paddy fields it has risen to 13-14 per cent, on average. Meanwhile, the industrial tax is only 4-6 per cent."[32] Nguyen Huu Tho, Vice-Chairman of the Council of State, recently acknowledged that "agricultural tax ... is still high, [and this] unlikely encourages the peasants to produce".[33] What is more, apart from the official agricultural tax, local authorities "still seek to introduce many kinds of [mandatory] contributions other than those [officially] stipulated, that are beyond the peasants' endurance".[34]

As a result of all these kinds of overt and disguised taxes, members of co-operatives ultimately generally get only "13 or 15 per cent of the crops" in present socialist Vietnam where peasants are supposed to be "liberated" from the "semi-feudal and colonial yoke" whereas, according to the peasants themselves, in the former "semi-feudal" regime where they had supposedly been mercilessly exploited, they "still got about 20 per cent of the crop" after paying the land rent and other contributions.[35]

The unequal terms of trade between the agricultural products sold by the farmers and the industrial inputs bought by the latter from state-trading agencies (the "price scissors" phenomenon) also got worse during the period under review.[36]

In a speech delivered at the first Peasants' Congress, Nguyen Van Linh admitted that in 1988 "the originally irrational relationship between the prices of agricultural products and industrial goods has become even more irrational",[37] and this, naturally, at the expense of the peasants. The industrial inputs sold to farmers were not only overpriced (this overpricing, in Vietnam as in many communist countries, represents, in fact, a very important disguised form of supplementary agricultural tax) but also not delivered on time and in sufficient quantity. Generally, farmers received only 30 per cent of the fertilizers they needed.[38] The Party newspaper reported that farmers in the Mekong delta, for instance, got only 30-50 per cent of the fertilizers and pesticides they needed.[39] This shortage of industrial inputs (due particularly to an acute shortage of foreign currency) was one of the main causes of stagnation in agricultural production during the past years. Another important cause of agricultural stagnation was the "end-product contract" system described earlier which lasted roughly until the 1988 winter-spring crop.[40]

All the abovementioned factors manifestly contributed to dampen the peasants' enthusiasm for work because they went against their legitimate economic interests.[41] The Party newspaper admitted that:

> ... for a long time now, many of our policies have ... remained inhibitive and inequitable, thus depriving peasants of enthusiasm and the material conditions for production. This is an important cause of the slow development of agriculture ....[42]

In his report delivered at the first Peasants' Congress (March 1988), Pham Bai, a member of the Party Central Committee, also acknowledged that

> many state and party policies concerning the socio-economic issues [related to agriculture] still display a lack of common sense .... As a result, some peasants and their dependants do not show interest in the countryside and agricultural production.[43]

In another passage of his report, he pointed out:

> Agricultural production is not developing ... quickly, and still fails to meet ... society's demand for food staples and to supply sufficient raw materials for the industrial sector and farm products for export .... Efforts to carry out intensive cultivation and multicropping, to increase labour productivity, and to develop cultivation and animal husbandry have brought poor results.

Table 4.1 gives some figures which are indicative of the evolution of agricultural production during the first three years of the Fourth FYP. The table shows that after increasing in 1986, compared with 1985, total food staples decreased by 4 per cent in 1987. This situation was caused not only by natural calamities but also, and "mainly", as Vo Van Kiet admitted in his annual economic report,

> by our own doing: [agricultural] planning still followed the old-fashioned way; investment ... remained inadequate; production was not assured of necessary material conditions [particularly of industrial inputs] ....; policy on prices for the selling of [agricultural products] and buying of [industrial inputs] between the state and peasants was not based on mutual agreement [as officially proclaimed] but was imposed on the farmers; and many injustices remained in the distribution of income within the agricultural cooperatives. All this did not encourage the farmers to produce.[44]

Following the decline of food staples production in 1987, a *famine* broke out in the northern provinces of the country in the first semester of 1988 during the interval between two harvests, despite the mobilization of 260,000 tons of rice from the south, and the importation and donations of rice from foreign countries.[45] According to Vietnamese press reports, this famine "hit 10 million people and claimed at least 26 lives".[46] The food shortage had a serious effect on children in particular, with some of them receiving less than half the average daily allowance for food. According to the National Institute of Nutrition in Hanoi, in some areas, children received only from 1,100 to 1,300 calories a day when the necessary daily intake for children was 2,300 calories. A UNICEF

TABLE 4.1
Agricultural Production, 1986–88

	1986	1987 Est.	1988
	(In millions of dong at 1982 prices)		
Gross Output	95,428	94,498	98,372[a]
Crop cultivation			
of which:	72,342	69,669	
(A) Food crops	(49,702)	(46,549)	
(B) Non-food	(22,640)	(23,120)	
Animal husbandry	23,085	24,829	
	(In thousands of metric tons)		
Food staples			
of which:	18,379	17,651	19,0
(A) Paddy	16,002	15,286	
(B) Subsidiary crops	2,377	2,365	
Paddy average yield (ton/ha)	2.81	2.53	

[a] Calculation based on data mentioned in Vo Van Kiet's annual economic report.

SOURCES: *Nien Giam Thong Ke 1986* (Hanoi: Tong Cuc Thong Ke, 1988), pp. 32, 36, 38; *Tap Chi Cong San*, no. 6 (1988), p. 20; and *Nhan Dan*, 14 December 1988 (Vo Van Kiet's annual economic report); IMF, *Vietnam—Recent Economic Developments* (SM/88/103), 11 May 1988, p. 9 (data provided by the Vietnamese authorities).

representative in Vietnam pointed out at that time that "if they continue[d] on 1,100 calories a day for four months they would be crippled".[47] In connection with this famine, Vo Van Kiet admitted that

> the major shortcoming ... of the Council of Ministers consisted of its failure ... to anticipate the food shortage in late 1987 and early 1988 ...; and consequently, it failed to take the special measures required ... to closely monitor the state of food shortage in some localities, and to decide at an early date the need to import grain to make up for the shortage and build up grain reserves.[48]

It should be stressed that the fundamental cause of this famine was the Party's self-defeating policy *vis-à-vis* the farmers (as described earlier) which dampened the latter's enthusiasm for work, and consequently slowed down agricultural production while the population continued to grow rapidly.[49] The natural calamities in 1987 were only the subsidiary cause of this famine. For "even in normal years", confessed Vo Van Kiet, "some 5-10 per cent of the peasants (about 2-3 million people) in the countryside, especially in the North, suffered from food shortage due to local crop failure ...."[50] (This statement manifestly belies the official proclamation of the so-called food sufficiency in 1983, and again in 1985.)

During the second semester of 1988 the food staples situation, however, improved significantly, compared with the first semester. Overall, food staples production reportedly amounted to 19 million metric tons in 1988, that is, an increase by 7.6 per cent compared with 1987.[51]

If population growth is compared with the increase in food staples, in 1987 (the latest year for which the population figure was available at the time of writing) the population grew by 4.4 per cent whereas food staples production decreased by 3.1 per cent, compared with 1985, the last year of the previous FYP.[52]

It should be noted that the food staples output shown in Table 4.1 refers to gross production, and the losses resulting from storage, especially food staples stored in collectively and state-owned warehouses, have to be deducted from this figure. According to the Party newspaper, "dilapidated storage facilities and cluttered loading areas have resulted in rice losses at a rate of 15–20 per cent due to excessive humidity and 5-10 per cent due to rats, termites, weevils, and theft by dishonest elements".[53]

The average per capita gross food staples production has evolved as follows:[54]

    1986 : 300.8 kg
    1987 : 280.0 kg
    1988 : 297.8 kg

In 1988, the average per capita food staples production was still below the amount required for human consumption only (to say nothing of seeds, etc.) which is officially set at 300 kg — "a bare minimum [which] approaches the limits of hunger".[55]

The Party newspaper recently acknowledged that Vietnam "is still a long way from resolving the food staples problem".[56] According to Nguyen Khac Vien, a well-known publicist in Hanoi "if one wants rice in abundance, one has to liberate the peasants. And there is only one way to do it: to dissolve the co-operatives which the peasants do not want any more. This is undoubtedly the case in 3/4 of existing cooperatives ...."[57]

As long as the food staples problem — which represents the most important among the three major economic programmes mentioned earlier — is not basically solved, it would be difficult for the Party leadership to "stabilize the socio-economic situation" in general, which is the overall objective of the Fourth FYP.

Industry and Handicrafts

Regarding the production of consumer goods which represents the second major economic programme of the Fourth FYP, Vo Van Kiet pointed out that its implementation necessitated in-depth investments, ensured supply of raw materials, and encouragement of all economic sectors — particularly the non-public sectors — to turn their potentials to good account.[58]

In-depth investments should aim at fully utilizing the production capacity of all existing enterprises, including heavy industrial enterprises and national defence enterprises in order to boost consumer goods production. However, the share of state investment outlays in light industry in 1986 (the latest year of available data) represented only 9.1 per cent whereas that of heavy industry amounted to 26.6 per cent (compared with 7.3 and 22.2 per cent respectively in 1985) in total gross state investment (calculated at 1982 constant prices).[59]

Concerning the supply of raw materials, Kiet pointed out that exploitation of all sources of local raw materials should be accelerated through investments, incentive policies, and technological innovations. Besides raw materials imported from the COMECON countries, additional foreign exchange should be used to import materials from the non-socialist countries. Another way to alleviate the shortage of raw materials, according to Kiet, was to engage in production based on foreign-supplied materials and/or production co-operation with foreign countries.

In order to exploit the potential of all economic sectors for the production of consumer goods, Kiet emphasized that

> equal treatment must be given to all of them; uniform tax rates and credit loan rates must be applied; fair treatment must be carried out regarding the purchase of materials ...; and all narrow-minded prejudices and discriminatory regulations [against private sectors] must be abolished so that all potentials of small-scale industry and handicrafts ... can be brought into full play.[60]

Concerning specifically the public sector which is supposed "to play the leading role" in the chorus of all economic sectors, he stressed that

> state-run consumer goods enterprises must shift to economic accounting and ensure that their business operations are profitable ...; [however] enterprises that prove to be inefficient and incapable of improvement must be dissolved or shifted to other forms of ownership.[61]

In connection with state-run enterprises, the important Resolution of the Third Central Committee Plenum of the Sixth Party Congress (August 1987) deals with shifting the operations of grass-roots public enterprises from state-subsidization to "economic accounting", in conjunction with "renovating the mechanism of state economic management", that is, the central planning mechanism.

The main goal of renovating the economic management mechanism, both at the micro (grass-roots state-run enterprises) and the macro (central planning) levels, reminiscent of Deng Xiaoping's urban reform, is, according to the Third Plenum communiqué:

> the creation of a strong impetus to liberate all production potentials, ... and develop the commodity economy in the direction toward socialism ... in order to serve immediately the three major economic programmes. In renovating the economic management mechanism [one] must generally enforce the system

of... [economic] laws of socialism [which play] a guiding role ... in conjunction with the law of value and other laws of commodity production under socialism.[62]

This renovation, it was said,

> is a process which encompasses many ... steps. The main aim of the steps to be taken from [1987] until 1990 is the shifting of activities of economic units to socialist business operations [that is, economic accounting]. To do this, [one] must implement the system of autonomy in production and business for grassroots economic units — especially the state-run ones — along with basically renovating a step further their ... operating procedures .....[63]

As regards the autonomy of grass-roots state-run enterprises — which are, in any case, "under centralized and unified state control" — this Third Plenum issued new regulations which superseded the former Politburo's "Draft Resolution No. 306", and served as a basis for working out a specific management mechanism for all state-owned economic units.[64]

Following these new regulations the Council of Ministers issued, at the end of 1987, the important Decree No. 217-HDBT,[65] which superseded Decree No. 76- HDBT issued in June 1986.

Generally, according to the new regulations, state-run enterprises which are assigned mandatory targets or which have received orders for producing commodities by state agencies must receive, at least in theory, a guarantee for their inputs in terms of materials, and the sale of their products. If they conduct business profitably, they can independently use additional funds for developing their production and business. They can also independently organize their production and decide upon their labour and wages policy, which would depend on the performance of the enterprises.

The state agencies will not interfere in the daily operations of the enterprises which are to be decided by the congress of workers. Relations between state agencies and grass-roots state-run enterprises are based on the plans, the socio-economic policies and the state laws which are binding to both of them. The state also encourages direct links between the state-run enterprises, and between the latter and other economic sectors and/or foreign enterprises. Generally, by granting autonomy to the grass-roots state-run enterprises, and linking closely responsibility and benefits, the Party hopes to create a driving force for their production and business, and consequently enable them to really play a leading role in the national economy.

The government has decided that from January 1988 onwards the Decree No. 217-HDBT would come into force. However, one wonders how the managers of state-run enterprises can implement this Decree given that prices are still "irrational" and highly unstable as a result of a four-digit inflation.[66] This viewpoint was confirmed by Premier Do Muoi when he admitted that "it is extremely difficult to step up economic accounting in each enterprise as well as throughout the national economy considering the high rate of inflation at present [December 1988]".[67] Vo Van Kiet also acknowledged that "Inflation is still serious . . . . Prices are still high and have upset the macro-economic balance reckoned in monetary terms, and [consequently] the yardsticks and criteria for economic accounting are confused".[68]

The fact remains that, despite repeated exhortations to shift from state subsidization to "economic accounting", the share of state subsidies (for basic consumer goods, exports and to cover losses of public enterprises) in the total budget expenditure has not fallen, but increased from 11.4 per cent in 1985 to 29.33 per cent in 1986, and then to 41.34 per cent in 1987![69] Foreign Minister Nguyen Co Thach, admitted in a news conference held in New Delhi that "up to [1988], 37 per cent of the budget expenditure had gone on [state] subsidies".[70]

Renovating the management of state-run enterprises requires renewed methods of central planning. In this connection, the Third Plenum communiqué specified that state agencies at all levels should completely assign the function of production and business management to grass-roots state-run enterprises, and "stop managerially controlling their production and business".[71] "The functions of the state machinery", it was stipulated, "are to enhance the effectiveness of centralized and unified leadership by the central government, which is reflected in the formulation of socio-economic and technological strategies; provide guidance and leadership in the implementation of economic policies and essential economic-technical norms; exercise control over all economic activities; and ensure ... observance of law and economic management ... at all echelons [including] grassroots [state-run] enterprises".[72]

Thus, one can see that the Party does not "abandon centralized planning in favour of managerial decision-making at the factory in state enterprises", as an American journalist wrote.[73] In the Party's view, the fact of granting autonomy to grass-roots state-owned enterprises in running their production and business allows the central planning authority "to play a truly central role",[74] that is, to focus more efficiently on restricted but vital issues at the macro level. One should therefore view the relationship between the new role of central planning and the autonomy of grassroots enterprises in a dialectical way in order to correctly grasp the meaning of the Third Plenum's Resolution.

Alongside state-run enterprises which represent the public sector, the Party now strongly encourages the development of all the other economic sectors, especially the small private sectors and handicrafts, with a view to boosting commodity production in general. In this connection the Politburo issued, in July 1988, an important Resolution — known as Resolution No. 16 — dealing with the renovation of policies and managerial mechanism *vis-à-vis* non-public sectors. The latter includes activities carried out by co-operatives, families and individuals, joint state-private enterprises and national capitalists in the domains of small-scale industry, industrial services, construction and small-scale transport.

At the beginning of 1988 these activities were performed by nearly two million people, including rural craftsmen. They reportedly turned out 60 per cent of the gross local industrial output, and 40 per cent of the gross national industrial output.[75] The Party acknowledged, ten years after its brutal "socialist transformation" campaign (described earlier in Chapter 2) that its

> greatest mistake toward the [non-public] economic sectors during the past was the collectivization of production ... in a formalistic manner [that is, collectivization for collectivization's sake] without paying adequate attention to consolidating and

developing the productive forces. As a result, ... the latter were weakened, and many sources of existing potential — in terms of materials and equipment, raw materials, capital and social skilled labour — were wasted instead of contributing to the expansion of commodity production.

The Party Resolution admitted that after collectivization "the quality of equipment in almost all production units has degraded; product quality and production efficiency were poor; [and] workers' incomes were low".[76]

It took the Party leadership ten years to realize that "the mechanism of management over non-public sectors was unsuitable, and this has made it impossible for production to develop rapidly".[77] Hence, the Politburo's Resolution No. 16 which aims "first of all, at most satisfactorily tapping the production potential of [the non-public sectors], and successfully bringing into full play the synergy of all economic sectors for the benefit of [national] socio-economic development".[78] This Resolution pointed out in particular two important points:

> First: while consolidating and developing the state-run sector to make it truly assume the leading role and fostering the collective sector, it is necessary to vigorously develop the family-based sector, joint state-private sector, and enterprises run by *small* entrepreneurs and *individual* capitalists in both the urban and rural areas. All prejudices ..., discriminations, or unequal treatment ... with regard to these economic sectors should be abolished.
>
> Second, ... it is necessary to fully respect the principle of self-management and the right of the production units in these sectors to choose their form of organization ..., decide on their plan of production and business operations . . ., and adopt various regulations concerning labour, finance, and credit. The state should ... safeguard their legitimate interests, including the right to ownership and inheritance of small entrepreneurs and national capitalists engaged in industrial production.

The respect of their self-management should, however, go together with the "supervision and control over their activities".

It is worth noting that besides the encouragement of individual and capitalist enterprises, Resolution No. 16 also emphasized the need "to transform all of them into important parts of the national economy operating *along the line of transition to socialism*" (emphasis added).[79] In other words, they are now encouraged to develop their activities, but only on a small-scale and "in accordance with state policy".[80] Their business operations should, however, stay "within the orbit of socialism".[81] In this connection, it might be useful to recall here the Sixth Party Congress's Resolution: "we should make use of private capitalist economy (*small* capitalists) in some branches while transforming them step by step through various forms of state capitalism".[82] This viewpoint was reiterated recently by Nguyen Van Linh when he pointed out: "We are in the first phase of building socialism, and we have many [small] capitalists. They have the right to hire labour but they must obey the labour laws. It is like Lenin's New Economic Policy using local and foreign capitalists. However, Vietnam will bypass any developed capitalist stage".[83]

One has to bear all this in mind, and not to jump to conclusions like that of one Western journalist who wrote that Vietnam "is moving [down] the capitalist road [in the classic sense of the term]."[84]

* * *

The emphasis laid upon the expansion of the consumer goods industry does not imply, however, the neglect of heavy industry during this Fourth FYP. The tasks set forth in this connection, according to Vo Van Kiet, included "the optimum use of all existing enterprises by intensifying in-depth investment ..., and the building of new essential enterprises within the permissible investment capacity".[85] The Party also advocated "the expansion of international cooperation ..., particularly in the fields of metallurgy, engineering, and electronics".

Regarding the energy sector, Kiet said that "concentrated investments should continue to be made with the aim of putting into operation all four generator groups at the Tri An hydroelectric project in 1989, and the three generator groups at the Hoa Binh hydroelectric project in 1990 .... Electricity output was set at 8.3 billion kWh in 1990". He also pointed out that the construction of a number of important coal mines would be completed; and the coal production was set at 7.5 million tons in 1990. Investment in petroleum and natural gas production was also planned to increase significantly. Engineering output was also expected to increase, on average, by 13 per cent during the 1988-90 period. Vietnam is "broadening cooperation with CMEA countries in engineering and electronics production, and trying to attract capital and technology from [non-socialist] countries to reinforce [its] engineering and electronics sectors".[86]

Intensive investments are being made in the existing steel combines and tin mines to increase their output. In addition, the production of phosphate fertilizers and cement was set at 600,000 tons and 2.6 million tons respectively in 1990.

* * *

Industrial and handicraft production in the first three years of the Fourth FYP are given in Table 4.2. The table shows that the gross industrial production (that is, industrial plus handicrafts production) increased by 25.6 per cent in 1988 compared with 1985, the last year of the previous FYP. It should be noted that handicraft production still represented 43.1 per cent of gross industrial production in 1986.[87] Heavy industry and light industry increased by 14.1 and 31.2 per cent respectively in 1988 compared with 1985.

The specific share of heavy industry in total gross industrial production, however, tended to decrease: 29.7 per cent in 1988, compared with 32.7 per cent in 1985, whereas that of light industry tended to increase correlatively: 70.3 per cent compared with 67.3 per cent respectively.[88]

Industrial production in the centrally managed industries increased less than that in the locally managed enterprises — 13 and 16.3 per cent respectively in 1987, compared with 1985 — reflecting the shortage of imported raw materials experienced by the former.

Electricity production increased by 18.7 per cent in 1987 (to 6.19 billion kWh) compared with 1985.[89] This substantial increase

TABLE 4.2
Industrial and Handicraft Production, 1986–88
(In millions of dong at 1982 prices)

	1985	1986	1987 Est	1988[a]
Gross industrial production	105,340	112,451	121,410	132,336
By sector: Heavy industry	34,463	35,862	37,625	39,335
Light industry	70,877	76,589	83,785	93,001
By type of management: Central management	35,618	38,423	40,275	
Local management	69,722	74,028	81,135	
By industrial branches:				
Energy, combustibles	6,048.6	7,059	7,714	
Metallurgy	1,353.8	1,594	1,567	
Machinery	14,677	16,178	18,221	
Chemical industry	11,209	10,815	11,736	
Construction material, earthenware, porcelain, glassware, wood, forest products, cellulose, paste, and paper industries	21,065	22,962	23,670	
Food and foodstuffs	28,906	30,495	32,732	
Weaving, leather, sewing, dyeing, printing and cultural products	17,770	18,835	20,116	
Other industries	3,927	4,058	5,169	

[a] Calculations based on percentages mentioned in Kiet's report.
SOURCES: *Nien Giam Thong Ke 1986*, pp. 129–30; Data provided by the Vietnamese authorities, quoted in IMF, *Vietnam — Recent Economic Developments*, 1 May 1988, p. 11; *Nhan Dan*, 14 December 1988 (Vo Van Kiet's report).

was largely due to the commissioning of the first of the four turbine generators at the Tri An hydropower station in the South.

Coal production grew by 21.4 per cent in 1987 (to 6.8 million tons), compared with 1985, exceeding the 1983 output for the first time. After the testing period of exploitation in 1986, crude oil production at Vung Tau amounted to 0.2 million tons in 1987, and it is planned to increase this to 2 million tons in 1990.

Despite the overall increase in gross light industrial production in 1987, compared with 1985, the performance with regard to individual products was mixed: the production of bicycle tires, porcelain, paper, salt, tea and fish sauce increased, whereas that of bicycle tubes, glass products, matches, sea fish, sugar, cigarettes, and cotton fabrics fell. Meanwhile, shortages in the supply of consumer goods generally persisted. In spite of the significant increase in gross industrial production during the period under review, the per capita output of the major industrial products was still very low.[90]

Regarding industrial management, Premier Do Muoi pointed out in an address to the National Assembly (December 1988) that "because of poor organization and management ... labour productivity, product quality, and production efficiency have all been on the decline; materials consumption and circulation fees have all exceeded the set norms; loss, waste, and misappropriation of, as well as damage to state-owned materials and goods have reached an alarming level".[91] In a speech delivered at the Sixth Trade Union Congress (October 1988), he confessed "I have a headache because at present equipment and machinery have been operating at only 50 per cent of their capacity, and workers' labour productivity is very low".[92] The under-utilization of capacity was due to a shortage of energy, raw materials, spare parts and means of transportation[93] whereas the low labour productivity was due particularly to "the worsening of the living conditions of the working people" whose "wages cannot ensure the minimum living standard"[94]

Production costs, according to Vo Van Kiet, "remained high, making it difficult for many enterprises to market their products, and resulting in a shortage of capital for production".[95] He also pointed out that "the state still has to compensate for losses to maintain the [state-run] enterprises" despite repeated exhortations to stop state subsidization and shift to "economic accounting". "A matter of concern", stressed Kiet, "is that the quality of many industrial goods has deteriorated".[96] In a directive on product quality control issued by the Council of Ministers in 1988, it was stated that "many consumer goods have failed to satisfy even the lowest standards. Many export products were rated unsatisfactory ...."[97]

Lastly, it is worth noting that, in 1987, the specific share of industry and handicrafts in the Produced National Income (reckoned in 1982 prices) represented only 30.1 per cent whereas that of agriculture amounted to 48.2 per cent, compared with 28.2 and 50.8 per cent respectively in 1985.[98] Vietnam still remains a predominantly agricultural country.

Foreign Economic Relations

In this section, only three topics will be examined, namely, the economic co-operation between Vietnam and other CMEA countries, the new law on foreign investment, and Vietnam's foreign trade.

Economic Co-operation between Vietnam and Other CMEA Countries

In 1986, the Sixth Party Congress' Resolution pointed out that

> [Vietnam] should broaden and heighten the effectiveness of [its] external economic relations, promote export to meet the need for import, widen [its] participation in the international division of labour, first of all and mainly by promoting the all-sided relations in labour division and cooperation with the Soviet Union, Laos and Kampuchea, and with other member countries of the CMEA (Council for Mutual Economic Assistance). [Vietnam] should [co-operate] with the fraternal countries in charting and implementing the CMEA programme for assistance to Vietnam, and the CMEA General Programme for Scientific and Technical Progress till the year 2000. [Furthermore, Vietnam] should actively develop economic and scientific-technical cooperation

with other [that is, non-Socialist] countries, [and] with international organizations and private organizations abroad [that is, in the West] on the principle of equality and mutual benefit".[99]

Elaborating on this, Foreign Minister Nguyen Co Thach, in a recent interview, stressed that Vietnam would "take advantage of favourable external conditions ..., and concentrate its efforts as best it can on stabilizing [its] economy step by step, and create the basis for further economic development within the next 20 to 30 years".[100] In another part of his interview, he emphasized:

> International specialization and cooperation has become the economic development law of each country in particular, and of the world economy as a whole. Nowadays, a closed-door policy is suicide, and opening doors is one of the necessary conditions for economic development (...).
>
> We must not allow local, transient problems to distract us from the direction of [our] basic objective [that is, "building socialism and defending the country's independence"] nor must we allow ourselves to be tricked by our enemies who want to see us distracted ..., and incapable of ... concentration on stabilizing and developing [our] economy.[101]

Thus, compared with the previous periods, Vietnamese leaders seem to be now more conscious of the fact that the country needs a friendly international environment if it wants "to broaden [its] relations with the outside world for the purpose of [economic] development".

As regards specifically Vietnam's "comprehensive and long-term cooperation" with other CMEA countries, the Party and government have always been considering it as "the cornerstone of its policy in international relations" as Deputy Premier Tran Duc Luong and Vietnamese permanent representative at the CMEA pointed out recently.[102] It might be helpful to recall that in October 1987, the 43rd extraordinary session of the CMEA adopted a multilateral co-operation programme between the CMEA European members on the one hand, and Vietnam, Cuba, and Mongolia on the other for the 1991–2005 period[103] with a view to gradually raising the level of economic development of the latter to that of the former. It was emphasized, however, that this multilateral co-operation should be carried out in a new way. It was decided that henceforth, 1) large-scale assistance should not be rendered before the recipient country can make effective use of it; 2) assistance should not be indiscriminate, but should take into account the economic-potential, and the level of development of each particular recipient country; and 3) an end should be put to the inefficiency and departmentalism of the central planning bodies — which frequently lead to a lack of co-ordination between bilateral and multilateral projects or their overlapping — in order to enhance long-term planning co-operation.

Two levels of co-operation were devised in the relation between states with different levels of socio-economic development: state-to-state relations, and direct links between enterprises or amalgamated enterprises located in different CMEA countries. As a consequence, two interconnected levels of management of foreign trade and economic relations have to be set up. The first level of co-operation remains, however, the most important one because of the existence of bilateral long-term programmes and agreements, such as the long-term programme of economico-technical assistance between the USSR and Vietnam. As for the second level of co-operation, in October 1987 the USSR and Vietnam signed agreements on the fundamental principles for establishing and operating joint enterprises, combines, and international organizations, as well as on direct production, and scientific-technological relations between Soviet and Vietnamese enterprises and organizations, thereby setting up a legal framework for direct links between enterprises in the USSR and Vietnam.[104]

The specific types of assistance between other CMEA countries and Vietnam include the following: in the field of energy, the USSR and other CMEA countries (East Germany, Bulgaria, and Czechoslovakia) have helped Vietnam build a number of large (such as the Pha Lai, Hoa Binh and Tri An power plants) as well as small and medium-sized power plants, power lines and transformer stations. The USSR is assisting Vietnam in designing a general scheme for the development of electricity up to the year 2000. It has also helped Vietnam to build coal mines while Poland and other socialist countries have supplied Vietnam with coal mining equipment and machinery.

In 1987, the Vietnam-USSR joint venture, Vietsovpetro, established in the framework of the Vietnam-USSR Treaty on Oil and Gas Prospection and Exploitation on the continental shelf of southern Vietnam, reportedly produced the first ton of crude oil. The first oil refinery and petrochemical complex is also under construction with Soviet assistance.

Co-operation between other CMEA countries and Vietnam in non-ferrous and ferrous metallurgy is also developing. The USSR, Bulgaria, Hungary, Czechoslovakia and East Germany have also co-operated with Vietnam in bauxite prospecting in the South.

In the area of mechanical engineering and electronics, some CMEA countries are assisting Vietnam in building new enterprises and modernizing the existing ones with a view to boosting the production of mechanical equipment for agriculture and forestry. In March 1987, Vietnam and other CMEA countries signed agreements on the joint production of machine-tools, and on building and repairing sea-going vessels.

In the chemical industry, the USSR is helping Vietnam to expand the Lao Cai apatite mine, and to upgrade the Lam Thao superphosphate plant. Vietnam is also co-operating with other CMEA countries in producing chemicals for export.

In the field of light industry, East Germany and Hungary have helped Vietnam build spinning mills, whereas Bulgaria and Poland have provided Vietnam with more equipment for textile and spinning mills. Vietnam has been producing garments, knitwears, leather goods, footwear, and so forth with materials supplied by other CMEA countries. The USSR and Vietnam have signed agreements on the joint production of large quantities of such items.

The CMEA countries, particularly the USSR, have also been supplying Vietnam with fertilizers, insecticides, tractors, means of transport and other important industrial inputs, including fuels and lubricants, to help it carry out its "food staples programme". On the other hand, Vietnam has been supplying tropical products to some of the CMEA countries.

As regards scientific-technical co-operation, suffice it to mention that since the signing of a multilateral agreement in 1981 between a number of CMEA countries and Vietnam research on food plants, animal husbandry, tropical medicine and prospection of bauxite have been carried out. At present, together with other CMEA countries, Vietnam is also carrying out 42 out of 93 priority projects contained in the CMEA's comprehensive programme for technological and scientific progress up to the year 2000.[105]

Overall, since it became a full member of the CMEA (June 1978), Vietnam has received much collective assistance from the former. However, as a Soviet economist pointed out "'since Vietnam's interests were given top priority [whereas] the requirements of other CMEA countries [were given only] secondary consideration, the latter were not as interested in the results of cooperation as could otherwise have been expected".[106] The same economist advocated that "mutual benefit [should] serve as a linchpin for the new model of cooperation [between Vietnam and other CMEA countries]". He also suggested that, besides the CMEA, Vietnam should forge closer links with other countries in Southeast Asia. "Vietnam", he said, "would be the first to benefit from this approach, because such 'mixed' regional integration would give it access to advanced technology, [thanks to] the multilateral ties connecting CMEA, Vietnam and [other] countries in Asia and the Pacific".[107]

* * *

Among the CMEA countries, the Soviet Union remains the biggest aid donor to Vietnam. According to Yegor Ligachev, the Soviet economic aid to Vietnam in the Fourth FYP will amount to 8–9 billion rubles, that is, more than double that provided for the previous FYP, and equivalent to the total of Soviet economic aid during the last thirty years.[108]. If reckoned in U.S. dollars it would amount to US$11.7–13.2 billion.[109] (Here again one should remember that this amount is overestimated because rubles are over-valued in relation to the U.S. dollar at the official exchange rate). Ligachev warned, however, in his greetings at the Vietnamese Sixth Party Congress that "every socio-economic project undertaken in Vietnam with Soviet economic assistance [should] be put into use on schedule and yield the biggest possible efficiency".[110]

The meeting between Nguyen Van Linh and M. Gorbachev in Moscow in May 1987 marked an important turning point in the economic relations between Vietnam and the USSR. In the joint Soviet–Vietnamese statement, it was stressed that

> the new approaches to questions of each respective country's socio-economic development elaborated by the 27th CPSU Congress (February 1986) and the Sixth CPV Congress (2 December 1986) persistently require an increase in the effectiveness of co-operation in the direction of socialist integration, the international division of labour, coproduction and specialization of production, and a more active use of the principle of socialist economic management.[111]

According to Foreign Minister Nguyen Co Thach, Vietnam and the USSR are

> resolved to bring Vietnamese-Soviet economic relations from relations of trade and unilateral assistance to a higher form of socialist international labour division — that is, cooperation in production for *mutual benefit* ....; eliminate the old relations of the bureaucratic system of subsidization and definitely shift to socialist business and accounting; diversify the various procedures and forms of co-operation such as establishing joint ventures, cooperating in fulfilling contracts ..., and achieving co-operation at all three levels: government, [economic] sector, and enterprise (emphasis added).[112]

And he added: "With a great determination and effort of all the parties ..., Vietnam and the Soviet Union will ... achieve the objective set by Comrade M.S. Gorbachev: Vietnam must be strong, (and) the Soviet Union must be strong".

Needless to say that the implementation of the abovementioned principle of mutual benefit implies that henceforth Vietnam has to make more strenuous efforts than before in the area of economic co-operation with the USSR.

It was reported that with Soviet economic aid, Vietnam "had built, restored, and upgraded or brought into full play more than 300 projects of different economic branches".[113] However, nowadays there would appear to be few illusions about the effectiveness of past aid. One Soviet economist has reportedly said to Western journalists:

> Before we didn't have cooperation — we just advanced money ... Many of our long-term construction projects are just standing there. Some work at 50% capacity ... We've put in billions of rubles, and we've got back around 10% of that ...
>
> In Vietnam ... some comrades still want a state monopoly of production and to develop through rapid industrialisation ... But we were mistaken in the past to believe that they were ready for this.[114]

Hanoi officials have also begun complaining to foreign visitors that "they are frequently overcharged for often outmoded Soviet technology, while receiving below-market prices for their exports of fruit and vegetables, seafood and industrial crops". A recent article in *Tien Phong* magazine reported that a common problem in many Soviet factories is that their production tools are obsolete and they break down frequently.[115]

Regarding Soviet-Vietnamese trade, it was reported that in 1986 and 1987 Soviet exports to Vietnam reached 1,318.4 and 1,454.5 million rubles respectively, whereas Soviet imports from Vietnam amounted to only 294.3 and 318.9 million rubles respectively.[116] Compared with 1985, Soviet exports increased by 24.8 per cent in 1987, whereas Soviet imports were augmented by 13.5 per cent. The Soviet trade surplus also increased by 28.3 per cent during the same period.

The USSR remains Vietnam's main trading partner: the volume of goods exported to the Soviet Union accounted for 60 per cent of Vietnam's total exports (and 80 per cent of its exports to the CMEA countries).[117] Vietnam's exports to the USSR consist mainly of raw materials, finished products, and subcontracted goods (woollen carpets, ready-to- wear clothes, and shoe uppers) whose value in the Fourth FYP is expected to increase by 70–80 per cent over the previous FYP. Sixty-eight per cent of Vietnam's imports from the USSR were products such as petroleum, cotton, rolled steel, fertilizers, non-ferrous metals, and so forth ..., and 20 per cent were equipment for Soviet-funded projects.[118] It was reported, however, that the Vietnamese privately complained that the Soviet Union had recently almost doubled the price of goods it exported to

Vietnam. They also "find particularly irksome the Soviet practice of increasing by several times the price of goods purchased for Vietnam in Singapore, Thailand, India and other countries".[119] On the other hand, the Soviets complained that the planned Vietnamese exports to the CMEA countries, including the USSR, were not fulfilled in 1987, in spite of the fact that the Vietnamese press boasted that Vietnam's foreign trade turnover had exceeded the plan for that year.[120] They also complained of the poor quality of Vietnamese natural rubber, etc . . . .[121]

New Law on Foreign Investment

As said earlier, since the Sixth Party Congress, Vietnam has decided to, as Premier Do Muoi put it, "truly open [its] door to mingle with the modern world, develop mutually beneficial economic, cultural, scientific, and technical cooperation with all nations, organizations, and individuals".[122] Foreign Minister Nguyen Co Thach has also stressed:

> we must put an end to the policy of autarky and closing our door to the outside world. We must act fast to incorporate our economy into the world economy and occupy an optimum position in the international division of labour. Only by so doing shall we bring about fast economic progress .... In order to participate in the international division of labour, and turn to account our strong points — skilled and cheap labour, abundant natural resources — we are undertaking a gradual change over from an autarkic to a commodity economy. We have promulgated the law on foreign investment ....[123]

The new Law on Foreign Investment — demonstrably more liberal than the 1977 law[124] — was passed by the National Assembly on 29 December 1987, and promulgated on 9 January 1988.[125] It is designed, in the Party's view,

> to create further conditions for exploiting satisfactorily all potentials [of the country, and] broaden commercial relations, and economic, scientific, technical cooperation with the outside world in order to serve the cause of socialist construction.[126]

This 42-article law was regarded by *The Economist* as "one of the most liberal in all Southeast Asia".[127] According to one foreign observer, it "goes far beyond anything the Communist Party [of Vietnam] has ever offered to foreign capitalists".[128] Concretely, this Law has several aims, namely:

1. to attract foreign capital and high technology (see, in particular, Article 3 concerning economic sectors in which investment is encouraged; Article 8 regarding the proportion of foreign capital contribution to a joint venture; and Article 11 concerning the percentage of products for export in a joint venture);
2. to learn advanced economic management and train economic cadres and skilled labour (see, in particular, Article 12 regarding the setting up of a board of management as the leading body of a joint venture);
3. to strengthen Vietnam's economic potential and role within the framework of the international division of labour, especially in COMECON;
4. to effectively explore natural resources;
5. to increase employment (see Article 3, section 3 regarding labour-intensive production using raw materials and natural resources available in the country);
6. to promote export and foreign currency-earning services; and
7. to increase capital accumulation for socialist industrialization.

To attain the above-mentioned aims Vietnam wants to give foreign investors favourable conditions and ensure the security of their capital and interests; guarantee that their enterprises will not be nationalized, and that they get at least the same profits as they may earn in the neighbouring countries; and allow them to remit capital and profits to third countries.

According to Article 4, there are three forms of investment: 1) contractual business co-operation such as production and management sharing; 2) joint venture between foreign investors and Vietnamese economic organizations; and 3) ventures wholly-owned and operated by foreign investors. While there are no upper limits, the share of foreign capital contribution should be no less than 30 per cent (see Article 8). As for the duration of a joint venture and a private enterprise with 100 per cent foreign capital, it should not exceed twenty years (see Article 15). However, where necessary, it may be extended for a longer period.

According to Article 11, Vietnamese and foreign partners in a joint venture must mutually agree upon the percentage of products for export. Foreign currency earnings from exports and other sources should be at least sufficient to meet all foreign exchange needs and ensure normal operation of the joint venture and the benefits of the foreign partner. Each partner to the joint venture shall appoint its nominees to the Board of Management in proportion to the capital contribution, provided, however, that each of them will have at least two nominees. The General Director or the first Deputy Director of the Board of Management should be a Vietnamese. The most important matters related to the operation of the joint venture should be decided by the Board of Management on the principle of unanimity. Wages and other allowances of the Vietnamese personnel should be payable in dong originating from foreign currencies.

According to Article 26, the rate of income tax is set at 15–25 per cent of the earned profits. However, for oil and gas, and some other valuable resources, the income tax is higher. In fact, income tax in Vietnam seems to be lower than that of the neighbouring countries, except the People's Republic of China.

According to Article 3, foreign organizations or persons may invest in different sectors of the Vietnamese economy. However, they are encouraged to invest in sectors which are carrying out the "major three economic programmes" mentioned earlier; in high-technology industries using skilled labour; in labour-intensive production; in infrastructure; and in foreign currency-earning services such as tourism, ship repair, airport, seaport and other services .

On 5 September 1988, the Council of Ministers promulgated a decree detailing the implementation of this Law. This decree supplements the broad provisions of the Law with a comprehensive list of 113 articles dealing with potential problems faced by foreign investors.[129] The provisions for corporate independence, taxes and wages contained in this decree are particularly encouraging, analysts said.

Regarding taxes on profits, for example, this decree stipulates that some joint ventures will be subjected to a lower rate, ranging from 10 to 14 per cent (they usually range from 15 to 25 per cent) in order to "encourage investment" or in "exceptional cases". Others will be exempted "for an extended period of years and enjoy a tax cut of 50 per cent for four years after the enterprise becomes profitable". Profits repatriated abroad are subject to a 10 per cent tax; however, this can drop to 5 per cent in the case of foreign interests "holding more than 50 per cent of the capital or investing more than US$10 million". Imports of raw materials or equipment related to the business are also exempted from tax.[130]

Direct foreign investment, however, can only take place *pari passu* with a systematic development of the endogenous private sector. It also needs an adequate supportive national and international environment. Regarding the internal environment, however, the spiralling inflation, an irrational tax system, the rigid banking system, the underdeveloped infrastructure (electricity, transportation and communications), the lack of a local contingent of businessmen, and economic and technical experts, and secrecy regarding basic economic information, are likely to deter prospective investors

As for the external environment, it is safe to say that as long as the Kampuchean issue is not resolved a large increase in foreign investment cannot be expected in Vietnam.[131] At the end of 1988, Deputy Premier Vo Van Kiet claimed that the promulgation of the Law on foreign investment "has resulted in more than 50 projects with low capital, mainly in the fields of petroleum and natural gas, marine products, tourism and so forth".[132] Premier Do Muoi has also recently pledged "to make all-out effort to solve the problems of inflation, rate of exchange as well as to improve the systems of road transport, communication and services, etc, with a view to paving the way for more effective [foreign] investment in Vietnam".[133]

Foreign Trade

"The export program" represents one of the "three major economic programs" during the current Fourth FYP. In order to implement this programme the Party has advocated the reorganization of the production of export goods, the concentration of capital and inputs on commodities of high economic value, on areas of specialized crop cultivation, on key export items, and the streamlining of the export-import network.

The Party also stressed that it was necessary

> to renovate the buying mechanism of export goods (the State will buy export goods at actual market prices and also sell materials and commodities to the producers at actual market prices) with a view to eliminating the use of foreign exchange in commercial dealings at home, limiting the State subsidization of losses in exports, and, at the same time concentrating all sources of export goods.[134]

Regarding the management of foreign exchange, Vo Van Kiet pointed out that its mechanism should also be renovated

> in order to ensure the needs of the whole country, and at the same time the right of business organizations to use foreign exchange for production purposes. The general guideline would be [that all business organizations should] buy foreign exchange at the State bank, and reserve foreign exchange mainly for the import of materials and equipment".[135]

In December 1987, the National Assembly had passed an "Import–Export Law" (more precisely, a law on import and export taxes on commercial goods), which was promulgated by the State Council on 11 January 1988. This Law stipulates that all economic organizations allowed to export and import goods must pay taxes for their products. Goods exported or imported by foreign-invested enterprises, or by joint ventures are also subject to taxes fixed by this Law. Tax on goods for export and import is classified into two categories: minimal (for commercial partners enjoying a favoured status) and universal tariffs (for the rest of Vietnam's commercial partners). This Law also defines cases in which taxes are reduced or exempted.

Regarding import taxes, the State has decided to exempt taxes or apply low tax rates for such items as machinery, equipment, raw materials, and fuel with a view to encouraging the development of production, and creating conditions for various economic sectors to tap all domestic production potentials. Low tax rates are also prescribed for staple consumer goods not yet, or insufficiently, produced in the country. However, high taxes are levied on "luxury items" to limit their import. Concerning export taxes, it is claimed that they are applied to only a few items, and are designed "to rationally adjust income among various [economic] sectors and export organizations".[136]

How has foreign trade evolved during the first three years of the Fourth FYP? Table 4.3 shows that in 1987, exports reckoned in U.S. dollars increased by 18 per cent, whereas imports grew by 37.8 per cent, compared with 1985. In 1987, exports covered only 36.5 per cent of imports. Exports to the non-convertible area (CMEA countries) increased by 9.7 per cent in 1987, compared with 1985, whereas that to the convertible area grew by nearly 28 per cent (in part because of the start of petroleum exports). Imports from the non-convertible area increased by 52.6 per cent in 1987,[137] compared with 1985, whereas that from the convertible area rose only 1.3 per cent. In 1987, more than 78 per cent of Vietnam's imports came from the non-convertible area.

Despite numerous exhortations to increase exports, the trade deficit remained large: US$1,311 million in 1987, compared with 844 million in 1985, that is, an increase of 55.3 per cent. In 1987, this trade imbalance was particularly pronounced with respect to the non-convertible area (US$1,311 million) where imports amounted to as much as 3.8 times the level of exports. The continuation of the large trade imbalance has been, as usual, made possible by the availability of large amounts of aid from the CMEA countries. The trade deficit with the convertible area (amounting to only US$35 million) in 1987, however, was constrained by the limited amount of financing available, a constraint that has become stronger in recent years as Vietnam's arrears have risen.

Developments in commodity exports (carried out by centrally-managed enterprises only) in 1987 were mixed, compared with 1985. Coal exports fell sharply because of transportation difficulties and problems in securing contracts with traditional purchasers such as Japan and South Korea. Exports of agricultural and forestry products grew significantly whereas that of marine products, handicrafts and light industrial goods declined, in particular the latter.

TABLE 4.3
Vietnam's Foreign Trade, 1985–87
(In million US$)[1]

	1985	1986	1987
Exports, total	746	785	880
Convertible area	336	307	430
Non-convertible area	410	478	450
Imports, total	–1,590	–2,155	–2,191
Convertible area	–459	–453	–465
Non-convertible area	–1,131	–1,702	–1,726
Trade Balance (Deficit)	844	1,370	1,311
Convertible area	123	146	35
Non-convertible area	721	1,224	1,276

Trade with the non-convertible area (that is, CMEA countries) is conducted in terms of "transferable rubles" (TR). The Vietnamese authorities' practice consists of adding data expressed in "transferable rubles" to data expressed in U.S. dollars. This probably implies an exchange rate of US$1 = TR1, which differs from the rate quoted by the "International Bank for Economic Cooperation", which was TR1 = US$1.6246 at the end of 1987.

SOURCE: Data provided by the Vietnamese authorities and IMF staff estimates, quoted from IMF, *Vietnam — Recent Economic Developments*, 11 May 1988, p. 32; and author's own calculations concerning the trade balance.

Petroleum was exported for the first time in 1987 (US$30 million). All exports went to Japan which has refineries capable of handling Vietnam's particular quality of crude as well as being able to supply essential inputs for production.

Table 4.4 gives some figures concerning major Vietnamese exports by commodity and by area of destination in the 1985–87 period (by centrally as well as locally managed enterprises). It is worth noting that, according to the long-term trade agreements and various accords signed with its commercial partners, Vietnam's 1986-90 export value should be double that of the 1981-85 period. However, in the first two years (1986 and 1987) of this Fourth FYP, it only attained little more than a quarter of this planned export value.[138]

TABLE 4.4
Vietnam: Major Exports by Commodity and by Area of Destination, 1985–87
(In million US$)[1]

	1985	1986	1987
I. *Central Enterprises*	636	665	720
Coal	40	34	12
Convertible area	35	29	10
Non-convertible area	5	5	2
Rubber	30	30	28
Convertible area	2	2	6
Non-convertible area	28	28	22
Tea	20	17	16
Convertible area	5	4	2
Non-convertible area	15	13	14
Coffee	16	16	28
Convertible area	2	2	24
Non-convertible area	14	14	4
Wood flooring (non-convertible area)	12	12	19
Marine products	80	82	73
Convertible area	60	70	73
Non-convertible area	20	12	—
Agriculture and forestry products	170	140	198
Convertible area	50	35	38
Non-convertible area	120	105	160
Handicrafts and light industrial goods	268	251	221
Convertible area	72	45	10
Non-convertible area	196	206	211
Petroleum (convertible area)	—	—	30
Unclassified	—	83	95
Convertible area	—	—	77
Non-convertible area	—	83	18

TABLE 4.4 (continued)
Vietnam: Major Exports by Commodity and by Area of Destination, 1985–87
(In million US$)[1]

	1985	1986	1987
II. *Local Enterprises (convertible area)*	110	120	160
Marine products	20	25	40
Agricultural products	70	75	100
Handicraft and light industrial goods	20	20	20
III. *Total*	746	785	880
Of which:			
Convertible area	336	307	430
Non-convertible area	410	478	450
IV. *Memorandum items*			
Proportion of exports to:			
Convertible area	45	39	49
Non-convertible area	55	61	51
Proportion of exports from:			
Central enterprises	85	85	82
Local enterprises	15	15	18

[1] Valuation of the ruble is at par with the U.S. dollar.
Sources: Data supplied by the Vietnamese authorities and IMF staff estimates, quoted from IMF, *Vietnam — Recent Economic Developments*, 11 May 1988, p. 34.

On the other hand, according to Deputy Premier Vo Van Kiet, "inappropriate prices and rates of exchange have resulted in a situation where the more [state corporations] exported, the bigger the losses [they] suffered".[139] The State had naturally to compensate for these losses.[140] The quality of a number of export goods was also regarded by Kiet as "poor".[141] Recently, the Party newspaper disclosed that "due to the slow and insufficient supply of materials and fuel as well as poor management, lack of transportation facilities, and shortage of gunny sacks and warehouses ... the volume of goods not meeting [required] standards delivered to various ports for export was substantial".[142]

As for major Vietnamese imports by centrally managed enterprises, the two largest single components remained capital and intermediate goods, particularly petroleum products and raw materials. They increased by 41 per cent in 1987, compared with 1985. This large increase, particularly from the non-convertible area reflected the adoption by the Vietnamese authorities of a more comprehensive coverage to include imports wholly financed by long-term loans from the CMEA countries. Consumer imports (which included food staples) also increased by 22 per cent in 1987, compared with 1985. Some figures concerning major Vietnamese imports by type of enterprise and by origin in the 1985–87 period are given in Table 4.5.

In 1988, according to the Minister for external economic relations, exports (reckoned in "rubles-US dollars") increased by 17.6 per cent (to socialist countries by 17 per cent, and to non-socialist countries by 18 per cent), and imports grew by 9 per cent compared with the previous year.[143]

A new feature that emerged in 1988 was that Vietnam "has switched from [pure] commercial operations to joint-ventures and specialization in production". It signed ten agreements with the USSR on specialization and co-operation in the production of rubber, coffee, tea, essential oils, garments, textiles, leatherware, and shoes, and on Soviet technical help to the coal industry.[144] It is worth noting that "due to [irrational] foreign exchange rates, and especially to the slow readjustment of the mechanism for controlling and fixing [internal] prices, [state export corporations] continue to suffer losses in exports".[145]

Vietnam's total external indebtedness (including arrears on interest) reportedly rose from US$7.65 billion at the end of 1986 to US$8.62 billion at the end of 1987 (including debt outstanding to the convertible area of US$2.50 billion).[146] Since 1980 the proportion of debt that has actually been serviced has fallen sharply. However, with rising exports and declining scheduled debt service obligations, the ratio of scheduled debt service to exports fell from a peak of 108 per cent in 1986 to 61 per cent in 1987. The proportion of Vietnam's export earnings that was devoted to servicing debt

TABLE 4.5
Vietnam: Major Merchandise Imports, 1985–87

	1985	1986[1]	1987
	(In million US$)[2]		
TOTAL IMPORTS	1,590	2,155	2,191
A. *By type of enterprise*			
Central enterprises	1,463	2,099	2,026
Consumer goods	200	288	244
Of which: Food grains	(87)	(85)	(60)
Other	(113)	(100)	(80)
Capital and intermediate goods	1,263	1,867	1,782
Machinery and equipment	(200)	(722)	(548)
Fuel and raw materials	(1,063)	(1,018)	(1,234)
Local enterprises	127	126	165
Consumer goods	52	51	70
Production goods	75	75	95
B. *By origin*			
Total imports	1,590	2,155	2,191
Convertible area	459	453	465
Non-convertible area	1,131	1,702	1,726
Consumer goods	252	339	314
Convertible area	181	239	234
Non-convertible area	71	100	80
Capital and intermediate goods	1,338	1,816	1,877
Convertible area	278	214	231[3]
Non-convertible area	1,060	1,602	1,646
	(In per cent of total)		
C. *Memorandum items*			
Proportion of imports from			
Convertible area	29	21	21
Non-convertible area	71	79	79
Proportion of imports by			
Central enterprises	92	94	92
Local enterprises	8	6	8

[1] The large increase in recorded imports from the non-convertible area reflects the adoption by the authorities of a more comprehensive coverage to include imports wholly financed by long-term loans from that area.
[2] Valuation of the ruble is at par with the U.S. dollar.
[3] Includes $30 million of imports for the joint Soviet-Vietnamese petroleum venture.

SOURCES: Data provided by the Vietnamese authorities and IMF staff estimates, quoted from IMF, *Vietnam — Recent Economic Developments*, 11 May 1988, p. 37.

was about 6 per cent in both 1986 and 1987.[147] Do Muoi recently acknowledged that besides the food staples shortage, "foreign debt has been a headache for [the government]".[148]

* * *

A broad view of the major aspects of Vietnam's economy has been presented in the previous pages. The following is a general picture of the economy by the end of 1988, which was the second year of "economic renovation". Addressing the National Assembly on 21 December 1988, Premier Do Muoi pointed out:

> Our country is facing great socio-economic difficulties ..., the greatest one is the acutely imbalanced economy, above all the disequilibrium between [national] economic growth and the growth rate of the population which is reaching an explosive stage. During the 1986-88 period, the population increased by 2.06 per cent annually.[149] Correlatively, with this rate of population growth, we must at least achieve a 8.2 per cent increase in Gross Social Product (GSP) and National Income (NI). However, during the past several years, our country achieved, on average an annual increase of 4-5 per cent in GSP and NI. For this reason, the per capita output of basic products was very low in our country. *Our per capita National Income was ranked as one of the poorest countries in the world.*
>
> The employment issue is becoming more and more acute. Overall, the number of unemployed and underemployed in our society in both urban and rural areas, now stands at several million. This is an important cause leading to negative socio-economic consequences at the present.
>
> The slowness of economic growth was due to the imbalanced [macro] economic structure: the producer goods industry [that is, heavy industry] is still minimal and cannot meet the requirements of agriculture and light industry. Almost all major equipment and materials have been imported from abroad, while payment depends chiefly on foreign loans because our exports can cover only one-third of our import requirements.
>
> Despite a huge trade deficit due to large imports, there is a great shortage of materials and equipment, fuel, and consumer goods in the country. [Besides the shortage of materials needed to increase the rate of utilization of the existing equipment

capacity from 50% to 70% in the industrial sector], there is [also] a shortage of spare parts for machinery and means of transportation. This is particularly true with the supply of spare parts imported from the capitalist countries.... The supply of consumer goods, first of all food staples, is still unstable. In 1989, even without the occurrence of major natural disasters, the state quota procurements of food staples are planned to reach 4.2 million metric tons only. The food staples stockpile reserves are still too small, and cannot cope with possible major natural disasters. Most other consumer goods are characterized by an imbalance between small supply and great demand. Alongside this situation, there is, however, a substantial stockpile of materials and goods which cannot be sold due to their low quality, high production cost, poor design, and a horde of other causes.

Because of their backwardness and serious deterioration, our communications and transportation systems and other infrastructure networks are not only hindering the economic development but are also seriously hampering our efforts to attract [foreign] investment and broaden co-operation with the outside world.

The already existing imbalances of the national economy have further worsened because of poor [macro-economic] management. A commonly seen fact is that labour productivity, product quality, and production efficiency have all been on the decline; that materials consumption [for production purposes] and circulation fees have exceeded the set norms; and that the loss, waste, and misappropriation of, as well as damage to, state-owned materials and goods have reached an alarming level .... In 1988, our economic-technical norms have regressed, compared with that set 15-20 years ago.

Due to the irrationality of the [macro] economic structure, the unfinished renovation of the economic management mechanism, and also the weaknesses of the financial and monetary sectors, a large budget deficit has been recorded for many years.... *National consumption has far exceeded Produced National Income, and has even taken up part of national capital and foreign loans* [which were destined, in principle, for productive investment purposes]. In the meantime, there were many cuts in those [budgetary] expenditures which were needed to guarantee minimum living conditions for the wage-earners; to recreate fixed assets and accumulate capital for expanding production; to modernize the technical equipment that have become so old and out of date; to maintain our educational, public health, and cultural activities. [Note that Premier Do Muoi did not apparently contemplate the cut of huge military and police expenditures which were nevertheless one of the principal causes of the large budget deficit!][150]

The State had no alternatives other than issuing more banknotes to cover its [budget] expenditures. [Consequently] inflation has reached an alarming rate; prices have continually soared [and] living conditions of the vast majority of the working people have *become more and more difficult with every passing day*"[151] (emphasis added).

After this gloomy picture painted by the Prime Minister himself, any further comment would be superfluous.... However, it should be recalled that thirteen years earlier, at the so-called Political Consultative Conference on National Reunification held in Ho Chi Minh City (November 1975), Truong Chinh had solemnly told the people, particularly those in the South that "the path to socialism [was] the only path that [would] lead our land to prosperity, and our entire people to happiness".[152] Le Duan had also declared at the Fourth Party Congress (December 1976) that "only under socialism can the age-old dream of the working people come true, i.e., liberation from ... poverty and backwardness, a life of plenty, ... a civilized and happy life .... Under socialism, our motherland will have a modern economy, advanced culture and science, etc."[153] The harsh reality concerning the country's economy and the working people's living conditions mentioned in the preceding pages has categorically refuted the demagogic promises of the Party leaders. Instead of a "modern" and "prosperous" economy, one witnesses, thirteen years after reunification, a moribund economy which is, according to the Party journal itself, engulfed in "a financial and monetary crisis which is deepening with every passing day",[154] and shaken by "an alarming inflation" and "a deepening recession" at the same time.[155]

Instead of "a happy life", "a life of plenty", the working people are experiencing unprecedented hardship, growing misery, even *famine*. The well-known Vietnamese publicist, Nguyen Khac Vien, recently exclaimed "our country is sinking into a real [socio-economic] crisis".[156] Compared with the naked truth described in the preceding pages, promises made by the Vietnamese leaders more than a decade ago look like not only an exercise of pure demagogy but also, *a great historical imposture*!

In 1975, flushed with military victory, the Party leadership thought, according to Nguyen Van Linh himself, that "it would not take much time for [Vietnam] to achieve socialist construction". The Party leadership also "simplistically believed that now that it had defeated [the USA] it would be *easy* ... to succeed in economic construction"[157] (emphasis added). Yet, thirty years later, Premier Do Muoi acknowledged:

> We understand ever more profoundly the lesson of experience for which we have had to pay a fairly dear price. That is, to gain independence and reunification is extremely hard, but it is *many times harder* to defend, and consolidate independence and reunification, advance toward socialism, make the people rich and the country strong, [and] 'make our homeland more prosperous and more beautiful' as instructed by Uncle Ho...[158] (emphasis added).

In April 1977, during his official trip to Paris, the then Premier Pham Van Dong had asserted that Vietnam would set an example to the Third World not only in the military field but also in the economic field (see Chapter 2). Today, after more than a decade, Socialist Vietnam has indeed set an example, but unfortunately, not a positive but rather a negative one. "The Vietnamese Communists", a Western journalist aptly pointed out, " are by now widely recognized in Asia as the region's premier example of how not to run a country".[159] At a meeting of writers, artists and cultural workers held in Hanoi in October 1987, a courageous Vietnamese writer bluntly told the audience, "We have won the war [against the U.S]. But we have not won any victory in economic construction in peace time. We have to squarely face this reality".[160]

Mr Le Phuong, Chief Editor of *Vietnam Courier*, a state-owned magazine, has also commented to a Western journalist: "We look at Singapore, South Korea, Taiwan, Hong Kong and Thailand, and we see that we are far behind them in economic development".[161] A knowledgeable Japanese Vietnam-watcher also aptly pointed out: "[Vietnamese leaders'] trial-and-error moves have plunged

TABLE 4.6
Key Economic Indicators, 1988

	Population Dec. 1988 (million)	GNP per capita (US$)	GDP Growth (%)	Exports 12 mths (US$ billion)	Surplus/Deficit Current Account (US$ million)	Foreign Debt (US$ billion)	Inflation CPI (%)
Brunei	0.2	17,000	2.0	2.3	N.A.	0.2	2.3
Cambodia	7.8	<130	0	0.1*	N.A.	0.6*	10*
China	1,088.8	280	9.3	34.1	−7,034	30.0	18.2
Hong Kong	5.7	8,227	13.6	53.3	2,480	8.3	8.3
India	815.3	270	1.5	11.3	−4,728	52.5	9.0
Indonesia	175.1	500	3.7	17.2	−3,936	47.3	8.0
Japan	122.9	23,533	4.2	262	78,844	112	2.1
Laos	3.8	135	4.5*	0.1	−129	0.6*	65
Malaysia	17.1	1,800	6.9	20.3	2,336	17.5	2.7
Pakistan	105.6	350	7.7	4.3	−1,600	16.2	6.3
Philippines	59.4	650	6.2	6.8	−743	28.4	8.8
Singapore	2.6	7,550	10.9	33.0	479	4.3	3.6
South Korea	42.9	2,800	12.1	60.0	13,713	33.5	5.5
Sri Lanka	16.7	400	1.5	1.4	−412	4.6	7.7
Taiwan	20.0	5,275	7.1	60.5	16,105	12.7	1.4
Thailand	55.0	881	9.3	11.9	−69	15.5	4.3
Vietnam	67.1	130	4.5*	0.7*	−1,111	7.9*	700

Note: Compiled from national and multilateral statistics, updated from official estimates for current rates of change. Figures marked with an asterisk (*) are less reliable due to a lack of recent or trustworthy data, or to official information that differs from market estimates.

SOURCE: *Asiaweek*, 13 January 1989, p. 6.

the economy into great confusion, a dismal performance in stark contrast to the ASEAN countries' progress in the same period".[162]

In Table 4.6 one can compare the economic performance of Socialist Vietnam with that of the neighbouring countries.

Referring to the great disparity in per capita GNP between Vietnam and the neighbouring Asian countries, Tran Bach Dang, a veteran Party member, bitterly remarked in the Party journal that Vietnam "is ashamed" of its derisory position.[163] Recently, Premier Do Muoi himself raised the alarm: "If we let the [economic] situation continue as it did in recent years, we will encounter a more difficult situation and will lag even farther behind neighbouring countries with regard to growth rate, national income, and people's average standard of living".[164]

NOTES

1. *Nhan Dan*, 20 October 1986; and *Vietnam Courier*, no. 12 (1986), pp. 4–5. See also Nguyen Van Linh's speech at the Ho Chi Minh City Party branch, in *Nhan Dan*, 25 October 1986; and Nayan Chanda, "Back to Basics. Vietnam's leaders admit their policies have failed", *Far Eastern Economic Review*, 13 November 1986, pp. 108; 110.
2. See articles published in *Nhan Dan* from 5 November 1986 to 20 November 1986, and reprinted in *Tim Hieu Nghi Quyet Dai Hoi VI. Mot So Van De Thuoc Quan Diem Kinh Te* (NXB Thanh Pho Ho Chi Minh, 1986).
3. *6th National Congress of the Communist Party of Vietnam. Documents* (Hanoi: Foreign Languages Publishing House, 1987), pp. 44–45.
4. Ibid., pp. 45;188.
5. Ibid., pp. 45–48; 51–117. See also Vo Van Kiet, "Phuong Huong, Muc Tieu Chu Yeu Phat Trien Kinh Te, Xa Hoi Trong 5 Nam 1986–1990",*Tap Chi Cong San*, no. 1 (1987), pp. 86–115. Regarding specifically the readjustment of the macro-economic structure, see Tran Thanh, "Ve Xay Dung Co Cau Kinh Te Hop Ly", *Tap Chi Cong San*, no. 2 (1987), pp. 67–71.
6. *Nhan Dan*, 20 December 1987. See also ibid., editorial, 21 December 1987 and editorial in *Tap Chi Cong San*, no. 1(1988) pp. 14–18.
7. Vo Van Kiet's report in *Nhan Dan*, 28 December 1987; and "Nhung Tu Tuong Chi Dao Lon Cua Ke Hoach Phat Trien Kinh Te, Xa Hoi 5 Nam 1986–1990 Va Nam 1988", *Tap Chi Cong San*, no. 2 (1988), pp. 1–7.
8. Vo Van Kiet's report in *Nhan Dan*, 29 December 1987.

9. *6th National Congress of the Communist Party of Vietnam*, p. 51.
10. Linh said: "The guiding conception of the economic plans and policies is to liberate all existing production capacity, tap all late potentials of the country, and effectively use international assistance to vigorously develop productive forces along with building and consolidating *socialist* relations of production" (emphasis added), *Nhan Dan*, 29 March 1988.
11. *L'Unita*, 21 June 1987. See also Linh's address at the opening ceremony of the Nguyen Ai Quoc Higher Party School, Hanoi Radio, Domestic Service, 6–7 May 1987.
12. On the "renovation", see, in particular, Hong Chuong, "Ve Cuoc Van Dong Doi Moi", *Tap Chi Cong San*, no. 2 (1988), pp. 25–31; Tran Ho, "Su Lac Hau Ve Nhan Thuc Ly Luan Kinh Te", ibid., pp. 20–24; Vu Nhat Khai, "Nang Cao Chuc Nang Phe Phan, Cai Tao Cua Ly Luan Mac-Lenin", ibid., pp. 32–36; Nguyen The Phan, "Nhan Thuc Lai Ve Chu Nghia Xa Hoi", ibid., no. 8 (1988), pp. 47–52; Truong Son, "Su Dung Va Cai Tao Dung Dan Cac Thanh Phan Kinh Te", ibid., no. 1 (1988), pp. 30–34; 61; Duong Phu Hiep, "Chu Nghia Xa Hoi Can Duoc Nhan Thuc Lai", *Triet Hoc*, no. 1 (1988), pp. 12–20; E. Bogatova and M. Trigubenko, "The 6th CPV Congress on the Strategy of Vietnam's Socio-Economic Development", *Far Eastern Affairs*, no. 3 (Moscow, 1987), pp. 1–13; E. Bogatova, "Vietnam: The Search for Avenues to Renovation", ibid., no. 6 (1988), pp. 39–44; Ma Zongshi, "Perestroika in Vietnam. A Balance Sheet", *Indochina Report*, no. 17 (Singapore, October-December 1988), pp. 1–18; Nguyen Duc Nhuan, "Signes de renouveau au Vietnam", *Le Monde Diplomatique* (Paris Janvier, 1988), pp. 18–19; Vo Nhan Tri, "Vietnam in 1987: A Wind of Renovation", *Southeast Asian Affairs 1988* (Singapore: Institute of Southeast Asian Studies, 1988), pp. 305–12; and Vo Nhan Tri, *The Renovation Agenda: Groping in the Dark?* (Paper delivered at the International Conference on Vietnam Today: Assessing the New Trends, Bangkok, 1–3 September 1988).
13. *6th National Congress of the Communist Party of Vietnam*, p. 52.
14. Ibid., p. 53. For more details, see Nguyen Huy, "Bao Dam Cho Nong Nghiep That Su La Mat Tran Hang Dau . . . ", *Nghien Cuu Kinh Te*, no. 1 (1987), pp. 40–49.
15. See Vo Van Kiet's report in *Nhan Dan*, 28 December 1987. See also Le Hong Tam et al., "Gop Phan Nghien Cuu Xac Dinh Chuong Trinh Luong Thuc-Thuc Pham", *Nghien Cuu Kinh Te*, no. 2 (1987), pp. 9–12, 60; Van Tung, "Nhung Bien Phap Kinh Te — Ky Thuat Nong Nghiep Chu Yeu Phuc Vu Chuong Trinh Luong Thuc—Thuc Pham", *Ke Hoach Hoa*, no. 4 (Hanoi, 1987), pp. 13–17; and Vo Tong Xuan's interview in *Nhan Dan*, 21 January 1987.
16. See the full text of this Law in *Nhan Dan*, 9 January 1988; and also Ton Gia Huyen, "Luat Dat Dai — Dau Hieu Moi Trong Quan Ly Cua Nha Nuoc Ta", *Tap Chi Cong San*, no. 3 (1988), pp. 18–22.
17. Editorial in *Nhan Dan*, 12 April 1988. For a full text of this Resolution, see ibid. (English translation in *Foreign Broadcast Information Service* [FBIS-EAS-88-088], 6 May 1988, pp. 38–52). See also Vo Chi Cong's articles

commenting on this Resolution in *Nhan Dan*, 9–11 May 1988; and "Thuc Hien Nghi Quyet Cua Bo Chinh Tri Ve Doi Moi Quan Ly Kinh Te Nong Nghiep", *Tap Chi Cong San*, no. 5 (1988), pp. 1–6.
18. "Thuc Hien Nghi Quyet Cua Bo Chinh Tri Ve Doi Moi . . .", pp. 1; 4.
19. Regarding the necessity to produce a marketable agricultural surplus, see Nguyen Dinh Nam, "Xay Dung Co Cau San Xuat Nong Nghiep Hang Hoa", *Tap Chi Cong San*, no. 3 (1988), pp. 23–26; 37.
20. For more details on "Khoan gon", see Huu Tho's article in *Nhan Dan*, 18 and 19 July 1988; Vu Dinh Tu's article in *Tap Chi Cong San*, no. 8 (1988), pp. 65–70; and Luu Van Sung's article in *Nghien Cuu Kinh Te*, no. 4 (1988), pp. 25–29.
21. Full text of the Politburo's Resolution No. 10 in *Nhan Dan*, 12 April 1988.
22. *Doan Ket*, nos. 405–6 (Paris, September-October, 1988), p. 14. (This first demonstration was followed by a bigger one on 9 November 1988). See also Murray Hiebert, "Collective Anger", *Far Eastern Economic Review*, 19 January 1989, p. 19.
23. *Nhan Dan*, 10 September 1988; and editorial in ibid., 12 September 1988. See also Le Phuoc Tho's article in *Nhan Dan*, 22–23 September 1988.
24. M. Hiebert wrote: "Hanoi reverses collectivisation drive in face of protests" (*Far Eastern Economic Review*, 17 November 1988, p. 110). Alan Dawson said: "He [Linh] ordered reversal of collectivisation", *Straits Times*, 1 December 1988.
25. *Nhan Dan*, 8 December 1988.
26. For more details, see Tran Duc, "Mot So Van De Nong Hoi Trong Hop Tac Hoa O Nuoc Ta", *Tap Chi Cong San*, no. 12 (1988), pp. 26–31.
27. Document of the International Monetary Fund (IMF), *Vietnam — Recent Economic Developments*, SM/88/103, 11 May 1988, p. 50; 52. (All the percentages are based on 1982 prices).
28. Nguyen Dinh Nam, "Xay Dung Co Cau . . .", p. 23. See also *Tap Chi Cong San*, no. 5 (1988), p. 2; Tran Thi Que, "Tham Canh San Xuat Nong Nghiep . . . ", *Nghien Cuu Kinh Te*, no. 3 (1988), pp. 19; 21.
29. See Premier Do Muoi's article on land utilization in *Nhan Dan*, 26 May 1988.
30. *Nhan Dan*, 23 December 1988. See also Vu Oanh, "Giai Cap Nong Dan Tap The Tren Mat Tran Nong Nghiep", *Tap Chi Cong San*, no. 5 (1987), p. 40; Nguyen Dinh Nam, "Xay Dung Co Cau . . . ", p. 24; and Nguyen Van Ky's article in *Nghien Cuu Kinh Te*, no. 4 (1988), pp. 16–17.
31. See his speech at the Sixth Trade Union Congress, *Nhan Dan*, 18 October 1988.
32. *Saigon Giai Phong*, 15 May 1987.
33. Ibid., 25 November 1988.
34. According to a radio correspondent, Hanoi Radio, Domestic Service, 5 July 1988. On the same score, see also Hoang Cong Thi, "Cac Chinh Sach Thue . . . ", *Tap Chi Cong San*, no. 11 (1988), p. 19; Huy Hung, "Tu Nan Doi Giap Hat Ma Tim Bien Phap Khac Phuc Nan Doi", ibid., no. 9 (1988), pp. 37–38; and Vo Tong Xuan's interview in *Nhan Dan*, 21 January 1987.
35. Thai Duy, "Nong Dan Phai Duoc Lam Chu Nong Thon", *Lao Dong* (Hanoi),

24 March 1988. According to *Nhan Dan*, 20 July 1987, peasants actually receive only 16–17 per cent of the output (see Nguyen Thanh Van's article). See also Le Dien, "Chi Mong Sao Duoc Cong Bang, Dan Chu", *Dai Doan Ket* (Hanoi), 1 September 1987.
36. For more details, see Vu Oanh, "Giai Cap Nong Dan Tap The . . . " p. 41; Le Ngoc, "Nong Dan Da Duoc . . . ", *Thong Ke*, no. 9 (1987), pp. 24–25; Duy Hung, "May Van De Ve Loi Ich . . .", *Nghien Cuu Kinh Te*, nos. 1 and 2 (1988), p. 59; and Xuan Kieu, "Ve Chinh Sach Cung Ung Vat Tu . . .", *Tap Chi Cong San*, no. 6 (1987), p. 54.
37. *Nhan Dan*, 29 March 1988.
38. Tran Thi Que, "Tham Canh San Xuat Nong Nghiep . . . ", p. 19.
39. See M. Hiebert, "Less cooperation in store", *Far Eastern Economic Review*, 28 April 1988, p. 76.
40. Hence, the necessity to initiate the new "Khoan Gon" contract system which was tested in many localities for the 1987 winter-spring crop; and starting from the 1988 winter-spring crop, it was applied extensively in the whole country (see Nguyen Hong Son, "The problem of distribution of products in agricultural cooperatives", *Vietnam Courier*, no. 5 [1988], p. 15).
41. For more details, see Duy Hung, "May Van De Ve Loi Ich . . ." pp. 54; and Vu Oanh, "Giai Cap Nong Dan Tap The . . . , p. 41.
42. Editorial in *Nhan Dan* , 28 March 1988. See also Nguyen Van Ky's article in *Nghien Cuu Kinh Te*, no. 4 (1988), pp. 18; 19.
43. Hanoi Radio, Home Service, 28 March 1988.
44. *Nhan Dan*, 28 December 1987.
45. Vo Van Kiet's report in *Nhan Dan*, 28 June 1988.
46. Agence France Presse (AFP), quoted in *Straits Times*, 11 July 1988.
47. Quoted in *Straits Times*, 31 August 1988.
48. *Nhan Dan*, 28 June 1988.
49. See Thai Duy's article in *Dai Doan Ket*, 26 March 1988, p. 3; Huy Hung, "Tu Nan Doi Giap Hat . . . ", pp. 35–38.
50. *Nhan Dan*, 28 June 1988.
51. However, Vo Van Kiet said it had increased by 8.5 per cent, compared with 1987. (See *Nhan Dan*, 14 December 1988.) Had it so increased, the total food staples production would have reached 19.151 million metric tons, and not 19 million as he had mentioned in his report (ibid).
52. Calculation based on population data mentioned in *Vietnam Courier*, no. 7 (1988), p. 20, and on food staples data mentioned in *Nien Giam Thong Ke 1986*, (Hanoi: Tong Cuc Thong Ke, 1988), p. 40, and in Table 4.1.
53. See Nhat Ninh's article in *Nhan Dan*, 20 May 1988; and Nguyen Thanh Bang, "Thu Ban Ve Van De Luong Thuc O Nuoc Ta Trong May Nam Truoc Mat" *Tap Chi Cong San*, no. 6 (1988), p. 23. Regarding tubers, the rate of loss amounted to approximately 40–50 per cent *(Nhan Dan*, 11 November 1987).
54. *Nien Giam Thong Ke 1986*, p. 41; and Vo Van Kiet's reports in *Nhan Dan*, 28 December 1987 and 15 December 1988.
55. See Viet An's article in *Vietnam Courier*, no. 2 (1987), p. 19.

56. *Nhan Dan*, 19 March 1988.
57. Nguyen Khac Vien, "Coi Troi Cho Nong Dan", *Lao Dong*, 26 May 1988. See also Nguyen Thanh Bang, "Thu Ban Ve Van . . . ", p. 23. According to a Vietnamese economist 75 per cent of the agricultural producers' co-operatives managed to produce only enough food staples for their own consumption. Hence, there was a very small agricultural marketable surplus for the whole country (see Nguyen Van Ky's article in *Nghien Cuu Kinh Te*, no. 4 [1988], p. 20).
58. *Nhan Dan*, 29 December 1987.
59. IMF, *Vietnam — Recent Economic Developments*, 11 May 1988, p. 50 (data provided by Vietnamese authorities).
60. *Nhan Dan*, 29 December 1987.
61. Ibid. For more details on the "consumer goods program", see Tran Ngoc Trang, "Mot Vai Suy Nghi Ve Chuong Trinh Hang Tieu Dung", *Ke Hoach Hoa*, no. 5 (Hanoi, 1987), pp. 6–8; and the journal *Cong Nghiep Nhe*, no. 225 (Hanoi, April 1987), pp. 1–2.
62. *Nhan Dan*, 1 September 1987.
63. Ibid.
64. See the full text of the Resolution of the Third Plenum (Part II), ibid., 12 September 1987. See also Vu Huy Tu's article in *Nghien Cuu Kinh Te*, nos. 5 and 6 (1987), pp. 19, 26.
65. See the full text of Decree no. 217-HDBT and editorial in *Nhan Dan*, 16 December 1987. See also Pham Hung's article, ibid., 14 December 1987; and Tran Duc Luong's interview, Hanoi Radio, Domestic Service, 23 and 24 December 1987.
66. Vo Nhan Tri, "Vietnam in 1987. A Wind of Renovation", p. 308.
67. *Nhan Dan*, 23 December 1988.
68. Ibid., 14 December 1988. On the same score, *Nhan Dan* (19 November 1987) wrote for instance: "the capital allocated at the beginning of the year was equivalent to the prices of materials at that time. Now the prices have increased 10 times, reducing the capital to 1/10 of its previous value. If the policies on prices, finance and banking are applied too slowly and not in a synchronized way, cost accounting in enterprises will be confused, driving many state enterprises into trouble, because the value of sold goods cannot cover the purchase of materials to restart the production cycle. This also means upsetting the planning task". For more details on the prerequisites for "economic accounting", see *Thong Ke*, nos. 5–6 (Hanoi, 1987), p. 35. Regarding the connection between "economic accounting", autonomy of grassroots enterprises and central planning, see: Nguyen Thanh Ha, "Ve Moi Quan He Giua Ke Hoach Va Hach Toan Kinh Doanh O Nuoc Ta Hien Nay" *Nghien Cuu Kinh Te*, no. 3 (1988), pp. 7–12; 17; and Danh Son, "Hach Toan Kinh Te Va Viec Bao Dam Quyen Tu Chu San Xuat . . . ", ibid., no. 3 (1987), pp. 7–14.
69. Calculations based on data provided by Vietnamese authorities and IMF staff estimates mentioned in IMF, *Vietnam — Recent Economic Developments*, 11 May 1988, p. 21.

70. *Reuter*, quoted in the *Straits Times*, 28 January 1989.
71. *Nhan Dan*, 1 September 1987.
72. See the full text of the Resolution of the Third Plenum (Part II), *Nhan Dan*, 12 September 1987. See also Vo Chi Cong's article on the renovation of the central planning mechanism in *Nhan Dan*, 18 September 1987.
73. B. Crossette's article in *International Herald Tribune*, 30 December 1987.
74. *Nhan Dan*, 1 December 1987.
75. See the full text of this Resolution in *Nhan Dan*, 19 September 1988, and also the editorial.
76. Ibid.
77. *Nhan Dan*, 23–25 August 1988.
78. See the full text of this Resolution in *Nhan Dan*, 19 September 1988.
79. Ibid.
80. *Nhan Dan*, 26 July 1988.
81. See Tran Trong Tan's article in *Nhan Dan*, 7 June 1988.
82. *6th National Congress . . .* , p. 192. Note that the term "state capitalism" here should be understood in the Leninist-Maoist sense, as described in Chapters I and II. Regarding the reason for the restoration of the private sector, see Duong Phu Hiep's article in *Triet Hoc*, no. 11 (1988), p. 15; Hong Chuong's article in *Tap Chi Cong San*, no. 2 (1988), pp. 28–29; and Tran Dinh Nghien's article in ibid, no. 3 (1988), pp. 34–36.
83. See his interview with Chris Ray in *Vietnam Today* (Newsletter of the Australian-Vietnam Society), February 1988, p. 6.
84. See M. Hiebert's article in *Far Eastern Economic Review*, 7 May 1987, p. 101.
85. Vo Van Kiet's report in *Nhan Dan*, 29 December 1987.
86. Ibid.
87. *Nien Giam Thong Ke 1986*, p. 129.
88. Ibid., p. 132 (for 1985), and own calculations for 1988.
89. These calculations as well as the following ones are based on data mentioned in IMF, *Vietnam — Recent Economic Developments*, 11 May 1988, pp. 12–13, 60, unless otherwise stated.
90. For details, see *Nien Giam Thong Ke 1986*, p. 152.
91. *Nhan Dan*, 23 December 1988.
92. Quoted by a radio correspondent, Hanoi Radio, Domestic Service, 24 October 1988.
93. "This is particularly true with the supply of spare parts imported from the capitalist countries and such construction materials as iron, steel, and cement", stressed Do Muoi (see *Nhan Dan*, 23 December 1988).
94. See the confession of Pham The Duyet, ex-Chairman of the Party-controlled Vietnamese Trade Union Federation, in *Tap Chi Cong San*, no. 10 (1988), p. 11.
95. *Nhan Dan*, 14 December 1988.
96. Ibid., 28 December 1987.
97. Hanoi Radio, Domestic Service, 10 August 1988. On the same score, see *Nhan Dan* (editorial), 28 May 1987 and 22 September 1987; and Hoang Manh Tuan,

"Tang Cuong Quan Ly Chat Luong San Pham", *Tap Chi Cong San*, no. 4 (1988), pp. 32–36.
98. See IMF, *Vietnam — Recent Economic Developments*, 11 May 1988, p. 7; and *Nien Giam Thong Ke 1986*, p. 27.
99. *6th National Congress* ... , p. 191.
100. *Nhan Dan*, 1 January 1989.
101. Ibid.
102. Ibid., 29 June 1988; and *Vietnam Courier*, no. 9 (1988), p. 21.
103. *Pravda*, 15 October 1987.
104. For more details, see *Nhan Dan*, 23 November 1987 (full text of the joint enterprise agreement); and also M. Tribugenko, "Cooperation between CMEA and Vietnam: Checking the Slow Down", *Far Eastern Affairs*, no. 4 (Moscow 1988), pp. 25–29.
105. See *Nhan Dan*, 29 June 1988; and *Vietnam Courier*, no. 9 (1988), p. 21. See also M.E. Trigubenko, "Cong Hoa Xa Hoi Chu Nghia Viet Nam Va Hoi Dong Tuong Tro Kinh Te ... ", *Nghien Cuu Kinh Te*, no. 3 (1988), pp. 24–32; Nguyen Van Binh, "Quan He Kinh Te Va Thuong Mai Cua Viet Nam Voi Cac Nuoc Hoi Dong Tuong Tro Kinh Te", *Ngoai Thuong*, no. 2 (1988), pp. 11–14; and Nguyen Khac Vien, "Sev Va Quoc Te Hoa Kinh Te Xa Hoi Chu Nghia", *Tap Chi Cong San*, no. 6 (1987), pp. 47–52.
106. See Tribugenko's article in *Far Eastern Affairs*, no. 4 (Moscow, 1988), p. 25 and 29.
107. Ibid., p. 33.
108. *Pravda*, 19 December 1986. One Vietnamese source disclosed that during the 1986–90 period the USSR is assisting Vietnam with 8.7 billion rubles (*Nong Nghiep* [Hanoi], 5 November 1987).
109. *Nihon Keizai Shimbun*, 19 December 1986; *Le Monde*, 20 December 1986; and *The Economist*, 10–16 January 1987 ("US$11–13 billion at official exchange rates", p. 21).
110. Vietnam News Agency (VNA) (Hanoi), 15 December 1986.
111. *Pravda*, 22 May 1987; and *Nhan Dan*, 22 May 1987.
112. See Nguyen Co Thach's article in *Nhan Dan*, 2 November 1988.
113. Ibid.
114. Quoted in Sophie Quinn-Judge and Murray Hiebert's article in *Far Eastern Economic Review*, 10 November 1988, p. 23.
115. Ibid.
116. *Vnechniaia Torgovlia*, no. 3 (1988) (in Russian)
117. *Vietnam Weekly* (Hanoi), no. 46 (14 November 1988). For details concerning Soviet-Vietnamese trade during the period under review, see A. Yampolsky, "USSR-Vietnam: Improvement of Trade and Economic Ties", *Foreign Trade*, no. 5 (Moscow, 1988), pp. 5–8; Doan Duy Thanh, "Quan He Kinh Te Thuong Mai Viet Nam Lien Xo Ngay Cang Phat Trien", *Kinh Te Doi Ngoai*, no. 10 (Hanoi, 1988), pp. 1–4. See also his article in *Ngoai Thuong*, no. 3 (1988), pp. 1–2; and Thang Tam, "Vietnam-USSR Trade and Shipping Relations grew steadily," *Vietnam Courier*, no. 7 (1988), p. 9. For an overview of Soviet-

Vietnamese economic co-operation in general, see *Quan He Huu Nghi Va Hop Tac Toan Dien Viet Nam — Lien Xo*, (Hanoi: NXB Su That, 1988).
118. *Vietnam Weekly* (Hanoi), no. 46, 14 November 1988.
119. Nayan Chanda, "A Troubled Partnership", *Far Eastern Economic Review*, 9 June 1988, p. 17.
120. A. Yampolsky, "USSR-Vietnam . . . ", p. 5.
121. *Izvestia*, 4 August 1987.
122. See his speech delivered at the National Assembly, in *Nhan Dan*, 23 December 1988.
123. See his interview with *Vietnam Courier's* correspondent, VNA, 31 December 1988.
124. See Nguyen Duc Thinh, "Nhung Dieu Khoan Moi Cua Luat Dau Tu Nuoc Ngoai Tai Viet Nam So Voi Dieu Le Dau Tu 1977", *Ngoai Thuong*, no. 5 (1988), pp. 8–10; 13.
125. For the full text of this Law, see *Vietnam Courier*, no. 3 (1988), pp. 9–13. See also Luu Van Dat, "Ve Luat Dau Tu Nuoc Ngoai Tai Viet Nam", *Tap Chi Cong San*, no. 6 (1988), pp. 24–27; and "Luat Dau Tu Nuoc Ngoai Tai Viet Nam . . . ", *Ngoai Thuong*, no. 1 (1988), pp. 10–13.
126. *Nhan Dan* (editorial), 12 January 1988.
127. *The Economist*, 19 December 1987, p. 25.
128. "Vietnam's Quest for Foreign Investment — A Bold Move", *Indochina Issues*, no. 80 (March 1988), p. 1. On this Law, see also M. Hiebert's articles in *Far Eastern Economic Review*, 4 February 1988, pp. 78–80, and 17 March 1988, pp. 22–23.
129. See the full text in *Vietnam Weekly* (VNA), no. 39 (Hanoi, 26 September 1988).
130. For more details, see AFP, Hong Kong, 29 September 1988.
131. Concerning the obstacles to foreign investment in Vietnam, see Nguyen Xuan Oanh's article in *Saigon Giai Phong*, 7 January 1988; Fumo Goto, "Hanoi's Open Door Policy: Beyond the New Investment Law" (Paper delivered at the International Conference on "Vietnam Today: Assessing the New Trends", Bangkok, 1–3 September 1988), p. 8ff.; and Alan Dawson's article in *Bangkok Post*, 9 February 1988.
132. *Nhan Dan*, 14 December 1988.
133. See his interview in *The Nation* (Bangkok), 9 January 1989.
134. *Tap Chi Cong San*, no. 2 (1988), p. 3. Concerning "the export program", see also Nguyen The Uan, "May Van De Co Ban Ve Chuong Trinh Xuat Khau", ibid., no. 6 (1987), pp. 21–25; 30; Vo Van Kiet, "Phai Giai Phong Nang Luc San Xuat De Tang Nhanh Xuat Khau", *Ngoai Thuong*, no. 1 (1988), pp. 3–4; and Phan Xuan Gia, "Ve Viec Doi Moi Co Che Quan Li Ngoai Thuong", *To Quoc*, no. 11 (Hanoi, 1987), pp. 26–30.
135. *Nhan Dan*, 29 December 1987. See also "Chi Thi Cua Chu Tich Hoi Dong Bo Truong Ve Mot So Van De Cap Bach Trong Cong Tac Xuat Nhap Khau (So 182/CT, 14 June 1988), *Ngoai Thuong*, no. 6 (1988), pp. 3–6.
136. *Nhan Dan* (editorial), 13 January 1988. For the full text of the law, see "Luat Thue Xuat Khau, Thue Nhap Khau Hang Mau Dich", *Ngoai Thuong*, no. 2

(1988), pp. 1–2 (translated in *Foreign Broadcast Information Service* [FBIS-EAS-88-013], 21 January 1988, pp. 68–70).
137. This sharp increase in imports from the non-convertible area could be explained by the fact that until 1986, imports of certain commodities, mainly equipment and machinery, that were wholly financed by loans or transfer from the socialist countries, were excluded from recorded imports. But from 1986 these imports and receipts began to be recorded, resulting in an apparently large increase in imports.
138. Kiet's report in *Nhan Dan*, 29 December 1987.
139. Ibid., 28 December 1987.
140. For reasons of state subsidization in this particular case, see Ngo Van Hai's article in *Nhan Dan*, 22 July 1988.
141. Ibid., 29 December 1987.
142. Ibid., 24 October 1987 (editorial); and also ibid., 9 November 1987.
143. Hanoi Radio, International Service in English, 29 December 1988.
144. Ibid.
145. *Nhan Dan*, 14 December 1988.
146. IMF, *Vietnam — Recent Economic Development*, 11 May 1988, p. 42.
147. Ibid.
148. Hanoi Radio, International Service in English, 30 December 1988.
149. Yet in May, he wrote in an article published in *Nhan Dan* (26 May 1988) that "the annual growth rate of the population at present is 2.2–2.3 per cent (an increase, on average, of 1–1.5 million people annually)". As for the Party's journal, it disclosed that the average growth rate of the population was 2.2 per cent annually (*Tap Chi Cong San*, no. 11 [1988], p. 27).
150. Nguyen Van Linh acknowledged in a speech delivered at a conference of the Ho Chi Minh Party Committee in February 1988 that "[Vietnam] has to feed an army which is the largest in the world if compared to the ratio between soldiers and population" (*Saigon Giai Phong*, quoted by Hanoi Radio, Domestic Service, 6 February 1988). Besides, there are more than a million public security agents (*Cong An*) in Vietnam.
151. Do Muoi's speech in *Nhan Dan*, 23 December 1988.
152. See his *Selected Writings* (Hanoi: Foreign Languages Publishing House, 1977), p. 803.
153. *Communist Party of Vietnam, 4th National Congress* (Hanoi: Foreign Languages Publishing House, 1977), p. 36.
154. Nguyen The Uan, "Tu Duy Moi Va Van De Thuc Tien", *Tap Chi Cong San*, no. 11 (1988), p. 53.
155. Huy Minh, "Thuc Trang Lam Phat O Nuoc Ta ... ", ibid., p. 29. Another Party economist complained that "since more than 40 years, there have not been any moment in which one finds the national economy so chaotic, [and] messy than that of the recent years" (see Tran Phung's article, ibid., p. 14).
156. See his article in *Lao Dong*, 10–17 December 1987.
157. Nguyen Van Linh's speech at the 5th Central Committee Plenum, *Nhan Dan*, 23 June 1988.

158. *Nhan Dan*, 23 December 1988. In 1981, Pham Van Dong also admitted that "waging a war is simple, but running a country is very difficult", quoted by *The Economist*, 20 December 1986 — 2 January 1987, p. 32.
159. *Asian Wall Street Journal*, 4 January 1988.
160. See Duong Thu Huong, "Doi Dieu Suy Nghi Ve Nhan Cach Cua Nguoi Tri Thuc", *Doan Ket*, no. 2 (Paris, 1988), p. 35.
161. Quoted in M. Richardson's article in *International Herald Tribune*, 19 December 1988.
162. Tadashi Mio, "Another Perspective on the Indochina Problem", *Japan Review of International Affairs* 1, no. 2 (Fall/Winter 1987): 208.
163. See his article in *Tap Chi Cong San*, no. 7 (1988), p. 43.
164. *Nhan Dan*, 23 December 1988.

Chapter **5**

Conclusion

"Today socialism can be discussed only on the basis of experience",[1] exclaimed Lenin after the Russian October revolution.

What then is the Vietnamese experience as far as the Party's economic strategy of development is concerned?

As said earlier, there were two *great* turning points in the Party's development strategy and economic policy since the reunification of the country. The first was the Sixth Central Committee Plenum in September 1979 (Fourth Congress) and the second, the Politburo meeting in August 1986, followed a few months later by the Sixth Party Congress which endorsed the Politburo's stand. Roughly speaking, the Stalinist-Maoist model of development was, in fact, implemented until late 1986 in spite of some piecemeal, makeshift measures adopted since the Sixth Plenum in 1979, which were regarded by a high-ranking Party official as only a "small surgery whereas the patient needed a great surgery".[2]

One of the main aspects of the abovementioned strategy of development concerned the Marxist "law of correspondence" between "relations of production" and "forces of production". It might be helpful to recall here K. Marx's stand on this:

> In the social production which men carry on they enter into definite relations that are indispensable and independent of

their will; these relations of production correspond to a definite stage of development of their material forces of production.[3]

In other words, the relations of production, which include not only the ownership system but also the economic management mechanism, and the income distribution system, must suit the level of the productive forces and *not* the reverse. However, until 1986, the Vietnamese leadership was much more influenced by Mao than by Marx. In 1960, summing up the prerequisites for successful institutional change and development, Mao emphatically said:

> All revolutionary history shows that the full development of new productive forces is not the prerequisite for the transformation of backward production relations. Our revolution began with Marxist-Leninist propaganda, which served to create new public opinion in favour of the revolution. After the old production relations had been destroyed, new ones were created, and these cleared the way for the development of the new social productive forces. With that behind us we were able to set in motion the technological revolution to develop social productive forces on a large scale.[4]

This viewpoint was criticized later on by a well-known Chinese economist in these terms:

> In the past two decades [the 1960s and 1970s] we have failed to grasp ... the dialectical relationship between the relations of production and the productive forces under China's specific conditions. Forgetting about the state [of underdevelopment] of the productive forces in the country, we exaggerated the extent to which a change in the relations of production might influence [read, boost] the development of productive forces; erroneously ... [believed that] the relations of production [were] lagging behind the requirements of the growth in productive forces, and drew the [wrong] conclusion that the higher the level of socialist public ownership, the better it would be for the growth in productive forces ... .
>
> As a result, [revolutionary] changes were made in the relations of production which *exceeded* the requirements of the growth in productive forces. Practice shows that a *hasty change* in the relations of production *cannot promote* but *retards* or even

undermines the development of productive forces[5] (emphasis added).

The same phenomenon also happened in Vietnam. After the fashion of Mao, Le Duan asserted in 1976 that "each transformation of the old relations of production and building of the new relations of production will promote the emergence and growth of new productive forces".[6] Basing on this erroneous ideological premise, the Party carried out the forced collectivization in the countryside; the brutal and overhasty "socialist transformation" of private industry, commerce and handicrafts in the cities; the rapid elimination of individual and private sectors, and correlatively, the deification of socialist ownership according to the belief that "the broader the scale, and the higher the degree of socialist ownership, the better", believing that, by doing so, "productive forces" could be *ipso facto* dramatically expanded. Unfortunately, as in Maoist China, this hasty revolutionary change in the "relations of production" did not pave the way for the development of "productive forces" as expected; on the contrary it *hampered* or even *undermined* their expansion. In fact, this self-defeating policy, based essentially on Party voluntarism, has delayed the development of productive forces in Vietnam for probably some decades.

It took the Party leadership ten years to realize, at last, at the Sixth Party Congress in December 1986, that

> [it] has not yet grasped and correctly applied the law of correspondence of production relations to the character and level of development of productive forces... . Practical experience has clearly shown that the productive forces are held back not only in the case of backward production relations, but also in case the production relations are ... far more advanced than the level of productive forces ... .
>
> Over the past ten years, the Resolutions of two National Party Congresses have recorded the task of basically completing the socialist transformation within the term of each Congress [that is, five years], yet this task has not been accomplished. Reality has taught us a bitter lesson, i.e., we should not be so impatient that we go counter to the objective laws. Now we must set it right as follows: It is a permanent and continuous task throughout the

period of transition to socialism to step up socialist transformation in appropriate forms and steps, making the production relations tally with the character and level of development of the productive forces ....[7]

Regarding specifically the economic management mechanism, the Party acknowledged in 1986 that

> the bureaucratic centralized management mechanism based on state subsidies, which [was] in force for many years, far from creating a driving force for development, has weakened the socialist [sector], limited the use and transformation of other economic sectors, put a brake on production, lowered labour productivity, product quality and economic efficiency, put distribution and circulation [of goods] in a state of chaos and given rise to numerous negative manifestations in our society. In that mechanism, the economy was managed mainly through administrative orders with detailed ... enforceable plans and quotas handed down from higher levels .... The [state-run] grassroots units had no right to autonomy ....
>
> That mechanism did not pay adequate attention to the commodity-money relationship [which "demands that production should be closely linked to the market ..., that all economic organizations and units should make up themselves for the expenses and should gain profits to realize enlarged reproduction"] and economic efficiency. This resulted in an [economic] management and planning style mainly based on ... [state] supply of materials [to grassroots enterprises which] realized cost accounting only for form's sake ....
>
> That mechanism has given rise to a cumbersome managerial apparatus ... indulging in a bureaucratic and authoritarian style of management.[8]

Thus, before 1986, as in Maoist China, economic planning and the market mechanism were mutually divorced. The socialist economy was regarded as a planned economy which was incompatible with a commodity economy (because a commodity economy and market forces were considered as capitalist).

Regarding the problem of income distribution, before the Sixth Party Congress, the Party leadership mistook socialist equality for "egalitarianism", and generally equated socialism with egalitarianism, once again as in Maoist China. Marxist equality refers to the principle of distribution of income according to work instead of according to capital, given that public ownership gradually replaces private ownership of the means of production in a socialist society. According to Marx, distribution of income according to work is real equality because "the equality consists in the fact that measurement is made with an equal standard, labour".[9] Distribution according to work recognizes the difference in work capacity of different individuals and, consequently, the difference in labour remuneration. Hence, it has nothing in common with "egalitarianism" which means equal pay regardless of actual performance. Egalitarian workpoints in agricultural producers' co-operatives and egalitarian wages applied in state-run industrial enterprises and other economic units have directly dampened the enthusiasm for work of the labouring people for a long time.[10]

Another important aspect of the Stalinist-Maoist strategy of economic development — which was in fact implemented until 1986 — was the top priority given to heavy industry at the expense of agriculture and light industry.

As said earlier, this policy could not but affect the growth of agriculture, and consequently, the peasants' standard of living. As agriculture and light industry slowed down, shortage of daily necessities grew dramatically, necessitating more dependence on foreign aid. Moreover, a huge amount of investment allotted to heavy industry at the expense of agriculture and light industry adversely affected the communications and transport systems which remain until now fairly backward. Overall, Vietnam's macro-economic structure is characterized by prolonged and acute imbalances resulting mainly from undue emphasis on heavy industry for such a long time. Recently, a high-ranking Party official, head of the theoretical department of the Marxist-Leninist Institute, bluntly said that "by stressing ideas such as the dictatorship of proletariat and developing heavy industry, [Vietnam's] economy has become worse and worse".[11]

Besides the endogenous aspects of the Stalinist-Maoist strategy of development it should also be recalled that the Party admitted that, until 1986, it did not "make effective use of the possibilities of expanding [Vietnam's] economic relations with foreign countries".[12]

Realizing all these errors, the Party decided at its Sixth National Congress (December 1986) to radically change its strategy of economic development with a view to developing to the maximum the "productive forces". Truong Chinh emphasized in his political report that:

> The practical conditions of our country require that importance be attached to intermediate and transitional economic forms, from a lower level to a higher one, from a small-scale to a larger one. In each step of socialist transformation, it is imperative to accelerate the building of the material and technical basis, create new productive forces, and *on this basis* continue to shape the production relations into new and appropriate forms and scale so as to further develop the productive forces[13] (emphasis added).

And "in order to strongly develop the productive forces", he pointed out,

> ... we must correctly determine the structure of [various] economic sectors [which include the state sector, the collective sector, the household economy, the "small commodity production" sector (individual farmers, handicraftsmen, etc. ...), the private capitalist sector, the "state-capitalist" sector, and the "subsistence economy" of some ethnic minorities in mountainous regions]. [The use of these various economic sectors] is a solution of *strategic significance*, helping to liberate and exploit all potentialities for the development of productive forces[14] (emphasis added).

Following this general statement, the Party Politburo recently issued, *inter alia*, Resolution No. 10 on renovating economic management in agriculture (April 1988) and Resolution No. 16 on renovating policies concerning non-public sectors, particularly in the small-scale industry and handicrafts sectors (July 1988) (see Chapter 4) "with the aim of expanding production and business operations to meet the needs of society and creating a new driving force to resolve [the] country's socio-economic problems".[15]

As regards the renewal of the macro-economic management mechanism, the current principle consists of, at least in theory, combining central planning — which is still regarded as "the number one characteristic of the economic management mechanism" — with "the correct use of the commodity–money relationship",[16] that is, market forces. Truong Chinh stressed in his political report that:

> We are managing in a planned way a commodity economy having the characteristics of the transitional period [to socialism]. The full and correct use of the commodity–money relationship in planning the national economy is an objective necessity (...). Planning must always be closely linked with a judicious use of economic levers. The economy must be managed mainly by economic method.[17]

As for the State Planning Commission and other central bodies entrusted with administrative-economic management, he continued,

> once released from routine work, [they] must ... concentrate on studying the socio-economic strategy, on working out long and medium-term plans, on ensuring the overall and balanced [aggregates] in the economy, and on the making of economic policies and laws .... The State uses economic levers both in direct and indirect planning to ensure the implementation of the guidelines and targets of national economic plans.[18]

Concerning the system of income distribution, he advocated

> a radical reform of the wage system in such a way as to ensure the reproduction of labour, to do away with egalitarianism, step by step abolish the remaining subsidized part in the wage system, apply the forms of remuneration closely linked to the results of labour and economic efficiency.[19]

The Party also proclaimed at its Sixth National Congress that it would radically readjust the overall economic structure as well as simultaneously restructure the state investment outlay. Compared with the previous period, in the Fourth FYP the Party has completely reversed, at least in theory, the order of priority. Henceforth, agriculture is given top priority, followed by light industry and lastly by heavy industry.[20] This restructuring was concretized in two of the "three major economic programmes" already described in Chapter 4.

Concerning Vietnam's external economic relations, Truong Chinh stressed in his political report that "whether the task of stabilizing and developing the economy ... as well as the cause of science and technological development and socialist industrialization in our country will be carried out rapidly or not depends to a large extent on the expansion and ... the effectiveness of our external economic relations". And he continued: "in the whole area of external economic relations, the most important task is to boost exports".[21] Hence, the importance of the "export programme" as the third component of the abovementioned "three major economic programmes" which altogether account for "almost 70% of total [state investment]" during the current Fourth FYP.[22]

It is worth noting that henceforth production units engaging in exports on a relatively large scale are allowed to deal directly with foreign customers, albeit under the control of the Ministry of Foreign Economic Relations.

Besides expanding exports and imports, and securing foreign loans, Vietnam also applies diversified forms of operation (subcontracting, production sharing, joint ventures, direct investments, etc. ...) in expanding its external economic relations, "on the basis of mutual benefit".

In December 1987, the Vietnamese National Assembly passed the Foreign Investment Law which was, as said earlier, regarded as "one of the most liberal in all Southeast Asia". The Vietnamese leadership realizes at last that, as Foreign Minister Nguyen Co Thach put it,

> autarky and closed-door policy is the path to backwardness and poverty. To cope with the challenge of history, the only path for us is to associate the Vietnamese economy with the world economy. That was the lesson drawn by the Sixth Party Congress .... [Henceforth, Vietnam is] determined to broaden its [economic] relations with the outside world for the purpose of development.[23]

He also let it be understood that Vietnam had already missed the opportunity "to take advantage of the rapid development in science and technology and the internationalization of the world economic life" once, and that now it is "determined not to miss the opportunity again". "If we miss it this time around", he emphasized, "the extremely great danger to the future of our nation will be unfathomable".[24]

However, according to Do Muoi,

> the expansion of [economic] relations with the outside world ... is not simple if it is to be carried out effectively, for not a few difficulties and obstacles still remain. We still have to resolve many specific problems concerning rules and institutions, organization of cadres, infrastructure, domestic capital, and so forth so as to really attract and make the most of foreign investment.[25]

***

What is the overall situation after two years of economic renovation? Premier Do Muoi acknowledged in a speech delivered before the National Assembly in December 1988 that "satisfactory achievements have been few and far between ...; the Council of Ministers' macro-economic management has been sluggish, inconsistent, perfunctory, and still marked by the old way of thinking and style of work in various aspects".[26] He also said:

> The new mechanism and policies related to [macro] economic management ... are not synchronized yet. Some newly promulgated policies have displayed some inadequacies and shortcomings. The old mechanism of bureaucratic centralism and state-subsidization ... which exists alongside the new, incipient mechanism of economic accounting, has caused not a few stumbling blocks in the process of management at both macro and micro-levels, and given rise to many new problems such as that ... between economico-administrative management and business management, between central government and localities, between state and non-state economic sectors, etc. (...). Our country is facing great socio-economic difficulties ... (and), the greatest one being the acute disequilibria in the national economy.[27]

Secretary-General Nguyen Van Linh also admitted, at the conference of the Ho Chi Minh Party Committee in February 1988 that:

We [the new party leadership] have erroneously believed that with these Resolutions [the Sixth Party Congress' Resolution and those of the Central Committee's second, third and fourth plena], we could change the situation immediately.[28] However, the actual socio-economic situation has not been improved yet. Worse still, some problems have become more acute. Here we have objective causes .... Yet, basically, subjective causes [that is, party and government policies] are the main culprit .... More time is needed before we can effect new changes.[29]

"It takes time", he said, "for a bedridden patient to recover as there is no miraculous medicine that can make him rise up overnight".[30] The predicament in which he found himself by the end of 1988, he thought, stemmed from the fact that the previous Party leadership had set forth "erroneous strategic policies concerning the [overall] economic structure, the mechanism of [macro] economic management and the socialist transformation"[31] which were characterized by Truong Chinh as "errors of leftist infantilism".[32]

On the whole, it might be said that Socialist Vietnam's experience is not only *catastrophic* in economic terms but also very *costly* in human terms. Indeed, one may recall innumerable victims of the land reform in the late 1950s and a sizeable number of people who slowly died in jails and in so-called new economic zones, or were driven mad as a result of the anti-bourgeoisie campaign in the 1970s, to say nothing of an incalculable number of "boat people" who perished in the sea following the brutal "socialist transformation" drive, etc..(the list of casualties is too long to enumerate here). Apart from these victims, regarded as "class enemies" by the Party, mention should also be made of other categories of victims who, paradoxically, represent the mainstay of the revolutionary regime, namely, the workers, civil servants, intellectuals, and soldiers. Their living standard and their health have been deteriorating continuously since reunification[33] due, *inter alia*, to the skyrocketting inflation. Their real wages have been falling while official statistics have boasted a steady increase in national production. In other words, it seems that in Socialist Vietnam human beings are sacrificed in order to produce material things!

Tran Bach Dang, a high-ranking Party official admitted, in an uncommon interview published in the *International Herald Tribune* (23 January 1989), that "It is fair to say that Marxism as it came [in Vietnam] lacked a human character". Paraphrasing Dang, it might also be asserted that "socialism", as it has been applied in Vietnam until now, desperately lacks a human character. Despite some recent liberalization measures with incipient "renovation", Vietnamese "socialism" still remains, by and large, a "socialism" without a human face.

NOTES

1. V.I. Lenin, *Collected Works*, Vol. 27, p. 514 (quoted in *Far Eastern Affairs*, no. 5 [Moscow, 1988], p. 69).
2. Tran Bach Dang, "Doi Moi: Thuc Chat Va Thoi Trang", *Dat Nuoc*, no. 5 (June 1987); reprinted in *Doan Ket*, no. 394 (August 1987), p. 25.
3. K. Marx, "A Contribution to the Critique of Political Economy", *Selected Works*, Vol I. (London: Lawrence and Wishart, 1963), p. 356.
4. Mao Zedong, *Critique of Soviet Economics*, translated by Moss Roberts (New York: Monthly Review Press, 1977), p. 51.
5. Xue Muqiao, *China's Socialist Economy* (Beijing: Foreign Languages Publishing House, 1981), pp. 236–37.
6. *Communist Party of Vietnam. 4th National Congress* (Hanoi: Foreign Languages Publishing House, 1977), p. 52. See also *Gop Phan Tim Hieu Duong Loi Kinh Te Cua Dang* (Hanoi: NXB Su That, 1981), p. 39: Revolutionary change in relations of production "always (*sic*) bring about a development of productive forces".
7. *6th National Congress of the Communist Party of Vietnam. Documents* (Hanoi: Foreign Languages Publishing House, 1987), pp. 22; 64–66. See also Tran Ho, "Su Lac Hau Ve Nhan Thuc Ly Luan Kinh Te", *Tap Chi Cong San*, no. 2 (1988), p. 21; Tran Dinh Nghiem, "Ve Che Do So Huu Xa Hoi . . .", ibid., no. 3 (1988), p. 34; Truong Son, "Su Dung Va Cai Tao Dung Dan . . .", ibid., no. 1 (1988), pp. 30–31; and Le Sy Thang, "Kinh Nghiem Lich Su Cua Con Duong Phat Trien Phi Tu Ban Chu Nghia . . .", *Triet Hoc*, no. 3 (1988), pp. 9–10. See also Soviet academician Bogomolov's critical remark in the preface of his book entitled *Economicheskye Problemy Perokhoda K Socialismy Stran C Hepazvitoy Ekonomikoy (Materialy Sovietko-Vietnamskogo Simpoziuma)* (Moskva: Nauka, 1986), p. 189 (in Russian): ". . . Some Marxists used to have illusions about the

people's government and socialization of the basic means of production which, in their view, should *automatically* ensure a substantial improvement of the people's well-being and growth of productive forces" (emphasis added).

8. *6th National Congress* .... pp. 71–72.
9. K. Marx, "Critique of the Gotha Programme", in *Selected Works of Karl Marx and Frederick Engels*, Vol. III (Moscow: Progress Publishers, 1983), p. 18.
10. Regarding the negative consequences of egalitarian wages, see, for example, Tran Bach Dang, "But Ky Kinh Te", *Tap Chi Cong San*, no. 7 (1988), pp. 49–50.
11. Quoted in Murray Hiebert's article in *Far Eastern Economic Review*, 19 January 1989, p. 19.
12. See *6th National Congress* ..., p. 19.
13. Ibid., p. 65.
14. Ibid., pp. 62–64.
15. Vo Van Kiet's report in *Nhan Dan*, 14 December 1988.
16. See *6th National Congress* ..., p. 73.
17. Ibid., pp. 73–74.
18. Ibid., p. 79. For more details on the renewal of the macro-economic management mechanism, see Vo Chi Cong's article in *Nhan Dan*, 18 September 1987. By the same author, see "Mot So Van De Co Ban Ve Doi Moi Co Che Quan Ly Kinh Te...", *Tap Chi Cong San*, no. 12 (1987), pp. 5–12; and Che Viet Tan, "Mot So Quan Diem Ve Phat Trien San Xuat Hang Hoa O Nuoc Ta", *Tap Chi Cong San*, no. 4 (1988), pp. 21–26.
19. See *6th National Congress* ..., pp. 83–84.
20. Ibid., pp. 51–57.
21. Ibid., pp. 95–96.
22. Vo Van Kiet's report in *Nhan Dan*, 29 December 1987.
23. Ibid., 1 January 1989.
24. Ibid.
25. Ibid., 23 December 1988.
26. Hanoi Radio, Domestic Service, 22 December 1988.
27. *Nhan Dan*, 23 December 1988.
28. *Saigon Giai Phong*, quoted by Hanoi Radio, Domestic Service, 6 February 1988.
29. *Nhan Dan*, 23 June 1988.
30. See *Saigon Giai Phong*, quoted by Hanoi Radio, Domestic Service, 6 February 1988.
31. See *Nhan Dan*, 23 June 1988.
32. *Nhan Dan*, 20 October 1986. See also Le Duc Thuy's (Deputy Director of the Institute of Economy in Hanoi) remark in *Tap Chi Cong San*, no. 8 (1988), p. 58.
33. Premier Do Muoi admitted, for instance, before the National Assembly that "the living conditions of a vast majority of the labouring people have become more and more difficult with every passing day" (*Nhan Dan*, 23 December 1988). Earlier, he had also acknowledged that the "wages of workers in state-

run enterprises and civil servants were seriously reduced" (*Nhan Dan*, 17 August 1988).

On the other hand, Duong Xuan An, General Secretary of the Vietnamese Trade Union Federation, told the 6th Trade Union Congress in Hanoi in October 1988 that "the situation of workers had worsened over the past five years", notably in terms of living standards and working conditions (Agence France Presse, Hanoi, 18 October 1988). On the same score, see also Pham The Duyet's article in *Tap Chi Cong San*, no. 10 (1988), p. 11.

THE AUTHOR

Dr VO NHAN TRI was born in Vietnam, went to secondary school there, and completed his education in Paris, Grenoble (France) and Birmingham (U.K.). He holds a Diploma from the Ecole Nationale d'Organisation Economique et Sociale (Paris, 1952), an Ingenieur Commercial degree (Grenoble, 1956), and received his Doctorate in Law from the University of Grenoble (1955). He was a former student of the Institut d'Etudes Politiques (University of Paris) and of the Ecole Pratique des Hautes Etudes (Sorbonne) in the early 1950s. He has also read for the Ph.D. programme at the University of Birmingham (1956–57).

He was head of the World Economy department at the Institute of Economics, Hanoi, from 1960 to 1975, and then Senior Research Fellow at the Institute of Social Sciences in Ho Chi Minh City from 1976 to 1984. He left Vietnam in 1984. Since then, he has been a Visiting Fellow at the Institute of Development Studies (University of Sussex, Brighton, 1985) and the Institute of Developing Economies (Tokyo, 1986), and a Senior Research Fellow at the Institute of Southeast Asian Studies, Singapore (1987–89). Currently, he is a Research Associate at the Centre National de Recherche Scientifique, Paris.

Among the many books and papers he has authored are *Croissance Economique de la Republique Democratique du Vietnam, 1945–65* (Hanoi: ELE, 1967); *U.S. Aid and the Vietnam War* (in Vietnamese) (Ho Chi Minh City: Institute of Social Sciences, 1980), and *Socialist Vietnam's Economy: An Assessment* (Tokyo: Institute of Developing Economies, 1987). He has also done many studies on the economic problems of North and South Vietnam, published in various Vietnamese, Soviet, French and Swedish journals.